D0193547

SOUL
SURVIVOR

ALSO BY PHILIP YANCEY

Reaching for the Invisible God
Meet the Bible (with Brenda Quinn)
The Jesus I Never Knew
What's So Amazing About Grace?
The Bible Jesus Read
Where Is God When It Hurts?
Disappointment with God
The Student Bible (with Tom Stafford)
Church: Why Bother?
Discovering God
Finding God in Unexpected Places
I Was Just Wondering

BOOKS BY DR. PAUL BRAND AND PHILIP YANCEY

Fearfully and Wonderfully Made
In His Image
The Gift of Pain

SOUL SURVIVOR

*How Thirteen Unlikely Mentors
Helped My Faith Survive the Church*

PHILIP YANCEY

GALILEE

DOUBLEDAY

New York London Toronto Sydney Auckland

WATERBROOK PRESS

Colorado Springs

A Galilee Book
PUBLISHED BY DOUBLEDAY
a division of Random House, Inc.

A hardcover edition of this book was published in 2001 by Doubleday.

GALILEE and DOUBLEDAY are registered trademarks of Random House, Inc., and the portrayal of a ship with a cross above a book is a trademark of Random House, Inc.

WATERBROOK and its deer design logo are registered trademarks of WaterBrook Press, a division of Random House, Inc.

THIS BOOK IS COPUBLISHED WITH WATERBROOK PRESS
2375 Telstar Drive, Suite 160,
Colorado Springs, CO 80920, a division of Random House, Inc.

First Galilee edition published November 2003

Book design by Pei Loi Koay

The Library of Congress has cataloged the hardcover edition as:
Yancey, Philip.
Soul Survivor: how my faith survived the church / by Philip Yancey—1st ed.
p. cm.
1. Christian biography. 2. Faith. I. Title.

BR1700.2.Y36 2001
270'.092'2—dc21
[B]   2001028890

ISBN 0-385-50275-3 (Doubleday)
ISBN 1-57856-818-8 (WaterBrook)

Copyright © 2001 by SCCT

All Rights Reserved

PRINTED IN THE UNITED STATES OF AMERICA

10 9 8 7 6 5 4 3 2

Kathryn Helmers went far beyond an agent's job description in this project. In many ways the book would not exist apart from her. She helped form and refine the vision in my mind, then spurred me along at every step, offering both encouragement and direction. Sentence structure, thematic organization, cover choices, jacket copy, contract legalese—she cheerfully entered into every phase of the publishing process. At various places I mention the "psychosis" of the writing process; Kathryn helped lower that at least to the level of a neurosis, and even coaxed out a few moments of health.

My editor at Doubleday, Eric Major, offered the same calming, supportive presence that I came to know twenty years ago when he published the U.K. editions of books I wrote with Dr. Paul Brand. And my assistant, Melissa Nicholson, spent long hours staring at computer screens in the library and on the Internet to research and check facts.

These chapters profile people I have written about elsewhere, as a journalist. In each case I greatly expanded and changed the material, and added a more personal slant. But I did rely on the research, and sometimes the actual words, of previous versions. Articles on Martin Luther King, Jr., Dr. Robert Coles, Mahatma Gandhi, and Dr. C. Everett Koop appeared in *Christianity Today* magazine; articles on Annie Dillard, Frederick Buechner, Leo Tolstoy and Feodor Dostoevsky, and Shusaku Endo appeared in *Books and Culture*. In addition, I wrote reflections on G. K. Chesterton as a foreword for an edition of *Orthodoxy,* on Dr. Paul Brand as a foreword for *The Forever Feast,* on Henri Nouwen for a chapter in *Nouwen Then,* and on John Donne for a collaborative work titled *Reality and the Vision.* And a few of my thoughts on King, Donne, Endo, and Tolstoy also showed up in my books *Reaching for the Invisible God, What's So Amazing About Grace?* and *The Jesus I Never Knew.* I thank the caretakers of these publications for allowing me to rummage through sentences and paragraphs to find some that fit this new purpose.

CONTENTS

Always this book will be associated in my mind with the events of September 11, 2001. The publisher had set the release date for September 20 of that year and scheduled media appearances in Washington, New York, and the Midwest the week of publication. Publicity people had worked hard on the media tour, only to find the media world—not to mention the travel world—in complete chaos in the wake of the terrorist attacks. Many television and radio programs had temporarily gone off the air, and those still broadcasting wanted to talk about one thing only, regardless of a book's content.

I had learned of the World Trade Center tragedy when my brother called me on the morning of an ordinary work day. "America is under attack," he said. "Turn on the television." Like almost everyone, I stopped what I was doing and sat glued to the television as the surreal events unfolded.

Three planes were missing, no, four—no, maybe six. They've hit the Pentagon. They're after the President. And then something no one could imagine took place live on network television. Two of the mightiest man-made monuments in the world simply vanished in a cloud of darkness before our eyes.

Ten days later I was sitting in one of the first planes permitted to resume the flight path over Lower Manhattan into LaGuardia Airport. Over the loudspeaker, the pilot had instructed us how to overpower a passenger by using pillows and blankets. Flight attendants, unusually subdued, wore pins depicting the four destroyed planes with the message IN OUR HEARTS FOREVER.

Lower Manhattan looked tragically incomplete. Where before, two of the tallest buildings in the world had stood, now I looked out on a gaping hole, with a plume of smoke still rising a half-mile high from the site. Wind was blowing the smoke to one side, and I could make out yellow bulldozers, like tiny toys, crawling over the mass of rubble. In an hour or so I would be at the site, for a friend in the Salvation Army had insisted I visit Ground Zero before my media engagements.

A driver named Eddie met me at LaGuardia. I told him my destination, the Salvation Army center near Ground Zero, and he said he knew it well. Eddie, a young Puerto Rican with a clean-shaved head, was impeccably dressed in a starched white shirt and tie, wearing gold bracelets and a diamond-studded ring. He had a perfect Brooklyn accent.

"Where were you on September 11?" I asked Eddie, making conversation. "Were you working?" He paused at least ten seconds before answering, no doubt weighing whether he wanted to tell the story once more, to a stranger.

"Actually, Mr. Yancey, I was parked just down from the World Trade Center."

"No! Tell me about it."

"I had picked up a ride at the airport, Mr. Firestone, and dropped him at the Millennium Hotel. I remember his name because I asked him if he owned the tire company, and he laughed and said no. He had a meeting scheduled at the WTC, and I planned to stay with the car and wait for him. I was sitting in this very car, reading the paper. I heard a roar like the sound jet engines make when the planes warm up. I live near LaGuardia, so I hear that roar every morning. Then the ground shook, the car shook, and I heard the explosion. What the . . . ? I jumped outside the car and saw people running everywhere.

"I was standing outside, by my car, when the second plane hit a few minutes later. My God, I've never seen a fireball like that. I knew I should get in the car and leave, but something glued me there. It's like when you see an accident, and you know you should drive past without looking, but you can't.

"You wouldn't believe the noise. Car horns were going off all over the place. Police, ambulance, and fire-truck sirens were coming closer. I quick called my wife in Brooklyn and told her, 'Honey, something big has happened down here. Turn on the news. I'm right in front of the Twin Towers, but I'm okay.'

"And then the people started streaming out. Thousands of people. Some screaming, some holding handkerchiefs over their faces, some covered with blood. I stood by the car as they ran past. I looked in the air and, oh my God, I saw little specks—people jumping. A man in a white shirt. A woman with her skirt flying up. A couple holding hands. A man trying to use his sports coat as a parachute. People would look up, try to figure where the falling bodies would land, and dodge them as they hit the sidewalk. I'll never forget that sight as long as I live.

"There was paper and debris and stuff—even furniture—flying everywhere, like a blizzard. I saw a boy, maybe fourteen, on the sidewalk doubled up, coughing, and when I went over to him, he pointed to his pocket. He couldn't speak. I reached in and pulled out an asthma pump, and he sprayed it and got his breath back.

"I was there forty-five minutes, I guess—I couldn't tell how long, but that's what they say now—until the first tower collapsed. A woman had fallen down on the sidewalk, an elderly woman. Everybody was running past her, not stepping on her or anything, but running right past her. I waited for a break in the people and went to her. 'Are you all right, ma'am?' I asked. 'I have some water in my car. Can I get you some?' She said she'd made it down something like fifty-eight floors, and I told her she was safe now.

"I could tell she was upset, so I asked if I could say a prayer for her. I'm Catholic, you know. It just seemed the thing to do. She looked relieved, and while I was kneeling there on the sidewalk holding her hand, I heard a noise louder than I thought possible. The entire giant building just collapsed, all hundred and ten stories. And I swear to God, Mr. Yancey, while I'm kneeling there holding that woman's hand, something falls from the sky—a piece of a computer or something—and hits that woman and she slumps over dead. Imagine—escaping from fifty-eight stories and then getting killed like that.

"I look behind me and see a cloud dark as night rushing right towards me. I let go her hand and take off running. It's like a cops-and-robbers cartoon. The faster I run, the closer the cloud gets. I realize I got no chance. I duck into a little space between two buildings to wait it out. When the cloud hits, it's darker than I knew dark could be. At night, even a cloudy night, at least you got space around you, air to breathe. This cloud was, like, solid. You couldn't see anything. You couldn't breathe. You were surrounded by dark you could feel."

Eventually, Eddie told me, he found his way back to his car. Police had already sealed off the area, but he wanted to get his limo out. It was covered with dust like volcanic ash, and he took off his white shirt and wiped the windshield until he could see out. He opened the doors and yelled, "Anybody want a ride outta here?" Eight people, strangers, piled in. He headed for the nearest bridge off Manhattan, crossing over just before the mayor ordered all bridges and tunnels closed.

When he finally got home, four hours after the attack, he found his wife hysterical and his two children huddled in a corner watching Mommy sob. After his phone call she had stood at her window in Brooklyn and watched the World Trade Center disintegrate, certain that her husband had been killed in the explosion and fire. Phone service was down, and she had not heard from him in four hours.

Eddie was so shaken that the next day he accepted a job to drive someone to Detroit. Airplanes were grounded, people were desperate to get home, and he wanted to get as far away from New York as he could. He drove straight through, took a two-hour nap in the car, and drove fourteen hours back to Brooklyn.

"Everything's different now, Mr. Yancey," Eddie said. "I go to my brother's house every night. We sit around, watch TV, play with the kids, play games. Stuff I never used to do. Family stuff. And I haven't missed Mass yet. I'll never be the same."

Outside the Salvation Army Center a tractor-trailer truck was parked. It came packed with supplies—blankets, food, clothing—from the State of Washington, clear across the continent from New York. When Salvationists opened the truck to unload it, they found inside a forty-foot banner which they unfurled and tacked to the side of the truck. Thousands of messages covered it, handwritten in grease pencil or permanent marker, and I stood and read them for probably ten minutes. Most were one sentence long. "You're in our hearts." "We're alongside you." "We love you." "You're our heroes." "You're our brothers and sisters." Some of the writers had drawn hearts, or angels, or other signs of companionship and hope. Third-graders had sent along homemade cookies in hand-decorated bags.

When we drove to a checkpoint manned by National Guard troops, the street was lined with New Yorkers—New Yorkers!—waving banners with similar messages. "We love you." "You're our heroes." "God bless you." "Thank you." A chaplain said that in the early days crowds ten-deep lined these streets at midnight, cheering every rescue vehicle that came by. Even after ten days, some still showed up to cheer.

The Salvation Army officer accompanying me was Incident Director for the city. He had been on the job barely a month when the planes hit. He worked thirty-six hours straight and slept four; forty hours and slept six; forty more hours and slept six. Then he took a day off. His assistant had an emotional breakdown early on, in the same van I was riding in, and may never recover.

After a few days the Salvation Army made a policy of accepting nothing but cash. They had nowhere to put the donations of food, clothing, and equipment brought to them by thousands of New Yorkers and others from out of state. Lines of people stretched around the block all day long, volunteers who wanted to help. The writer Chris de Vinck tells of a couple in his town who drove to Home Depot, bought $700 worth of shovels, and hand-delivered them to New York. A friend told me of firefighters in Chicago who jumped in a car, headed east, and got picked up going 108 mph in Indiana. When they explained their destination to the state trooper, he said, "Well, let's try to keep it under ninety," and gave them a flashing-light escort to the Ohio border.

America's ability to respond to a crisis is amazing. Less than two weeks after the tragedy, a rescue city had sprung up. Portable kitchens and toilets, tents, pallets full of plywood, cranes twenty-five stories high, refrigeration trucks, generators, bulldozers—they lined the streets approaching Ground Zero. As we neared the site, we switched from the van to an oversized golf cart. Soldiers wearing gas masks sprayed water and disinfectant on the tires—water to combat asbestos, disinfectant to fight the germs that flourish around a scene of death. They scrutinized each person's ID and waved us through.

As we got to Ground Zero, everything about the landscape changed. Sun was filtering down through the haze all the way to the sidewalks, no longer blocked by the towering buildings. At a plaza just across from the rubble, before they cordoned off the area, mourners had placed teddy bears, hundreds of teddy bears, maybe thousands, with flowers now dried and coated with dust. Occasionally I passed a wall plastered with photos of the missing, and poignant notes. "Please, Marcia, call your sister. I love you!" "We haven't given up hope, Sean. You'll always live in our hearts."

I had studied the maps in newspapers, but no two-dimensional representation could capture the scale of destruction. For about eight square blocks, buildings were deserted, their windows broken, jagged pieces of steel jutting out from floors high above the street. Thousands of offices equipped with faxes, phones, and computers sat vacant, coated in debris. On September 11, people were sitting there punching keys, making phone calls, grabbing a cup of coffee to start the day . . . and suddenly, apocalypse.

Just that morning the mayor had changed the mission away from rescue, in effect giving up hope that survivors would be found. No more bucket brigades, with meticulous removal of debris by hand. Giant machines were moving in. Measured by the buildings around it, the pile of rubble stood between ten and twelve stories tall. In the Rocky Mountains, I have seen how avalanches sweep whole mountainsides of snow and compress it into a pile as hard as concrete at the bottom of the slope. Still, I could not imagine that all the mass of 220 combined floors had compressed into this pile. Bulldozers crawled across the ugly mountain. Sparks shot up where welders worked to cut apart the girders.

Looking at Ground Zero, I thought of the garbage mountains outside Cairo and Manila, where armies of the poor make a living by combing through filth in search of neglected treasure: a plastic bag, a pencil, a piece of a telephone. Here in the most technologically sophisticated city in the world, a different kind of army was using the very best equipment to comb through rubble in search of treasure, in this case evidence of human beings: hair, flesh, body parts. Searchers sifted through the rubble before loading it onto a dump truck, forensic specialists checked it on the truck, and others examined it again when it arrived in the Bronx.

I studied the faces of the workers, uniformly grim. I didn't see a single smile at Ground Zero. How could you smile in such a place? It had nothing to offer but death and destruction, a monument to the worst that human beings can do to each other.

P art of the shock of that day was that common citizens were going about their daily routines—following baseball, watching the stock market, telling jokes about politics—and then innocent airplanes, the kind we ride on for trips to Disney World, morphed into agents of monstrous evil. No one had declared war, or given any warning. The very ordinariness of life was under attack.

"Everything's different," my driver Eddie had told me. Indeed, New York was a different place from the one I knew before September 11. To anyone who has spent time there, I need only mention one observation to mark that change. In a full day in Manhattan, I heard one car horn. "I don't know how to drive anymore," Eddie said. "I'm used to people honking at me, cutting me off, flipping me the bird. Now, they're so polite, I don't know how to act."

I wondered at the time how long the changes would last—for New York, for the nation, for me. We faced what most of us spend a lifetime ignoring: that all of us will die, and that many of us fill our lives with trivialities in apparent defiance of that fact. We learned, like Eddie, that playing games with kids may be more important than working late for overtime pay. We learned that even in a city known for its crusty cynicism, heroes can emerge. We learned that a Jay Leno comedy routine and major league sports, entertaining as they may be, are sometimes obscenely out of place. We learned that love for country and even for strangers can surge up with no warning. We learned that our nation, for all its flaws, has much worth preserving, and worth defending. And we learned that at a time of crisis, we turn to our spiritual roots: the President quoting Psalm 23, the cops and firemen stopping by their makeshift chapels, the Salvation Army chaplains dispensing grace and comforting the grieving loved ones.

I have never been especially patriotic. I've traveled too much overseas, I guess, and have seen from afar the arrogance and insensitivity of the United States. Sometimes I envy my friends who travel with a Canadian, rather than an American, passport. Our military, our Olympic athletes, even our tourists, walk with a swagger. I remember being in the Philippines around the time of the Sydney Olympics and asking my host if his country had ever won a gold medal. He hung his head. "We almost did once. And we have a chance for a bronze in boxing at this one." A nation of 90 million people had never won a gold medal.   Meanwhile, the Americans were furious if they didn't take home at least half the golds in swimming and track and field, and our winners strutted irreverently on the platform as an Australian band played our national anthem.

September 11 changed my attitude. I choked up when the Congress sang "God Bless America," and when the Buckingham Palace guard played "The Star-Spangled Banner," and when firemen told corny stories about their fallen comrades, and when a solitary bagpiper played "Amazing Grace" in Union Square, and when hundreds of New Yorkers walked around dazed with photos of their missing loved ones, sheltering candle flames in their cupped hands, and when Dan Rather had to be held and comforted on the air—by David Letterman of all people.

I felt a sudden surge of loyalty and unity with my country that was new to me. Scott Simon put words to it in a National Public Radio editorial after the WTC attacks. Patriotism is not based on a blind belief that the United States has no need to change, he said. God knows we need to change in many ways. Our love for America rests on the belief that the changes needed are more likely to occur here than anywhere else in the world.

I think of my own life. I grew up in a cloistered, fundamentalist environment in a South of legislated racism. Now I live two thousand miles away, in a place of exquisite beauty, with the ability to make a living reflecting in words on what matters most to me, rewarded and not punished for honesty and growth. Few countries in the world would allow for that kind of progression and mobility. The United States remains the land of promise and potential.

My wife and I had originally planned to leave just after September 11 for a vacation on a houseboat on Lake Powell with three couples from Illinois. When their flights were canceled, those plans changed. Instead, we took a three-day trip to Telluride, Colorado, and hiked in the mountains. The interlude pulled us away from nonstop television and gave an important reminder of the goodness and grace that exist in this world alongside the ugliness and evil. I have never seen the aspen trees so beautiful. They shone as gold, cascading down the sides of dark evergreen mountains like rivers of light. We took walks among them, stepping on a carpet of gold and listening to their papery rattle in the breeze. Fresh snow coated the mountain ranges, the pure white snow of early fall. After three days we returned from the healing isolation of nature to reenter a society in deep shock and mourning.

A massive shift in perspective happened to our country on September 11. As Eddie put it, "Everything's different now." For a time, at least, it made us look at our land, our society, and ourselves in a new way. Professional sports canceled all contests; comedies went off the air. We no longer saw ourselves as the lucky few on top of the world, but as a people vulnerable to hate and terror. That three thousand people could go to work as part of their daily routine and never come home made us all aware of our fragile mortality. Over the next months, the *New York Times* ran an obituary on every single person who died. Like most people in history, but not most Americans, we began to live in conscious awareness of death.

For me, the events of September 11 brought to the surface two haunting questions: Who am I? and Who do I want to be? They are quintessentially American questions. Unlike much of the world, we have the luxury of options—which, we discover, may turn into a burden. Rarely does an American man or woman unthinkingly follow in his or her parent's footsteps. We must define ourselves, carve out an identity. An event like September 11 speeds up the process by compressing time, chasing away distractions, and forcing us to focus on what matters most.

These two questions have caused me much soul-searching, long looks back at my past and projections forward into my future. For this reason, too, I will always associate this book in my mind with September 11. I had just finished putting to paper a record of that very process, an exploration of my own spiritual pilgrimage. I had the privilege of leisurely answering the question Who am I? as seen through a filter of thirteen people who have affected me most. I gain a glimpse of who I want to be through these same people.

I covet for everyone the experience I have had in writing this book. Since publication, letters have come from many readers who tell of their own search and their own survival, body and soul. We are not alone as we ask these questions—that, too, a truth revealed on September 11, 2001.

SOUL
SURVIVOR

Chapter 1

RECOVERING FROM CHURCH ABUSE

Sometimes in a waiting room or on an airplane I strike up conversations with strangers, during the course of which they learn that I write books on spiritual themes. Eyebrows arch, barriers spring up, and often I hear yet another horror story about church. My seatmates must expect me to defend the church, because they always act surprised when I respond, "Oh, it's even worse than that. Let me tell you my story." I have spent most of my life in recovery from the church.

One church I attended during formative years in Georgia of the 1960s presented a hermetically sealed view of the world. A sign out front proudly proclaimed our identity with words radiating from a many-pointed star: "New Testament, Blood-bought, Born-again, Premillennial, Dispensational, fundamental . . ." Our little group of two hundred people had a corner on the truth, God's truth, and everyone who disagreed with us was surely teetering on the edge of hell. Since my family lived in a mobile home on church property, I could never escape the enveloping cloud that blocked my vision and marked the borders of my world.

Later, I came to realize that the church had mixed in lies with truth. For example, the pastor preached blatant racism from the pulpit. Dark races are cursed by God, he said, citing an obscure passage in Genesis. They function well as servants—"Just look at how colored waiters in restaurants can weave among the tables, swiveling their hips, carrying trays"—but never as leaders. Armed with such doctrines, I reported for my very first job, a summer internship at the prestigious Communicable Disease Center near Atlanta, and met my supervisor, Dr. James Cherry, a Ph.D. in biochemistry and a black man. Something did not add up.

After high school I attended a Bible college in a neighboring state. More progressive than my home church, the school had admitted one black student, whom, to stay on the safe side, they assigned to a roommate from Puerto Rico. This school believed in rules, many rules, sixty-six pages' worth in fact, which we students had to study and agree to abide by. The faculty and staff took pains to trace each one of these rules to a biblical principle, which involved a degree of creativity since some of the rules (such as those legislating length of hair on men and skirts on women) changed from year to year. As a college senior, engaged, I could spend only the dinner hour, 5:40 P.M. until 7 P.M., with the woman who is now my wife. Once, we got caught holding hands and were put "on restriction," forbidden to see each other or speak for two weeks. Outside somewhere in the great world beyond, other students were demonstrating against the war in Vietnam, marching for civil rights on a bridge near Selma, Alabama, and gathering to celebrate love and peace in Woodstock, New York. Meanwhile we were preoccupied, mastering supralapsarianism and measuring skirts and hair.

Shortly after the turn of the millennium, in the spring of 2000, I experienced a fast-motion recapitulation of my life. The first day, I served on a panel at a conference in South Carolina addressing the topic "Faith and Physics." Though I have no expertise in physics, I got chosen along with a representative from Harvard Divinity School because I write openly about matters of faith. The panel was lopsided on the science end, for it included two Nobel prize-winning physicists and the director of the Fermilab nuclear accelerator near Chicago.

One of the Nobel laureates began by saying he had no use for religion, and in fact thought it harmful and superstitious. "Ten percent of Americans claim to have been abducted by aliens, half are creationists, and half read horoscopes each day," he said. "Why should it surprise us if a majority believe in God?" Raised Orthodox Jewish, he was now a confirmed atheist.

The other scientists had kinder words for religion but said that they restricted their field of view to what can be observed and verified, which by definition excluded most matters of faith. When my turn came to speak, I acknowledged the mistakes the church had made and thanked them for not burning us Christians at the stake now that the tables had turned. I also thanked them for rigorous honesty about their own nontheistic point of view. I read from Chet Raymo, an astronomer and science writer who has calculated the odds of our universe resulting, as he believes it did, from sheer chance:

> If, one second after the Big Bang, the ratio of the density of the universe to its expansion rate had differed from its assumed value by only one part in 10^{15} (that's 1 followed by fifteen zeros), the universe would have either quickly collapsed upon itself or ballooned so rapidly that stars and galaxies could not have condensed from the primal matter . . . The coin was flipped into the air 10^{15} times, and it came down on its edge but once. If all the grains of sand on all the beaches of the Earth were possible universes—that is, universes consistent with the laws of physics as we know them—and only one of those grains of sand were a universe that allowed for the existence of intelligent life, then that one grain of sand is the universe we inhabit.

After the panel two more Nobel laureates, another in physics and one in chemistry, joined the discussion, along with some thoughtful Christians. One of the physicists asked to see the quote by Raymo, whom he knew as a personal friend. He pondered a moment, thinking out loud, "Ten to the fifteenth power, ten to the fifteenth . . . let's see there are 10^{22} stars in the universe—yeah, I can buy that. I'll take those odds." We then moved on to the critique of religion. Yes, it has done harm, but consider the good it has accomplished as well. The scientific method itself grew out of Judaism and Christianity, which presented the world as a product of a rational Creator and thus comprehensible and subject to verification. So did education, medi-

cine, democracy, charitable work, and justice issues such as the aboli-
tion of slavery. The atheistic physicists freely acknowledged that they
had no real basis for their ethics, and that many of their colleagues had
served Nazi and Communist regimes without a twinge of conscience.
We had a fascinating interchange, that rare experience of true dialogue
resulting from different perspectives on the universe.

A day later, my wife and I got up early and drove a hundred miles
to the thirtieth reunion of our Bible college class. There, we listened
to classmates describe the last three decades of their lives. One told
of being delivered from arthritis after ten years when she finally dealt
with unconfessed sin in her life. Another extolled the advantage of
sleeping on magnets. Several were suffering from chronic fatigue syndrome, and others from severe depression. One couple had recently
put their teenage daughter in a mental institution. These did not seem
to be healthy people, and I felt sadness and compassion as I heard
their stories.

Paradoxically, in narrating their lives my classmates kept resurrect-
ing phrases we had learned at Bible college: "God is giving me the victory . . . I can do all things through Christ . . . All things work together
for good . . . I'm walking in triumph." I left that reunion with my head
spinning. I kept wondering how the skeptical scientists would have reacted had they sat in on the class reunion. I imagine they would have
pointed out a disconnect between the observable lives and the spiritual overlay applied to them.

The very next morning, a Sunday, we arose early again and drove
two hundred miles to Atlanta in order to attend the "burial" of the fundamentalist church I grew up in, the one with the many-pointed star.
After moving to escape a changing neighborhood, the church found itself once again surrounded by African-Americans, and attendance had
dwindled. In a sweet irony, it was now selling its building to an
African-American congregation. I slipped into the very last service of
that church, which had been advertised as a reunion open to all who
had ever attended.

I recognized acquaintances from my past, an unsettling time warp
in which I found my teenage friends now paunchy, balding, and

middle-aged. The pastor, who had served the same congregation for forty years, emphasized the church motto, "Contending for the faith." "I have fought the fight," he said. "I have finished the course." He seemed smaller than I remembered, his posture less erect, and his flaming red hair had turned white. Several times he thanked the congregation for the Oldsmobile they had given him as a love gift: "Not bad for a poor little pastor," he kept saying. During the expanded service, a procession of people stood and testified how they had met God through this church. Listening to them, I imagined a procession of those not present, people like my brother, who had turned away from God in large part because of this church. I now viewed its contentious spirit with pity, whereas in adolescence it had pressed life and faith out of me. The church had now lost any power over me; its stinger held no more venom. But I kept reminding myself that I had nearly abandoned the Christian faith in reaction against this church, and I felt deep sympathy for those who had.

That single weekend gave a snapshot reprise of my life. Where do I belong now? I wondered. Long ago I rejected the cultish spirit of the church I had just helped bury. Yet neither could I share the materialistic skepticism of the scientists on the panel. Though they may wager on one fantastic grain of sand arrayed against the forces of randomness, I cannot. Theologically, I probably fit most comfortably with the evangelical Bible college, for we have in common a thirst for God, a reverence for the Bible, and a love for Jesus. Nonetheless, I had not found there much balance or health. Sometimes I feel like the most liberal person among conservatives, and sometimes like the most conservative among liberals. How can I fit together my religious past with my spiritual present?

I have met many people, and heard from many more, who have gone through a similar process of mining truth from their religious past: Roman Catholics who flinch whenever they see a nun or priest, former Seventh Day Adventists who cannot drink a cup of coffee without a stab of guilt, Mennonites who worry whether wedding rings give evidence of worldliness. Some of them now reject the church entirely, and find Christians threatening and perhaps even repellent.

One of Walker Percy's characters in *The Second Coming* captures this attitude well:

> I am surrounded by Christians. They are generally speaking a pleasant and agreeable lot, not noticeably different from other people—even though they, the Christians of the South, the U.S.A., the Western world have killed off more people than all other people put together. Yet I cannot be sure they don't have the truth. But if they have the truth, why is it the case that they are repellent precisely to the degree that they embrace and advertise the truth? One might even become a Christian if there were few if any Christians around. Have you ever lived in the midst of fifteen million Southern Baptists? . . . A mystery: If the good news is true, why is not one pleased to hear it?

His last question rings loud. If the gospel comes as a *eucatastrophe,* J. R. R. Tolkien's word for a spectacularly good thing happening to spectacularly bad people, why do so few people perceive it as good news?

I became a writer, I now believe, to sort out words used and misused by the church of my youth. Although I heard that "God is love," the image of God I got from sermons more resembled an angry, vengeful tyrant. We sang, "Red and yellow, black and white, they are precious in his sight . . ." but just let one of those red, yellow, or black children try entering our church. Bible college professors insisted, "We live not under law but under grace," and for the life of me I could not tell much difference between the two states. Ever since, I have been on a quest to unearth the good news, to scour the original words of the gospel and discover what the Bible must mean by using words like *love, grace,* and *compassion* to describe God's own character. I sensed truth in those words, truth that must be sought with diligence and skill, like the fresco masterpieces that lie beneath layers of plaster and paint in ancient chapels.

I felt drawn to writing because for me it had opened chinks of light that became a window to another world. I remember the impact of a mild book like *To Kill a Mockingbird,* which called into question the apartheid assumptions of my friends and neighbors. As I went on to read *Black Like Me, The Autobiography of Malcolm X,* and Martin Luther King's "Letter from Birmingham City Jail," my world shattered. I felt the power that allows one human mind to penetrate another with no intermediary but a piece of flattened wood pulp. I saw that writing could seep into crevices, bringing spiritual oxygen to people trapped in air-tight boxes.

I especially came to value the freedom-enhancing quality of the written word. Speakers in the churches I frequented could *raise their voices!* and play on emotions like musical instruments. But alone in my room, controlling every turn of the page, I met other representatives of faith—C. S. Lewis, G. K. Chesterton, John Donne—whose calmer voices traversed time to convince me that somewhere Christians lived who knew grace as well as law, love as well as judgment, reason as well as passion. I became a writer because of my own encounter with the power of words, and I gained hope that spoiled words, their original meaning wrung out, could be reclaimed.

Ever since, I have clung fiercely to the stance of a pilgrim, for that is all I am. I have no religious sanction. I am neither pastor nor teacher, but an ordinary pilgrim, one person among many on a spiritual search. Unavoidably and by instinct, I question and reevaluate my faith all the time. When I returned from the head-spinning weekend among physicists, Bible college classmates, and Southern fundamentalists, I asked myself yet again, Why am I still a Christian? What keeps me pursuing a gospel that has come to me amid so much distortion and static, that often sounds more like bad news than good?

Every writer has one main theme, a spoor that he or she keeps sniffing around, tracking, following to its source. If I had to define my own theme, it would be that of a person who absorbed some of the worst the church has to offer, yet still landed in the loving arms of God. Yes, I went through a period of rejection of the church and God, a conversion experience in reverse that felt like liberation for a time. I ended up, however, not as an atheist, a refugee from the church, but as one of its advocates. What allowed me to ransom a personal faith from the damaging effects of religion?

The people profiled in this book go a long way toward answering that question. In thirty years as a journalist, I have had the freedom to investigate all sorts of people. I have met characters who belong in a Flannery O'Connor novel. I interviewed televangelist Jim Bakker at the height of his bizarre reign of oversold condos and air-conditioned doghouses at the extravagant PTL television studio and Christian theme park, and then watched as he publicly denied statements he had made to me on tape. I listened to a Las Vegas showgirl tell how she met God while on the operating table "to get my bustes enlarged," and under anesthesia had a dream of semi-tractor trailers made of human flesh—"ever'thing was made of flesh, even the mud flaps"—dumping a cargo of America's teenagers into a lake of fire.

For the most part, though, I tried to avoid such people, entertaining as they may be. They reminded me too much of my past, from which I was still trying to escape. Instead, I decided early on in my journalistic career to scout out people I could learn from, people I might want to emulate. Having grown up with mostly negative role models, I longed for some positive ones. I found some.

A millionaire entrepreneur named Millard Fuller grew disillusioned with the corporate rat race and, challenged by the radical minister Clarence Jordan, abandoned his life of luxury and founded an organization to build houses for those who cannot afford one; Habitat for Humanity recently celebrated its hundred thousandth completed home. A devout Presbyterian named Jack McConnell invented the Tine Test for tuberculosis, helped develop Tylenol and MRI imaging, and then came out of retirement to recruit retired physicians to staff free medical clinics for the poor. Dame Cicely Saunders enrolled in medical school in middle age because the authorities told her "in this profession, people only listen to doctors"; she never really practiced medicine, but instead ignited the modern hospice movement, ushering in a new way of care for the dying. Sir Ghillean Prance, while director of the New York Botanical Gardens and Royal Botanical

Gardens at Kew, England, began an institute with the oxymoronic name Economic Botany, which demonstrates to owners of the world's rain forests how they can make more money by harvesting products selectively and replanting than they can by clear-cutting. Interviewing each of these people at length, I came away impressed by the role that ordinary citizens, fueled by faith, can play in advancing the causes of justice and mercy.

"The glory of God is a person fully alive," said the second-century theologian Irenaeus. Sadly, that description does not reflect the image many people have of modern Christians. Rightly or wrongly, they see Christians rather as restrained, uptight, repressed—people less likely to celebrate vitality than to wag our fingers in disapproval. As a journalist, though, I have met people whose lives are indeed enhanced in every way by their faith. They have abundant life, and as I have spent time with such people, I have wanted to tap into that source of life for myself and then broadcast it to the rest of the world.

The people in this book are select representatives of those I have learned from and am challenged by. They hail from Japan, Holland, Russia, India, and England as well as North America. Not all are orthodox Christians and one, Mahatma Gandhi, decided against the Christian faith. Yet all were permanently changed by their contact with Jesus. Half of them I met in person and interviewed, in some cases developing a lifelong friendship. The other half I know only indirectly, through the writings they left behind. Strangely, those furthest from orthodox Christianity—Gandhi, Tolstoy, Dostoevsky, Endo—have best helped me understand my own faith, by shining light on it from an angle I had not considered.

Writers are parasites, leeching life from other people, and I am grateful to have had some share in these extraordinary lives. A few of them helped change history and the planet. Others faithfully responded to an inner call in a public arena. And some simply sat at home with a pad of paper, reflecting, sorting out, recording their lives and thoughts for posterity. Now I do the same, presenting these my mentors as if in a portrait gallery, in hopes of passing on their legacy to others.

The thirteen people you will meet here have one thing in common: their impact on me. For that reason, in each chapter I have asked myself what difference they made in my life. How have I changed because of my contact, direct or indirect, with this baker's dozen? Over time, the people I have profiled became shapers of my faith, my personal "cloud of witnesses." If I were invited to a convention full of skeptics, or representatives of another religion, and asked to explain my faith, these are the companions I would want along. I could simply point to them and say, "Christians are not perfect, by any means, but they can be people made fully alive. This is what they look like." Each stands at the top of his or her field, and credits personal faith as one of the reasons why.

I must say, writing these tributes has for me been an exercise of health and even joy. I did not set out with an agenda, to convert anyone, to defend the church or to critique it. I merely want to introduce others to a roomful of exceptional people whom I cannot, and have no wish to, get out of mind.

Fred Rogers, host of the children's television show "Mister Rogers' Neighborhood," draws upon a tradition every time he speaks. He asks the audience to pause for a minute of silence and think about all those who have helped them become who they are. Once, in a prestigious gathering at the White House, he was given only eight minutes to address children's issues, and still he devoted one of those minutes to silence. "Invariably, that's what people will remember," he says, "that silence." Usually a person from the past floats into mind—a grandparent, or elementary school teacher, or eccentric uncle or aunt. I have spent many minutes of silence pondering Mister Rogers' question. This book represents my answer. These are the ones who have helped restore to me the mislaid treasures of God.

The day I graduated from high school near Atlanta, I began a summer job digging ditches in order to save money for college. Our work crew consisted of four muscular black men and one skinny white kid—me. The white foreman dropped us off, parked his truck under a nearby shade tree, lit a cigarette, and began reading the sports pages. Although we started working just after sunrise, the air was already hot and muggy.

I dug in with gusto, rhythmically jamming my pointed shovel into the ground, pressing my foot down on the metal lip with a wiggle that loosened the dirt, then tossing it onto a pile a few feet away. *Thunk, swish; thunk, swish.* The four black men stood around watching this flurry of movement in amazement, as if I had invented an exotic new sport. Finally one of them said to me, "Son, you gon' kill yo'self like that. You won't last till water break. Watch me." He pushed the shovel blade into the ground, stepped on it, then paused to take a drag on a cigarette, leaning against the shovel handle. A minute or two later, he nonchalantly threw the dirt onto the pile I had made, set the shovel down, and took a few more drags. The other three men followed suit.

Anxious to impress the foreman on my first day, I compromised with a pace somewhere between theirs and mine. By water break, at ten o'clock, I knew without a doubt that my mentor had been right. My T-shirt was drenched in sweat and streaked with red Georgia clay. The joints in my feet hurt. It felt

Chapter 2

MARTIN

LUTHER

KING, JR.

A LONG

NIGHT'S

JOURNEY

INTO DAY

as if professional wrestlers had been jumping up and down on my arms. My back ached like an old man's, and I walked hunchbacked to the truck for water.

We lined up at the rear of the truck, taking turns to drink from a metal container that had been sitting in the hot sun all morning, which made the water even hotter than the air temperature. A single battered tin cup hung from a chain beside the water can and the men took turns drinking from it. Suddenly the foreman spied me in his rearview mirror. "Boy, whatcha doin'?" he said. "Come up here."

I dutifully reported to the truck cab. "Get in," he said, in a tone of disgust. "You ain't supposed to drink that stuff. That's nigger water! Here, I brung us some." He loosened the cap of a glass-lined thermos and poured ice water into a paper cup.

I was born in Atlanta, Georgia, in 1949, five years before the Supreme Court ruled in favor of integrated schools, fifteen years before a civil rights law forced restaurants and motels to serve all races, and sixteen years before the U.S. Congress guaranteed minorities the right to vote. Gas stations in those days had three labeled rest rooms: White Women, White Men, and Colored. Department stores had two drinking fountains, White and Colored. Many museums had one day a week reserved for Coloreds; otherwise they were barred entrance. When I rode the Atlanta buses, workmen and maids sat dutifully in the rear section and were required by law to give up their seats if white riders wanted them. In neighboring Alabama, blacks had to enter the front door to pay the driver, then exit the bus and walk outside back to the rear door. Mean-spirited drivers sometimes shut the rear doors early and drove off, stranding black customers who had already paid their fare.

My grandfather told us stories about the old days when his grandfather owned a plantation full of slaves, many of whom took the last name "Yancey" after emancipation. We would sometimes try to pick out the black Yanceys by their first names in the phone book. As a teenager he had seen bodies swinging from lampposts during the race

riot of 1906, when angry whites lynched nearly fifty black men after rumors of a sexual insult. He used to take my father and uncles on visits to the Confederate Veterans' Home where they would listen to the
old men reminisce about "the War of Northern Aggression," their term
for the Civil War. (One of those uncles would later pack up and move
his family to Australia after the courts forced schools to integrate.)
Each Christmas, as we sat at my grandmother's Southern feast of vegetables, mashed potatoes, biscuits, and ham and turkey, black em-
ployees from my grandfather's truck-body shop would appear at the
back door, knocking and then standing there awkwardly until he
dropped a few silver dollars into their hands as a Christmas bonus.

We lived in apartheid conditions. Although Atlanta had almost as
many black residents as whites, we ate in different restaurants, played
in different parks, and attended different schools and churches.
Sometimes I would see signs that read, "No dogs or Coloreds allowed."
By law black people could not serve on juries, send children to white
public schools, use a whites-only bathroom, sleep in a white motel, sit
on the main floor of a movie theater, swim in a white swimming pool.
(Because resorts in Alabama did not serve black people, Martin
Luther King, Jr., spent his wedding night in the closest thing to a public accommodation available, a funeral parlor owned by family
friends.) Our governor called for the Georgia Tech football team to forfeit their Sugar Bowl game invitation in 1955 when he learned that the
opposing team, Pittsburgh, had a black player on its reserve squad.
When a college professor applied to become the first of his race to enroll at the University of Mississippi, the authorities committed him to
the state mental institution on the grounds that only an insane Negro
would want to attend Ole Miss.

As a child I did not question the system we lived under because no
one around me questioned it. The most famous person in our church,
after all, was an occasional visitor named Lester Maddox, who sometimes spoke at the Men's Brotherhood meetings. A high school
dropout, Maddox owned the Pickrick, a fried chicken restaurant, and
placed ads in the Atlanta newspapers each week denouncing the federal government for trying to take away his property rights. When the

government insisted that he had to serve black diners and a group showed up to test their new privileges, his regular customers chased them away with ax handles while Maddox waved a .32 caliber pistol. He then closed his restaurant in protest, wrote even shriller newspaper ads, and opened a towering memorial to the death of free enterprise, which I visited. Funereal music played softly in the background as we mourners filed past a black-draped coffin in which reposed a copy of the U.S. Bill of Rights.

Maddox's museum sold souvenir pickax handles resembling those used by policemen to beat civil rights demonstrators. He offered three sizes, Daddy, Mama, and Junior, and I bought the Junior size with money earned from my paper route. It looked like a policeman's nightstick, and I kept it in my closet. (Maddox, a folk hero to Southern whites, went on to bécome Georgia's governor in 1967, and then because he could not succeed himself he got elected lieutenant governor and from that office campaigned as a candidate for president of the United States on the American Independent Party ticket in 1972.)

Black people gave us someone to look down on, someone to mock and feel superior to. My family moved every year or two when the rent went up, and lived sometimes in government projects and sometimes in trailer parks. Sociologically, we may have qualified as "poor white trash." But at least we were white.

Nowadays, historians who look back on the 1950s and 1960s in the South declare it a time ripe for social change. That depends on your perspective. Among my family, friends, neighbors, and church members, the time was most unripe. We viewed ourselves as under siege, our entire way of life threatened by outside agitators.

When the principal announced over the intercom system that President John F. Kennedy had been shot, some students in my high school stood and cheered. As the president who had proposed civil rights legislation and then backed it up by sending federal marshals to make the University of Mississippi accept its first black student, James Meredith, Kennedy represented an intolerable threat to our comfortable enclave of racism. Until then, Republicans like Eisenhower and Nixon had been the civil rights enemies; Democrats were beholden to Southern "Dixiecrats," who controlled three fourths of the congressional committee chairs and ruled in the Senate by filibuster. With Kennedy, though, an enemy of the South lived in the White House.

My high school was named for a Confederate general, John B. Gordon. In 1966, when I graduated from that school, no black student had ever set foot on campus. Black families had moved into the neighborhood, and whites on all sides were fleeing to Stone Mountain and points east, yet no black parents dared enroll their children in our school. We all believed then, and I have no reason to disbelieve now, that Malcolm, a short kid with a crew cut who wore metal taps on his shoes and loved to pick fights, singlehandedly kept them away. Reputed to be the nephew of the Grand Dragon of the Ku Klux Klan, Malcolm had put out the word that the first black student in our school would go home in a hearse.

The Ku Klux Klan had an almost mystical hold on our imaginations. I wrote school papers about it. It was an invisible army, we were taught, a last line of defense to preserve the Christian purity of the South. I remember as a child watching a funeral procession for a Dragon or Wizard or some such bigwig in the KKK. Caught trying to turn left across traffic, we had to wait until the entire motorcade passed. Dozens, scores, hundreds of cars slid past us, each one driven by a figure wearing a silky white or crimson robe and a pointed hood with slits cut out for eyes. The day was hot, and the drivers' sunburned elbows jutted from open car windows at acute angles. Who were they, these druids reincarnate? They could be anyone—the corner gas station attendant, a church deacon, my uncle—no one knew for sure. The next day's *Atlanta Journal* reported that the funeral procession had been five miles long.

I remember also a Fourth of July rally held at a fairgrounds racetrack. Sponsors had brought together such luminaries as George Wallace and a national officer of the ultra-conservative John Birch Society, as well as Atlanta's own Lester Maddox. We waved tiny rebel flags and cheered as the speakers denounced Washington for trampling states' rights. A group of twenty black men, showing bravery such as I had never before seen, attended that rally, sitting in a conspicuous dark clump in the bleachers, not participating, just observing.

I saw no one give a signal, but shortly after a rousing rendition of "Dixie," hooded Klansmen arose from the crowd and began an ominous climb down those bleachers, surrounding the cluster of black men. The blacks stood and huddled together, looking around in desperation, but there was no escape route. At last, frantic, a few of them started climbing a thirty-foot chain fence designed to protect spectators from the race cars, and the Klansmen scrambled to catch them. The speaker's bullhorn fell silent, and we all turned to watch the Klansmen pry loose the clinging bodies, as though removing prey from a trap. They began beating them with fists and with ax handles like the ones Lester Maddox sold. After a time, a few Georgia State Patrol officers lazily made their way over and made the Klansmen stop.

Although nearly four decades have passed, I can still hear the crowd's throaty rebel yells, the victims' pleas, and the crunch of the Klansmen's bare fists against flesh. And with much shame I still recall the adolescent thrill I felt—my first experience of the mob instinct—mixed in with horror, as I watched that scene transpire.

Today I feel shame, remorse, and also repentance. It took years for God to break the stranglehold of blatant racism in me—I wonder if any of us gets free of its more subtle forms—and I now see that sin as one of the most poisonous, with perhaps the most toxic societal effects. When experts discuss the underclass in urban America, they blame in turn drugs, changing values, systemic poverty, and the breakdown of the nuclear family. Sometimes I wonder if all those problems are consequences of a deeper, underlying cause: our centuries-old sin of racism.

These memories of racism from my youth all came flooding back as I read biographies of Martin Luther King, Jr., the Atlanta citizen whom Lester Maddox had labeled "an enemy of our country." In successive years, two long and incisive accounts of the King years won Pulitzer Prizes: David Garrow's *Bearing the Cross* in 1987 and Taylor Branch's *Parting the Waters* in 1989. Garrow's text runs for 723 pages and Branch's for 1,004, and the hours I pored over them gave me an odd sense resembling, but not exactly, déjà vu.

Although I was traveling familiar terrain—Selma, Montgomery, Albany, Atlanta, Birmingham, St. Augustine, Jackson—everything about the landscape had changed. The historians presented these names, and I too now viewed them, as the battlefields of a courageous moral struggle. When I grew up in the South of the 1960s, however, they represented a geography of siege. Troublemakers from the North, carpet-bagging students, rabbis, and ministers protected by federal agents, were invading our territory. And the person leading the march in each of those cities was our number-one public enemy, a native of my own Atlanta, whom the *Atlanta Journal* regularly accused of "inciting riot in the name of justice." Folks in my church had their own name for him: Martin Lucifer Coon.

King's appropriation of the Christian gospel galled us most. He was, after all, an ordained minister, and even my fundamentalist church had to acknowledge the integrity of his father, Daddy King, respected pastor of Ebenezer Baptist Church. We had our ways of resolving that cognitive dissonance, of course. We said that the younger King was a card-carrying Communist, a Marxist agent who merely posed as a minister. (Had not Khrushchev memorized the four gospels as a youth and Stalin attended seminary?) George Wallace cited FBI sources to accuse King of belonging to more Communist-front organizations than any man in the United States.

We said that Daddy King had raised Martin right, but that the liberal Crozer Seminary up north had polluted his mind. He followed the social gospel, if any gospel at all. (We never asked ourselves what conservative seminaries might have accepted Martin's application back then.) And when the rumors about King's sexual dalliances surfaced, the case against him was closed. Martin Luther King, Jr., was a fraud, a *poseur,* not a true Christian.

Recent biographies of King deal with these accusations in exhaustive detail. Most of the rumors trace back to leaks from FBI agents, for J. Edgar Hoover had a personal vendetta against King and, with Robert Kennedy's authorization, placed wiretaps on King and his associates.

President John Kennedy personally ordered King to break off contact with two close advisers because of alleged Communist ties. King himself never had Communist sympathies, although he sometimes tired of the injustices under democratic capitalism. True, some of his trusted advisers had belonged to the Communist Party years before, but King had friends across the political spectrum. He tended to judge people on the basis of their commitment to civil rights, and by that measure leftists had far more to offer than, say, Southern clergymen.

During King's time, the FBI looked with suspicion on white people who mixed easily with friends from a variety of races and economic groups. These were potential Communists. If only Christians, and not Communists, had fit that FBI profile, I now lament. Instead, we Southern Christians were, by and large, the foes of justice, and the truly Communist press overseas was trumpeting the story of segregation in "Christian America."

As for the other charge, accusations of King's sexual immorality reflect historical fact, not rumors. The FBI taped numerous episodes in King's hotel rooms, and thanks to the Freedom of Information Act historians can study the actual transcripts. Ralph Abernathy has revealed that King carried on extramarital affairs up until the eve of his death. One FBI agent (William Sullivan, who rose to become assistant director of the Bureau) sent King some of their recordings along with a note urging him to commit suicide: "You are done. There is but one way out for you. You better take it before your filthy abnormal fraudulent self is bared to the nation."

Besides the sexual immorality, King has been accused of plagiarism as well. He inserted into his graduate school thesis, his writings, and sometimes his speeches, long sections lifted without credit from other sources. Frankly, I find it easier to understand King's sexual failings, a sin in which he has much company, than his plagiarism. A master of riveting prose, why did he feel the need to steal someone else's?

Relentless pressures buffeted King from all sides. He faced death threats from segregationists as well as the FBI. A bomb went off in his home. Black churches were burning every week in the South. His volunteers were being threatened, beaten, and jailed, and some of them were dying. Often his Southern Christian Leadership Conference had to skip payroll, and his most effective fund-raiser was one of the advisers President Kennedy had demanded that he fire. Newspapers from the *Atlanta Journal* to the *New York Times* condemned his methods. The NAACP criticized him for being too radical, while SNCC (Student Nonviolent Coordinating Committee) accused him of timidity. Student demonstrators in a dozen cities pleaded with him to accompany them to jail; volunteers in Mississippi urged him to come risk his life with them. Should he concentrate on voting rights or on segregated restaurants? What unjust laws should he violate? What about defying court orders? Should he stick to civil rights or expand his focus to poverty? What about the war in Vietnam?

I better understand now the pressures that King faced his entire adult life, pressures that surely contributed to his failures. King's moral weaknesses provide a convenient excuse for anyone who wants to avoid his message, and because of those weaknesses some Christians still discount the genuineness of his faith. (These Christians might want to review the list of outstanding people of faith in Hebrews 11, a list which includes such moral deviants as Noah, Abraham, Jacob, Rahab, Samson, and David.) I certainly once dismissed him. Yet now I can hardly read a page from King's life, or a paragraph from his speeches, without sensing the centrality of his Christian conviction. I own a collection of his sermon tapes, and every time I listen to them I am swept up in the sheer power of his gospel-based message, delivered with an eloquence that has never been matched.

David Garrow builds his book around the scene of King's supernatural call, early in his career. "It was the most important night of his life," writes Garrow, "the one he always would think back to in future years when the pressures again seemed to be too great." King had been thrust into civil rights leadership in Montgomery, Alabama, after Rosa Parks had made her brave decision not to move to the back of the bus. The black community formed a new organization to lead a bus boycott and by default chose as a compromise candidate for its leadership the new minister in town, King, who at age twenty-six looked "more like a boy than a man." Growing up in middle-class surroundings, with a

kind of inherited religion from his preacher father, he hardly felt qualified to lead a great moral crusade.

As soon as King's leadership of the movement was announced, the
threats from the Klan began. Not only the Klan—within days King was
arrested for driving 30 miles per hour in a 25 mph zone and thrown into
the Montgomery city jail. The following night King, shaken by his first
jail experience, sat up in his kitchen wondering if he could take it anymore. Should he resign? It was around midnight. He felt agitated, and
full of fear. A few minutes before, the phone had rung. "Nigger, we are
tired of you and your mess now. And if you aren't out of this town in
three days, we're going to blow your brains out, and blow up your
house."

King sat staring at an untouched cup of coffee and tried to think
of a way out, a way to quietly surrender leadership and resume
the serene life of scholarship he had planned. In the next room
lay his wife Coretta, already asleep, along with their newborn
daughter Yolanda. Here is how King remembers it in a sermon he
preached:

> And I sat at that table thinking about that little girl and think-
> ing about the fact that she could be taken away from me any
> minute. And I started thinking about a dedicated, devoted and
> loyal wife, who was over there asleep. . . . And I got to the point
> that I couldn't take it anymore. I was weak. . . .
>
> And I discovered then that religion had to become real to
> me, and I had to know God for myself. And I bowed down over
> that cup of coffee. I never will forget it. . . . I prayed a prayer,
> and I prayed out loud that night. I said, "Lord, I'm down here
> trying to do what's right. I think I'm right. I think the cause that
> we represent is right. But Lord, I must confess that I'm weak
> now. I'm faltering. I'm losing my courage."
>
> . . . And it seemed at that moment that I could hear an inner
> voice saying to me, "Martin Luther, stand up for righteousness.
> Stand up for justice. Stand up for truth. And lo I will be with
> you, even until the end of the world." . . . I heard the voice of Je-

sus saying still to fight on. He promised never to leave me, never to leave me alone. No never alone. No never alone. He promised never to leave me, never to leave me alone.

(From sermon tape)

Three nights later, as promised, a bomb exploded on the front porch of King's home, filling the house with smoke and broken glass but injuring no one. King took it calmly: "My religious experience a few nights before had given me the strength to face it."

David Garrow weaves his narrative around that "visitation" at the kitchen table, returning to it again and again, because King drew strength from that memory at every hinge moment in his life. For him it became the bedrock of personal faith, an anointing from God for a particular task. As I read accounts of King's life, and his many references to that night, I am struck by the simplicity of the message he received: "I am with you." Those words convey an underlying theme of the Bible: the *Immanuel* ("God with us") presence of God. Over the next thirteen years of his career, King had other religious experiences, and many moments of crisis, but none to match what happened that night at his kitchen table. This one word sufficed.

Meanwhile, we in the Deep South viewed Martin Luther King, Jr., through a different religious lens. During my adolescence I attended two different churches. The first, a Baptist church with more than a thousand members, took pride in its identity as a "Bible-loving church where the folks are friendly," and in its support of 105 foreign missionaries, whose prayer cards were pinned to a wall-sized map of the world at the rear of the sanctuary. That church was one of the main watering holes for famous evangelical speakers. I learned the Bible there. It had a loose affiliation with the Southern Baptist Convention, a denomination formed in 1845 when Northern abolitionists decided that slave owners were unfit to be missionaries and the Southerners separated in protest. Even Southern Baptists were too liberal for most of us, though, which is why we maintained only a loose affiliation. Some of them smoked tobacco, and over fierce objections the convention had even endorsed recent civil rights legislation.

In the 1960s, as black students sought to integrate Atlanta's churches, our deacon board mobilized lookout squads who took turns patrolling the entrances lest any black "troublemakers" appear. I still have one of the cards the deacons printed up to give to any civil rights demonstrators who might appear:

> Believing the motives of your group to be ulterior and foreign to the teaching of God's word, *we cannot extend a welcome to you* and respectfully request you to leave the premises quietly. Scripture does NOT teach 'the brotherhood of man and the fatherhood of God.' He is the Creator of all, but only the Father of those who have been regenerated.
>
> If any one of you is here with a sincere desire to know Jesus Christ as Saviour and Lord, we shall be glad to deal individually with you from the Word of God.
>
> (Unanimous Statement of Pastor and Deacons, August 1960)

After the *Brown v. Board of Education* ruling, our church founded a private school as a haven for whites, expressly banning all black students. A few members left the church in protest when the kindergarten refused to admit the daughter of a black Bible professor, but most approved of the decision. A year later the church board rejected a Carver Bible Institute student for membership (his name was Tony Evans and he went on to become a prominent pastor and speaker based in Dallas, Texas).

The next church I attended was smaller, more fundamentalist, and more overtly racist (the one whose "burial" I recently attended). There I learned the theological basis for racism. The pastor taught that the Hebrew word *Ham* meant "burnt black," making Noah's son Ham the father of Negro races, and that in a curse Noah had consigned him to life as a lowly servant (Genesis 9). That is when I heard my pastor explain why black people make such good waiters and household servants. He acted out their moves on the platform, swiveling his hips as if to avoid a table, pretending to balance a tray of food above his head, and we all laughed at his antics. "The colored waiter is good at that job because that's the job God destined him for in the curse of Ham," he said. No one bothered to point out that the curse was actually pronounced on Noah's grandson Canaan, not Ham.

Around that same time, Mississippi's *Baptist Record* published an article arguing that God meant for whites to rule over blacks because "a race whose mentality averages on borderline idiocy" is obviously "bereft of any divine blessing." If anyone questioned such racist doctrine, pastors pulled out the trump card of miscegenation, or mixing of the races, which some speculated was the sin that had prompted God to destroy the world in Noah's day. A single question, "Do you want your daughter bringing home a black boyfriend?" silenced all arguments about race.

You can still read such twisted theology today, on Internet sites sponsored by white supremacists. Far fewer people accept it now, though, and one of the main reasons—for me, especially—is the prophetic role of Martin Luther King, Jr. It took a man of his moral force to awaken churches from what Reinhold Niebuhr called "the sin of triviality" to confront the broader claims of the gospel.

The word *prophet* comes to mind because King, like those Old Testament figures, endeavored to change an entire nation through a straightforward moral appeal. The passion and intensity of the biblical prophets has long fascinated me, for most of them faced an audience every bit as stubborn, prejudiced, and cantankerous as I was during my teenage years. With what moral lever can one move a whole nation? Studying the prophets, I note that virtually all of them followed a two-pronged approach.

First, they gave a short-range view of what God requires now. In the Old Testament, this usually consisted of an exhortation to simple acts of faithfulness. Rebuild the Temple. Purify your marriages. Help the poor. Destroy idols and put God first. The prophets never stopped there, however. They also gave a long-range view to respond to the people's deepest questions. How can we believe that God loves us in the face of so much suffering? How can we believe in a just God when the world seems ruled by a conspiracy of evil? Prophets answered such questions by reminding their audience of who God is, and by painting a glowing picture of a future kingdom of righteousness.

In true prophetic tradition, Martin Luther King, Jr., used that same two-pronged approach. For him, the short-range view called for one thing above all else: nonviolence. King matriculated to seminary the year that Mahatma Gandhi died, and from him, not from Christians in the United States, he gained a vision of how to change a nation. Gandhi, said King, was "the first person in history to live the love ethic of Jesus above mere interaction between individuals." Somehow Gandhi had found a way to mobilize a movement around Jesus' lofty principles of hope and love and nonviolence.

Like Gandhi, King looked to the Sermon on the Mount as a textbook for activism:

> When I went to Montgomery as a pastor, I had not the slightest idea that I would later become involved in a crisis in which nonviolent resistance would be applicable. I neither started the protest nor suggested it. I simply responded to the call of the people for a spokesman. When the protest began, my mind, consciously or unconsciously, was driven back to the Sermon on the Mount, with its sublime teachings on love, and to the Gandhian method of nonviolent resistance.
>
> (From *Stride Toward Freedom*)

King traveled with his wife to India in 1959 to observe firsthand the impact of a nonviolent revolution. "I left India," he reported, "more convinced than ever before that nonviolent resistance is the most potent weapon available to oppressed people in their struggle for freedom." For other models, he looked back to the biblical prophet Daniel and his three friends, who disobeyed the laws of Nebuchadnezzar, and to the early Christians, who faced hungry lions rather than submit to unjust laws of the Roman Empire. As he later articulated, "One who breaks an unjust law must do so openly, lovingly and with a willingness to accept the penalty."

The civil rights movement gave King many opportunities to test his nonviolent philosophy. A deranged woman stabbed him in New York, her weapon lodging a fraction of an inch from his aorta. A white man in Birmingham rushed the platform and pummeled King with his fists. ("Don't touch him!" King cried to his supporters, who surrounded the attacker. "We have to pray for him.") Southern sheriffs delighted in roughing up their famous adversary as they handcuffed him and hauled him away in paddy wagons. They clubbed his marchers with nightsticks, sicced German shepherd dogs on them, blasted them with water cannons that cracked ribs and sent bodies sprawling on the streets.

Half a century later, we may lose sight of how excruciatingly difficult it was for King to maintain his nonviolent stance. After you've been hit on the head with a policeman's nightstick for the dozenth time, and received yet another jolt from a jailer's cattle prod, and can point to no progress at all resulting from your suffering, you begin to question the effectiveness of meek submission. Many blacks abandoned King over this issue. Students especially, the intrepid heroes of the Freedom Rides through Alabama and Mississippi, drifted toward Black Power rhetoric after their colleagues kept getting murdered. SNCC, an organization with nonviolence in its name, moved toward armed revolt and derided King as "de Lawd." In Chicago, Black Power advocates booed King off the stage at a mass rally.

As riots broke out in places like Los Angeles, Chicago, and Harlem, King traveled from city to city trying to cool tempers and reminding demonstrators that moral change is not accomplished through immoral means. He had learned that principle from the Sermon on the Mount, and almost all his speeches reiterated the message. "Christianity," he said, "has always insisted that the cross we bear precedes the crown we wear. To be a Christian one must take up his cross, with all its difficulties and agonizing and tension-packed content, and carry it until that very cross leaves its mark upon us and redeems us to that more excellent way which comes only through suffering."

King clung to nonviolence because he profoundly believed that only a movement based on love could keep the oppressed from becoming a mirror image of their oppressors. He wanted to change the hearts of the white people, yes, but in a way that did not in the process harden the hearts of the blacks he was leading toward freedom. Nonviolence, he believed, "will save the Negro from seeking to substitute one tyranny for another."

When he accepted the Nobel Peace Prize in 1964, King referred yet again to the principles he had learned from the Sermon on the Mount: "When the years have rolled past and when the blazing light of truth is focused on this marvelous age in which we live, men and women will know and children will be taught that we have a finer land, a better people, a more noble civilization, because these humble children of God were willing to 'suffer for righteousness' sake.' "

Historians tell of King's tense encounter with Chicago's tough mayor Richard J. Daley. The movement supporters were feeling betrayed, believing they had reached an understanding with Daley that would permit them to march through Chicago with police protection in exchange for calling off a boycott. But Daley had double-crossed them by obtaining a court order banning further marches. As was his style, King sat silent through most of the contentious meeting, letting others air their views. The mood was hostile, and it looked as if the meeting would break apart in bitterness. King finally spoke up, with what one onlooker described as a "grand and quiet and careful and calming eloquence."

> Let me say that if you are tired of demonstrations, I am tired of demonstrating. I am tired of the threat of death. I want to live. I don't want to be a martyr. And there are moments when I doubt if I am going to make it through. I am tired of getting hit, tired of being beaten, tired of going to jail. But the important thing is not how tired I am; the important thing is to get rid of the conditions that lead us to march.
>
> Now, gentlemen, you know we don't have much. We don't have much money. We don't really have much education, and we don't have political power. We have only our bodies and you are asking us to give up the one thing that we have when you say, "Don't march."   (From *Bearing the Cross*)

King's speech changed the mood of the meeting, and ultimately led to a new agreement with Mayor Daley.

W*e have only our bodies,* King said, and in the end that was what brought the civil rights movement the victory it had been seeking so long. When I was in high school, the same students who cheered the news of President Kennedy's assassination also cheered King's televised encounters with Southern sheriffs, police dogs, and water cannons. Little did we know that by doing so we were playing directly into King's strategy. He deliberately sought out individuals like Sheriff Bull Connor and stage-managed scenes of confrontation, accepting jail, beatings, and other brutalities, because he believed a complacent nation would rally around his cause only when they saw the evil of racism manifest in its ugliest extreme.

In that goal, King succeeded spectacularly. A judge in DeKalb County, where I lived, required King to wear not only handcuffs but also leg and arm shackles in his courtroom as he sentenced him to four months at hard labor on a state road gang for driving a car registered in Alabama not Georgia. A Houston jury sentenced an SNCC volunteer to thirty years in prison for giving one marijuana cigarette to an undercover policeman. Mississippi courts jailed voter registration volunteers for "inciting a riot" when their homes and churches were shot up and bombed by the Klan. A bomb killed four little girls in Sunday School at a church in Birmingham.

"I have to do this—to expose myself—to bring this hate into the open," King explained after being knocked to the ground by a rock that struck him in the right temple. His own family sometimes questioned his wisdom. "Well, you didn't get this nonviolence from me," Daddy King said as his son faced yet another arrest in Birmingham. "You must have got it from your mama."

By exposing evil in cold light, King was attempting to provoke a national response of moral outrage—a concept my friends and I were not equipped to understand. Many historians point to one event as the single moment in which the movement attained at last a critical mass of support for the cause of civil rights. It occurred on a bridge outside Selma, Alabama, when Sheriff Jim Clark turned his policemen loose on unarmed black demonstrators. The mounted troopers spurred their horses at a gallop into the crowd of marchers, flailing away with their nightsticks, cracking heads and driving bodies to the ground. As whites on the sidelines whooped and cheered, the troopers shot tear gas into the panicked crowd. Most Americans got their first glimpse of the scene when ABC television interrupted its Sunday movie, *Judgment at Nuremberg*, to show footage. What the viewers saw broadcast from Alabama bore a horrifying resemblance to what they were watching about Nazi Germany. Eight days later President Lyndon Johnson submitted the Voting Rights Act of 1965 to the U.S. Congress.

We have only our bodies, King said. Not once in his career did an official of Selma or Jackson or Albany or Cicero respond to his entreaties by saying, "You know, Dr. King, you're right. We are racists, and these discriminatory laws are unjust, unconstitutional, unbiblical, and just plain wrong. We're sorry. We'll repent and start over." Not once. It took more than King's prophetic words to cut through the moral calluses of bigots like me. It took the bodies of the marchers in Selma and all the other places; it took King's own body in Memphis. Martin Luther King, Jr., did many things wrong, but one thing he did right. Against all odds, against all instincts of self-preservation, he stayed true to the short view. He did not strike back. Where others called for revenge, he called for love and forgiveness.

King recorded his struggle with forgiveness in "Letter from Birmingham City Jail," an amazing document scrawled on the margins of newspapers and on toilet paper, then smuggled out of his cell by friends. Outside the jail, Southern pastors were denouncing him as a Communist, mobs were yelling "Hang the nigger!" and policemen were threatening his unarmed supporters. In such circumstances King had to fast for several days in order to achieve the spiritual discipline necessary for him to forgive his enemies. As he explained, "We love men not because we like them, nor because their ways appeal to us, nor even because they possess some kind of divine spark. We love every man because God loves him."

The civil rights workers, however, needed something more than short-range admonitions toward love and nonviolence. They needed the long view of faith that the abuse they were taking would contribute to ultimate triumph. Already convinced of the justness of their cause, they wanted someone to lift their sights beyond the long string of disheartening failures. We now look back on the civil rights movement as a steady tidal surge toward victory. At the time, facing daily confrontations with the power structure and under constant intimidation from policemen, judges, and even the FBI, civil rights workers had no assurance of victory. We forget how many nights they spent in rank Southern jails. Most of the time the present looked impossibly bleak, the future even bleaker.

To such demoralized troops, King offered a vision of the world held in the hands of a just God. In 1961 he was performing the same role as had Old Testament prophets in 500 B.C.: he was raising the sights of God's people to the permanent things. Already, at that early date, students were getting restless, and here is what King told those students:

> There is something in this student movement which says to us, that we shall overcome. Before the victory is won some may have to get scarred up, but we shall overcome. Before the victory of brotherhood is achieved, some will maybe face physical death, but we shall overcome. Before the victory is won, some will lose jobs, some will be called communists, and reds, merely because they believe in brotherhood, some will be dismissed as dangerous rabblerousers and agitators merely because they're standing up for what is right, but we shall overcome. That is the basis of this movement, and as I like to say, there is something in this universe that justifies Carlyle in saying that no lie can live forever. We shall overcome because there is something in this universe which justifies William Cullen Bryant in saying truth crushed to earth shall rise again. We shall overcome because there is something in this universe that justifies James Russell Lowell in saying, truth forever on the scaffold, wrong forever on the throne. Yet that scaffold sways the future, and behind the dim unknown, standeth God within the shadow, keeping watch above His own.   (From *The New Yorker,* April 6, 1987)

For King, the long view meant remembering that, no matter how things appear at any given moment, God reigns. Later, when the famous march from Selma finally made it to the state capitol, the building which once served as the capitol of the Confederacy and from which the rebel flag still flew, King addressed those scarred and weary marchers from the steps:

> I know that you are asking today, "How long will it take?" I come to say to you this afternoon, however difficult the moment, however frustrating the hour, it will not be long, because truth pressed to earth will rise again.
>
> How long? Not long, because no lie can live forever.
>
> How long? Not long, because you still reap what you sow.
>
> How long? Not long, because the arm of the moral universe is long but it bends toward justice.
>
> How long? Not long, 'cause mine eyes have seen the glory of the coming of the Lord, trampling out the vintage where the grapes of wrath are stored. He has loosed the fateful lightning of his terrible swift sword. His truth is marching on.
>
> He has sounded forth the trumpets that shall never call retreat. He is lifting up the hearts of man before His judgment seat. Oh, be swift, my soul, to answer him. Be jubilant, my feet. Our God is marching on.   (From *The New Yorker,* April 6, 1987)

Speeches like these filled the movement with hope when there was little else to cling to. They are what inspired one seventy-two-year-old female volunteer to say with a weary smile, "My feets is tired, but my soul is at rest."

A prophet calls us to daily acts of obedience, regardless of personal cost, regardless of whether we feel successful or rewarded. And a prophet also reminds us that no failure, no suffering, no discouragement is final for the God who stands within the shadows, keeping watch above His own. A prophet who can convey both those messages with power just may change the world. While Martin Luther King, Jr., lived on earth, I, his neighbor, did not listen to what he said. I was quick to pounce on his flaws, and slow to recognize my own sin. But because he stayed faithful, in the short view by offering his body as a target but never as a weapon, and in the long view by holding before us his dream of a new kingdom of peace and justice and love, he became a prophet for me, the unlikeliest of followers.

I n 1974, ten years after the civil rights bill that spawned such conflict, I made my first visit to Mississippi, the heart of Southern resistance. I had moved away from the South and was trying to put my past behind me. Living in Chicago, I worked as the editor of *Campus Life*, a Christian magazine for young people, which took a progressive stance on social issues. Thanks to people like Dr. King, I saw that the Southern white church, my church, had stubbornly defended evil and not good. For a time I blamed God, and not the church, but my reading of the Old Testament prophets and of Jesus finally convinced me that God had always stood on the side of the oppressed, and for justice. I vowed, as a writer, to try and make amends.

I had heard about healing taking place between the races, especially in my home city of Atlanta, but wondered just how much had truly changed since my childhood. To find out, I accepted the invitation of John Perkins to visit the small town (population three thousand) of Mendenhall, thirty-two miles south of Jackson.

Perkins, a black minister, had lived through the worst nightmares of the civil rights movement. He knew most of the principal players on the Mississippi scene: Robert Moses, a soft-spoken philosophy student from Harvard, one of King's first volunteers, who went on to lead the SNCC voter registration drive in Mississippi, gaining almost legendary status for his calm persistence in the face of beatings, imprisonment, and dynamite and rifle attacks; Fannie Lou Hamer, "the lady who know how to sing," one of twenty children of an illiterate cotton picker, who signed on to register black voters in Sunflower County, Mississippi, and for her efforts was beaten senseless by local sheriffs, sustaining injuries from which she died, but not before leading an alternate delegation from Mississippi to the 1964 Democratic Convention; Medgar Evers, the NAACP field secretary who had first invited King to Mississippi and who was gunned down by an assassin in his driveway, just as his wife and daughters were running out to greet him.

I heard these stories and many more from John Perkins during the week I spent in Mississippi. I slept on a fold-out sofa in the living room of his home, which meant I got very little sleep since Perkins went to bed late and rose long before sunrise to read his Bible and pore over newspapers and journals piled on his kitchen table. But it also meant we had much time to talk, over coffee at the table, in his car as we drove through the cotton fields, in his office down the street. He told me of his own boyhood, of the night his older brother got shot dead by a police-man for making too much noise while standing in line in front of the Colored entrance of a movie theater, of his struggle to educate himself, and of his stint in the Army and his vow never to return to Mississippi.

Perkins kept that vow for a while, beginning a successful career as a union worker in greater Los Angeles. An unexpected conversion to Christianity, which he had always considered "the white man's reli-gion," derailed that career. Unable to get out of his mind the disad-vantaged neighbors he had left behind in Mississippi, he gradually felt a call from God to return, in June 1960.

At the time, most local ministers of Perkins's evangelical persua-sion stuck to preaching the gospel and left human needs to social workers and government agencies. Perkins did start a church and Bible institute, and launched a radio program called "Voice of Calvary." Yet he also accepted the broader mission proclaimed by Jesus:

> To preach the gospel to the poor
> To heal the brokenhearted
> To proclaim liberty to the captives
> And recovery of sight to the blind
> To set at liberty those who are oppressed
> To proclaim the acceptable year of the Lord.

Adopting that mission, Perkins began a rural health clinic, a co-op store, a vocational training center, a recreational center for Mendenhall's youth, a tutoring program and school, a housing program. Soon a few acres on unpaved streets on the wrong side of the tracks became a bustling center of services for the poor black families of Simpson County. Perkins tirelessly traveled the country, seeking financial support from white evangelicals—"I must have been the first person to integrate several hundred homes I stayed in," he says—and soliciting volunteer nurses, doctors, and teachers to serve a term in Mendenhall. With his stirring personal story, his plainspoken style, and his commitment to justice, Perkins captured the attention of evangelicals across the nation. He also captured the attention of local authorities.

White Mississippians did not mind the social services, but they resented the steady influx of Northerners, especially when Perkins began to lead a voter registration campaign. At the time only fifty black voters were registered in Simpson County, though blacks comprised 40 percent of the population. Such a ratio was typical: only 7,000 of Mississippi's 450,000 blacks were registered, due to the many legal barriers. Voters had to pay a poll tax, beyond the reach of most blacks. They had to interpret arcane sections of the Mississippi constitution to the satisfaction of all-white county registrars. As federal courts began dismantling these barriers, the state erected new ones: a requirement that names and addresses of applicants be printed in local newspapers (a convenience for harassment by the KKK, employers, and white neighbors), and a provision that allowed any registered voter in the county to challenge an applicant on grounds of character.

Perkins and his volunteers kept plugging away, eventually registering 2,300 voters in their county. When he led an economic boycott of downtown Mendenhall in protest of police brutality, however, he crossed a line. After a street demonstration in February 1970, a white staff member named Doug Huemmer and nineteen black student protesters from Tougaloo College were stopped by the Mississippi Highway Patrol and taken to a jail in nearby Brandon, the domain of a notorious sheriff. Huemmer called Perkins, who drove immediately to Brandon, walking right into a trap.

A dozen highway patrolmen and local policemen determined to

teach Perkins and Huemmer a lesson. "You're not in Simpson County anymore," one of them yelled. "You're in Rankin County, where we know how to treat smart niggers." They began kicking Perkins and hitting him with their fists—on the head, in the kidneys, in the groin—and stomping on his legs. He went unconscious, and when he came to in a pool of blood they poured moonshine whiskey over the sores on his head and pounded him again. They made him mop up his own blood. They put a fork up his nose and reamed it until the blood ran out, then did the same to his throat. Then they booked him on charges of contributing to the delinquency of minors. While they were taking his fingerprints, one of the officers put a gun to Perkins's head and pulled the trigger. The empty chamber clicked and everyone laughed at the cruel joke, then they beat him into unconsciousness again.

Perkins survived that night, although not long afterward doctors had to remove two thirds of his stomach as a result of the injuries. Over the next eighteen months of recuperation, he reconsidered his call from God to return to Mississippi. Was he really bringing good news to the people of Mendenhall? Black residents had more opportunities now, to be sure, but his efforts had hardened white attitudes. Reconciliation seemed more remote than ever. While recovering, he read books by Malcolm X, Rap Brown, and Eldridge Cleaver, all of whom had given up on the gospel and its message of reconciliation. Yet he could not deny that his own ministry had attracted some compassionate white volunteers: Doug Huemmer, who had suffered the very same treatment in the Brandon jail; Al Oethinger, who had come all the way from Germany to help out after reading books by Dr. King; Vera Schwartz, a missionary nurse who had joined the health center in Mendenhall instead of returning to Africa.

"That time was without a doubt my deepest crisis of faith," Perkins told me as we drove the back roads of Simpson and Rankin Counties, past the infamous jail and courthouse four years after the incident. "It was time for me to decide if I really did believe what I'd so often professed, that only in the love of Christ, not in power of violence, is there any hope for me or the world. I began to see how hate could destroy

me. In the end, I had to agree with Dr. King that God wanted us to return good for evil, not evil for evil. 'Love your enemy,' Jesus said. And
I determined to do it. It's a profound, mysterious truth, Jesus' concept
of love overpowering hate. I may not see it in my lifetime. But I know
it's true. Because on that bed, full of bruises and stitches, God made
it true in me. I got a transfusion of hope. I couldn't give up. We were
just getting underway in Mendenhall."

At that moment of crisis, Perkins came to believe with King that
"Hatred and bitterness can never cure the disease of fear; only love
can do that. Hatred paralyzes life; love releases it. Hatred confuses
life; love harmonizes it. Hatred darkens life; love illumines it."

Over the next decades, Perkins moved to Los Angeles, where he
founded a national organization for community development based on
what he had learned in Mendenhall, then returned to Mississippi to
spearhead a movement for racial reconciliation. He sometimes appears now with Thomas Tarrants, a KKK operative who served time for
murder, got converted in prison, and now pastors a multiracial church
in Washington, D.C.

When I visited Mendenhall in 1974, a sign welcomed me to town:
"White people unite, defeat Jew/Communist race mixers." I
asked John Perkins to show me an example of racism in action. "When
I write your story, people are going to tell me everything has changed,"
I said. "The civil rights bill was ten years ago. Is there still overt dis-
crimination?"

Perkins thought for a minute and suddenly his face brightened: "I
know—let's integrate the Revolving Table restaurant!" We drove to an
elegant restaurant famous for its mechanized Lazy Susan, which
slowly revolves in the center of a huge table, bearing platters of black-
eyed peas, squash, cabbage, sweet potatoes, chicken and dumplings,
and other Southern favorites. When we sat down, the white diners all
glared at us and then, as if at a prearranged signal, got up and moved
away to smaller tables. Except for Perkins and me, no one in the
restaurant spoke for the next hour. I ate uneasily, glancing over my

shoulder, expecting a nightstick. When I paid the bill and commented on the delicious food, the hostess took my money without responding or even looking me in the eye. I had the tiniest glimpse of the hostility Perkins had lived with all his life.

Two months later, when I published my article on John Perkins, the Mississippi branch of the Christian organization I worked for passed a resolution demanding that I be fired for stirring up bad memories. "Things have changed now," they said. "Why dig up the past?"

Why indeed? Almost three decades have passed since my Mississippi visit, and the great civil rights victories are nearing the half-century milestone. We live in a new century now, a new millennium even, and much has indeed changed. Nowadays, black patrons in Mississippi can eat wherever they want, drink from any water fountain, sleep in any motel. The victories that Martin Luther King, Jr., Medgar Evers, Bob Moses, John Perkins, and many others fought for were won—legally, at least—although they waited a full century after the Emancipation Proclamation. Progressive Southerners from Georgia, Arkansas, and Texas have served as president. Black visitors can attend white churches at will, though they seldom want to. All these dreams seemed unattainable to Martin Luther King, Jr., just four decades ago. As a token of the momentous changes, the nation now pauses each year to honor King himself, object of so much controversy during his lifetime, on a national holiday. He is the only African-American, the only minister, and indeed the only individual American so honored.

The victories did not come easily, and most did not come at all during his lifetime. Roy Wilkins of the NAACP, an uneasy rival of Dr. King, kidded him in 1963 that his methods had not achieved a single victory for integration in Albany or Birmingham. "In fact, Martin, if you have desegregated *anything* by your efforts, kindly enlighten me."

"Well," King replied, "I guess about the only thing I've desegregated so far is a few human hearts." He knew that the ultimate victory must be won there. Laws could prevent white people from lynching blacks, but no law could require races to forgive or love one another. The human heart, not the courtroom, was his supreme battleground. As one of those changed hearts, I would have to agree.

King had developed a sophisticated strategy of war fought with grace, not guns. He countered violence with nonviolence and hatred with love. King's associate Andrew Young remembers those turbulent days as a time when they sought to save "black men's bodies and white men's souls." Their real goal, King said, was not to defeat the white man but "to awaken a sense of shame within the oppressor and challenge his false sense of superiority. . . . The end is reconciliation; the end is redemption; the end is the creation of the beloved community." And that is what Martin Luther King, Jr., finally set into motion, even in born racists like me.

Despite the moral and social fallout from racism, somehow the nation did stay together, and people of all colors eventually joined the democratic process in America, even in the South. For some years now, Atlanta has elected African-American mayors, including civil rights leader Andrew Young. Even Selma, Alabama, has a black mayor, who in the year 2000 defeated the mayor who had held office since the notorious march. And old "Segregation forever!" George Wallace appeared in his wheelchair before the black leadership of Alabama to apologize for his past behavior, an apology he repeated on statewide television. When Wallace went on to apologize to the Baptist church in Montgomery where King had launched the movement, the leaders who came to offer him forgiveness included Coretta Scott King, Jesse Jackson, and the brother of the murdered Medgar Evers.

In 1995 the Southern Baptist Convention, 150 years after forming over the issue of slavery, formally repented of their long-term support of racism. (A pastor of the Abyssinian Baptist Church responded, "Finally we have a response to Martin Luther King's 'Letter from Birmingham City Jail' in 1963. Too bad it's thirty-two years too late.")

Even the large Baptist church I attended in my childhood learned to repent. When I attended a service several years ago, I was shocked to find only a few hundred worshipers scattered in the large sanctuary that, in my childhood, used to be packed with 1,500. The church seemed cursed. Finally the pastor, a classmate of mine from childhood, took the unusual step of scheduling a service of repentance. In

advance of the service he wrote to Tony Evans and to the shunned
Bible professor, asking their forgiveness. Then publicly, painfully, with
African-American leaders present, he recounted the sin of racism as it
had been practiced by the church in the past. He repented, and received their forgiveness. Although a burden seemed to lift from the
congregation after that service, it was not sufficient to save the
church. A few years later the white congregation moved out to the
suburbs, and today a rousing African-American congregation, the
Wings of Faith, fills the building and rattles its windows once more.

Observers of the South sometimes speak of it as "Christ-haunted."
Perhaps they should speak of it as "race-haunted" as well. All of us,
white or black, who grew up in those days bear scars. Some black people, like John Perkins and Bob Moses, bear physical scars. We whites
bear spiritual scars. Although I have not lived in the South for thirty
years, I live with its memories, like the medieval murderers who were
forced to wear the corpses of their victims strapped to their backs. The
entire nation bears scars. Who would suggest that we have achieved
anything like "the beloved community" King longed for?

I have visited King's old church in Atlanta, Ebenezer Baptist, and
sat in tears as I saw through new eyes the moral center of the black
community that gave them strength to fight against bigots like me. I
was on the outside in those days, cracking jokes, spreading rumors,
helping sustain a system of evil. Inside the church, and for a time only
inside the church, the black community stood tall. My eyes, blinded
by bigotry, could not see the Kingdom of God at work.

A few years before his death, King was asked about mistakes he
had made. He replied, "Well, the most pervasive mistake I have made
was in believing that because our cause was just, we could be sure that
the white ministers of the South, once their Christian consciences
were challenged, would rise to our aid. I felt that white ministers
would take our cause to the white power structures. I ended up, of
course, chastened and disillusioned. As our movement unfolded, and
direct appeals were made to white ministers, most folded their
hands—and some even took stands *against* us."

I once wrote a tribute to Martin Luther King, Jr., in the conservative journal *Christianity Today.* I spoke of him as a prophet, using some of the same words I have used here. I heard from many readers, some supportive and some angry. Two of the most thoughtful letters came from former college presidents, one from the president of Wheaton College, where I attended, and one from the president of the Bible college I also attended. "How can you call Dr. King a prophet?" both asked. A great moral leader, yes, an important agent of social change, certainly, but can a plagiarizer and womanizer be a Christian prophet? They balked at applying that label to a man with such obvious flaws.

I wrote detailed replies to both men, mentioning some of the flawed leaders God clearly used in biblical times. Solomon offers a good example: we honor his proverbs but not his lifestyle. Indeed, we are all in peril if the flawed messenger invalidates the message. I also cited King's powerful sermons, and mentioned that King required his volunteers to sign a strict pledge that committed them to daily meditation on Jesus' teaching, regular prayer, and walking and talking with love. And then the irony struck me. I had titled my article "Confessions of a Racist," yet almost all the letters focused on King's errors and not my own. How in the world could they question King's right to speak for God and not mine, given my spotted past?

Many of the Christians who still balk at seeing Martin Luther King, Jr., as God's instrument have no problem worshiping in churches that once portrayed him as the enemy, that opposed his ideals, and that either directly or indirectly perpetuated the sin of racism he fought with his own body. We saw the mote in his eye but not the beams in our own.

Only one thing haunts me more than the sins of my past: What sins am I blind to today? It took the greatness of Martin Luther King, Jr., to awaken the conscience of a nation in the last century. What keeps us in this new century from realizing the beloved community of justice, peace, and love for which King fought and died? On the wrong side of what issues does the church stubbornly plant its feet today? As King used to say, the presence of injustice anywhere is a threat to justice everywhere.

Occasionally, grace and power descend on great and flawed leaders to convict and lead us on. In the end, it was not King's humanitarianism that got through to me, nor his Gandhian example of nonviolent resistance, nor his personal sacrifices, inspiring as those may be. It was his grounding in the Christian gospel that finally made me conscious of the beam in my eye and forced me to attend to the message he was proclaiming. Because he kept quoting Jesus, eventually I had to listen. The church may not always get it right—and it may take centuries or even millennia for its eyes to open—but when it does, God's own love and forgiveness flow down like a stream of living water. Alas, by the time I tasted of that stream, King was already dead.

> Like anybody, I would like to live a long life. Longevity has its place. But I'm not concerned about that now. I just want to do God's will. And He's allowed me to go up to the mountain. And I've looked over, and I've seen the promised land.
>
> I may not get there with you, but I want you to know tonight that we as a people will get to the promised land.
>
> So I'm happy tonight. I'm not worried about anything. I'm not fearing any man. "Mine eyes have seen the glory of the coming of the Lord."
>
> (From King's last speech, in Memphis,
> the night before his assassination.)

GETTING STARTED WITH MARTIN LUTHER KING, JR.:

As an introduction to King's life, I recommend *The Autobiography of Martin Luther King, Jr.*, an AudioBook produced by Time Warner. Patched together from King's writings and read by LeVar Burton, the autobiography is incomplete and subjective, but the tapes include actual sermons and speeches delivered by King himself in his stirring, inimitable style, along with fine segues of gospel music. *A Testament of Hope: The Essential Writings and Speeches of Martin Luther King, Jr.*, draws together all the famous speeches, along with excerpts from most of King's writings. David Garrow's *Bearing the Cross* is the best single-volume biography of King; Taylor Branch's exhaustive *Parting the Waters* and *Pillar of Fire* expand the view to encompass other events going on in the civil rights movement. (Even in other countries, books can be purchased through the Internet. Try *www.amazon.com* for new or used books and *abebooks.com* for used books.)

If you had asked me during college years where I would end up, "Christian writer" would have fallen last on my list of options. I would have recounted the lies my church had told me about race and other matters, and poked fun at its smothering legalism. I would have described an evangelical as a socially stunted wannabe—a fundamentalist with a better income, a slightly more open mind, and a less furrowed brow. I would have complained about the furloughed missionaries at the Bible college I attended who taught classes in science and philosophy while knowing less about those subjects than my high school teachers. That school tended to punish, rather than reward, intellectual curiosity: one teacher admitted he deliberately lowered my grades in order to teach me humility. "The greatest barrier to the Holy Spirit is sophistication," he used to warn his classes.

At that same Bible college, however, I first encountered the writings of C. S. Lewis and G. K. Chesterton. Although separated from me by a vast expanse of sea and culture, they kindled hope that somewhere Christians existed who loosed rather than restrained their minds, who combined sophisticated taste with a humility that did not demean others, and, above all, who experienced life with God as a source of joy and not repression. Ordering tattered used copies through bookshops in England, I devoured everything I could find by these men, one an Oxford don and the other a Fleet Street journalist. As Lewis himself wrote after discovering Chesterton while

Chapter 3

G. K.

CHESTERTON

✻

RELICS

ALONG

THE

SEASHORE

recovering in a hospital during World War I, "A young man who wishes to remain a strong atheist cannot be too careful of his reading."

Their words sustained me, a lifeline of faith in a sea of turmoil and doubt. I became a writer, I have said, in large part because I realized the power of words in my own life, words that could sail across time and an ocean and quietly, gently, work a transformation of healing and hope. More time would pass before I fully returned to faith, but at least I had models of what life-enhancing faith could look like. Martin Luther King, Jr., had touched in me a moral chord of faith; these touched an aesthetic chord.

In his story of the prodigal son, Jesus does not dwell on the prodigal's motive for return. The younger son feels no sudden remorse nor burst of love for the father he insulted. Rather, he tires of a life of squalor and returns out of selfish motives. Apparently, it matters little to God whether we approach him out of desperation or out of longing. *Why did I return?* I ask myself.

My older brother, who played the role of prodigal more dramatically, demonstrated what could happen if I chose to leave everything behind. In an attempt to break the shackles of a confining upbringing, he went on a grand quest for freedom, trying on worldviews like changes of clothing: Pentecostalism, atheistic existentialism, Buddhism, New Age spirituality, Thomistic rationalism. He joined the flower children of the 1960s, growing his hair long and wearing granny glasses, living communally, experimenting with sex and drugs. For a time he sent me exuberant reports of his new life. Eventually, however, a darker side crept in. I had to bail him out of jail when an LSD trip went bad. He broke relations with every other person in the family and burned through several marriages. I got late-night suicide calls. Watching my brother, I learned that apparent freedom can actually mask deep bondage, a cry from the heart of unmet needs. The most musically gifted person I have ever known ended up tuning pianos, not playing them on a concert stage. I saw up close the destructive power of casting off faith with nothing to take its place.

At the same time, more positively, my career as a journalist gave me the opportunity to investigate people, such as those I have assembled in this book, who demonstrate that a connection with God can enlarge, rather than shrink, life. I began the lifelong process of separating church from God. Though I had emerged from childhood churches badly damaged, as I began to scrutinize Jesus through the critical eyes of a journalist, I saw that the qualities that so upset me— legalism, self-righteousness, racism, provincialism, hypocrisy—Jesus had fought against, and were probably the very qualities that led to his crucifixion. Getting to know the God revealed in Jesus, I recognized I needed to change in many ways—yes, even to repent, for I had absorbed the hypocrisy, racism, and self-righteousness of my upbringing and contributed numerous sins of my own. I began to envision God less as a stern judge shaking his finger at my waywardness than as a doctor who prescribes behavior in my best interest in order to safeguard my health.

"I am the man who with the utmost daring discovered what had been discovered before," G. K. Chesterton declared triumphantly. "I did try to found a heresy of my own; and when I had put the last touches to it, I discovered that it was orthodoxy." Guided in part by Chesterton, I landed in a similar place after a circuitous journey.

When someone asked Chesterton what one book he would want to have along if stranded on a desert island, he paused only an instant before replying, "Why, *A Practical Guide to Shipbuilding,* of course." If I were so stranded, and could choose one book apart from the Bible, I may well select Chesterton's own spiritual autobiography, *Orthodoxy.* Why anyone would pick up a book with that formidable title eludes me, but one day I did so and my faith has never recovered. *Orthodoxy* brought freshness and a new spirit of adventure to my faith as I found odd parallels between my own odyssey and that traveled by its author, a three-hundred-pound scatterbrained Victorian journalist.

Chesterton has sometimes been called "the master who left no masterpiece," perhaps the curse of his chosen profession. For most of his life (1874–1936) he served as editor of a weekly newspaper of ideas, in the process writing some four thousand essays on topics both trivial and important. He straddled the turn of the century, from the nineteenth to the twentieth, when such movements as modernism, communism, fascism, pacifism, determinism, Darwinism, and eugenics were coming to the fore. As he surveyed each one, he found himself pressed further and further toward Christianity, which he saw as the only redoubt against such potent forces. Eventually he accepted the Christian faith not simply as a bulwark of civilization but rather as an expression of the deepest truths about the world. He took the public step of being baptized into the Roman Catholic Church in a mostly Protestant nation.

As a thinker, Chesterton started slowly. By the age of nine he could barely read and his parents consulted with a brain specialist about his mental capacity. He dropped out of art school, and skipped university entirely. As it turned out, however, he had a memory so prodigious that late in life he could recite the plots of all ten thousand novels he had read and reviewed. He wrote five novels of his own as well as two hundred short stories, including a series of detective stories centered on "Father Brown"; tried his hand at plays, poetry, and ballads; wrote literary biographies of such characters as Robert Browning and Charles Dickens; spun off a history of England; and tackled the lives of Francis of Assisi, Thomas Aquinas, and Jesus himself. Writing at breakneck speed, getting many facts wrong, he nevertheless approached each of his subjects with such discernment, enthusiasm, and wit that even his harshest critics had to stand and applaud.

Chesterton traveled occasionally to Europe, and made it across the Atlantic to visit the United States (prompting the book *What I Saw in America*), but mostly he stayed at home, read widely, and wrote about everything that crossed his mind. The rollicking adventures took place inside his great, shaggy head. One can hardly overestimate his impact on others, though. Mahatma Gandhi got many of his ideas on Indian independence from Chesterton; one of his novels also inspired Michael Collins's movement for Irish independence; and C. S. Lewis looked to Chesterton as his spiritual father.

Chesterton had been dead more than thirty years when I first discovered him, but he resuscitated my moribund faith. As I look back now, and ask in what way he affected me, I see that he helped awaken in me a sense of long-suppressed joy.

Albert Einstein once articulated the most important question of all: "Is the universe a friendly place?" In childhood and adolescence I received mixed messages at best. Like the children of alcoholics— Don't talk, Don't trust, and Don't feel—I had responded by flat-lining emotionally. Even as my brother turned outward, launching his grand tour of freedom, I turned inward, sealing off one by one any avenue whereby people could get to me, either to manipulate me or cause pain. I read the novels of Sartre and Camus, whose heroes would stab themselves in the hand or murder someone on the beach just for the experience of it. Especially I read Nietzsche, who described a Superman impervious to suffering. I learned not to laugh or smile, and not to cry. I tried not to care or react: to cold or heat, to good smells or bad ones, to beauty or ugliness, to love or hate. In a perverted experiment, I broke my own arm against the metal frame of a bunk bed to test my mastery of pain.

I see now what I could not see then, that I was erecting a strong stone fortress against love, for I thought myself unlovable. In the most unlikely place, the Bible college I viewed as a kind of asylum, that inner fortress began to crumble. I found solace not in religion, where everyone around me claimed to find it, but in music. Late at night I would steal out of the dormitory and make my way to the chapel and its nine-foot Steinway grand. Living in the shadow of a brother preternaturally gifted in music, I never performed in public, but I could passably sight-read Mozart, Chopin, Beethoven, and Schubert, and that is how I spent many evenings, pressing some order into my disordered world. I was creating something, and in spite of myself it seemed beautiful as it echoed through the dark and empty chapel.

Then I fell in love. Janet and I drew together for all the wrong reasons—mainly we sat around and complained about the oppressive atmosphere of the school—but eventually the most powerful force in the universe, love, won out. I had found someone who pointed out everything right with me, not everything wrong. Hope aroused. I wanted to conquer worlds and lay them at her feet. For her birthday I

learned Beethoven's *Pathétique Sonata* and invited her, trembling, to
be the very first audience to hear me play. It was an offering to new
life, and to her who had called it forth.

"The worst moment for the atheist is when he is really thankful
and has no one to thank," wrote Chesterton. And also, "Joy, which was
the small publicity of the pagan, is the gigantic secret of the Christian." I know well that worst moment and know too the first stirrings
of joy that flapped fresh air into crevices long sealed off. Great joy carries within it the intimations of immortality. Suddenly I wanted to live,
even to live forever.

I dare not forget nature either. In childhood, nature had been my
place of refuge. We lived in a twelve by forty-eight-foot aluminum
trailer parked on church property, and home involved more tension
than peace, yet always I could find woods nearby where I could explore the squirrels' nests and bee swarms, the rotten logs full of exotic
beetles, and the marshes buzzing with the sound of dragonflies and
small frogs. I collected butterflies, beetles, and turtles, and worked
one summer studying mosquitoes and ticks at the Communicable Disease Center.

In Bible college too, and ever after, nature struck me as a symphony that plays on whether or not I stop to listen. If we cannot judge
for certain whether the universe is friendly, at least we can judge it a
font of limitless beauty. Climb the highest mountains where I now
live, in Colorado, and you will find the thin soil carpeted with tiny, del-
icate wildflowers, which thrive unattended regardless of whether anyone happens by. Dive the Great Barrier Reef and you will see coral and
tropical fish outfitted in color and design more brilliant than that displayed in any art museum in the world, not to mention a sea floor lit-
tered with seashells, the jewelry secretions of primitive animals.

I have stood in the mist of Iguaçù Falls in Brazil as gorgeous tropical butterflies, winged bearers of abstract art, landed on my arms to
lap up the moisture. I have crouched beside a bay in Alaska as a pod
of feeding beluga whales made shiny crescents of silver in unison
against the dark green water. I have sat under a baobab tree in Kenya
as giraffes loped effortlessly under sunset clouds and a line of half a

million wildebeest marched single file across the plain. Above the Arctic Circle, I have watched a herd of musk oxen gather in a circle like Conestoga wagons to protect the mothers and their young (who in wintertime must adjust to a 130°F. drop in temperature at birth). I have also sat in hot classrooms and listened to theology professors drone on about the defining qualities of the deity—omniscience, omnipresence, omnipotence, etc. Can the One who created this glorious world be reduced to such abstractions? Should we not start with the most obvious fact of existence, that whoever is responsible is a fierce and incomparable artist beside whom all human achievement and creativity dwindle as child's play?

I have mentioned sitting on a panel with three scientists, two of them Nobel laureates and professed atheists. We saw the world very differently, but agreed that religion, and not science, at least proposes an answer to two questions. (1) Why is there something rather than nothing? (Or, as Stephen Hawking put it, Why does the universe "bother to exist"?) (2) Why is that something so beautiful and orderly? It is no accident that the Old Testament was the first ancient literature to celebrate the glories of nature, for its authors recognized the Creator's handiwork.

Yes, but is it friendly? Another scientist, the naturalist Loren Eiseley, tells of an event he calls the most significant learning experience of his long life. Caught on a beach in a sudden rainstorm, he sought shelter under a huge piece of driftwood where he found a tiny fox kitten, maybe ten weeks old, which as yet had no fear of humans. Within a few minutes it had engaged Eiseley in a playful game of tug-of-war, with Eiseley holding one end of a chicken bone in his mouth and the baby fox pulling on the other end. The lesson he learned, said Eiseley, is that at the core of the universe, the face of God wears a smile.

I have had my own encounters with foxes, now that I live in Colorado. When three kits were born in a den across a ravine, I fancied myself a latter-day St. Francis and decided to befriend them. I sat near their den on a cushion and wrote my books and articles until soon the kits became accustomed to me. (The first time, I announced my undetected presence by saying, "Hi!" and they bolted in the air as if struck by lightning.) They peered at me inquisitively, golden eyes alert, ears twitching to every sound, their unscarred red coats glistening in the sun. Eventually the three began following me and I felt like the Pied Piper. If I stopped, they stopped, and hid behind a rock or bush. If I ran, they ran too. If I sat for a picnic lunch, they surrounded me and watched me eat.

As the summer progressed, I would stand in my driveway and whistle; on command, the three handsome young foxes came bounding across the ravine. They stalked butterflies in a patch of wildflowers, batting at them like a cat. They gave clumsy chase to wily squirrels. They dodged in and out of the spray of the sprinklers watering our grass. They stood on their hind legs and lapped water from our birdbath—once jumping back in alarm when a skim of ice reflected their own faces. If I threw a tennis ball, one would chase it down and take off running, the other two in hot pursuit.

All summer I had three companions. As I weeded the garden, cut the grass, or read the mail in a hammock, they followed my every move. If I ate lunch on our wooden balcony, they would climb the steps to join me. If I sat outdoors to write, they would observe me for a while, then curl up, white-tipped tails folded across their eyes, and go to sleep. I felt a thrilling flashback to Eden, when fear had not yet arisen between the species, and a flash-forward to heaven, when the lion shall lie down with the lamb and the fox shall curl up with the writer. I learned, like Eiseley, that at the heart of the universe a smile is found. "The beauty of the world," said Simone Weil, "is Christ's tender smile for us coming through matter." We glimpse it only rarely on this defaced planet, but that glimpse reveals as much reality as all theology books stacked together.

Gradually, music and romantic love and especially nature softened the incessant monotone of despair inside that had nagged me like a dull pain. I came to see the despair as a normal symptom of fallen humanity estranged from its Creator. Somehow, I must reconnect.

Chesterton had pointed to St. Francis, who learned his proper state from "Brother Sun" and "Sister Moon," and who saw inexhaustible beauty in the humblest weed, like a dandelion. In a memorable passage, Chesterton contrasts our state with that of God, who "is strong enough to exult in monotony. It is possible that God says every morning, 'Do it again' to the sun; and every evening, 'Do it again' to the moon. It may not be automatic necessity that makes all daisies alike; it may be that God makes every daisy separately, but has never got tired of making them. It may be that He has the eternal appetite of infancy; for we have sinned and grown old, and our Father is younger than we." Bit by bit, nature helped to rejuvenate in me that appetite of infancy.

I am not Francis, however, and unlike the saint of Assisi I keep finding mixed messages in nature. What glimpse of the Creator might I draw from the Cecidomyian gall midge, whose young hatch inside their mother and literally eat their way out, devouring the mother as they go? Or from the *Xenon peckii* fly, sightless and flightless, which spends its entire life inside the innards of a paper wasp, feeding on it? Or the tiny Amazon *Candiru* catfish that swims its way up the urethra of an unsuspecting bather, then extends its sharp spines, causing excruciating pain that can only be mitigated by surgical removal? Even my beloved foxes: eight times I have seen them catch a squirrel in my backyard, a bloody, shrieking affair that one does not easily put out of mind. Yesterday I watched a bull elk in rut, snorting, urinating, sweating, and crashing with horns lowered toward all males in sight, hardly a winsome image of romantic love.

Here, too, Chesterton proved a helpful guide. He countered pantheism and modern cosmic religion with the strong assertion in *Orthodoxy* that "Nature is not our mother; Nature is our sister." God created both the natural world and human beings as any artist creates, forming something separate from himself and then setting it free. "God had written, not so much a poem, but rather a play; a play he had planned as perfect, but which had necessarily been left to human actors and stage-managers, who had since made a great mess of it."

Chesterton viewed this world as a sort of cosmic shipwreck. A person in search of meaning resembles a sailor who awakens from a deep sleep and discovers treasure strewn about, relics from a civilization he can barely remember. One by one he picks up the relics—gold coins, a compass, fine clothing—and tries to discern their meaning. Fallen humanity lives in such a state. Good things on earth—the natural world, beauty, love, joy—still bear traces of their original purpose, but amnesia mars the image of God in us.

After *Orthodoxy* I read many of Chesterton's other works. (He wrote more than a hundred books, and as a writer it depressed me for weeks to learn that he dictated most of them to his secretary, and made few changes to the first drafts.) I was writing on the problem of pain at the time, and found much insight in his fictional treatment of that dark subject, *The Man Who Was Thursday*. Amazingly, considering their differences in style, he wrote it during the same year as *Orthodoxy*. He later explained that he had been struggling with despair, evil, and the meaning of life, and had even approached mental breakdown. When he emerged from that melancholy, he sought to make a case for optimism amid the gloom of such a world. He had been studying the biblical book of Job, and these two books resulted, one a book of apologetics full of unexpected twists and turns, the other best described as a combination spy thriller and nightmare.

In *The Man Who Was Thursday*, Chesterton does not diminish the incalculable mysteries of suffering and free will. Rather, he transforms them into a minimalist argument for faith. At its worst, at a bare minimum of goodness, with nature revealing only the back side of God, the universe offers reasons for belief. In God's own speech to Job, God pointed to the fierce wildness of nature—the hippopotamus and crocodile, thunderstorms and blizzards, the lioness and mountain goat, untamed oxen and ostriches—not its friendly side. If nothing else, nature reveals God as mysterious, incalculable, "wholly other," worthy of worship. We may have limited clues to the secrets of reality, but what wondrous clues they are. "Even mere existence, reduced to its most primary limits, was extraordinary enough to be exciting. Anything was magnificent as compared with nothing," Chesterton testified later. In his life also, nature and romantic love sounded as loud, reverberating grace notes.

For Chesterton, and also for me, the riddles of God proved more satisfying than the answers proposed without God. I too came to believe in the good things of this world, first revealed to me in music, romantic love, and nature, as relics of a wreck, and as bright clues into the nature of a reality shrouded in darkness. God had answered Job's questions with more questions, as if to say the truths of existence lie far beyond the range of our comprehension. We are left with remnants of God's original design and the freedom, always the freedom, to cast our lots with such a God, or against him.

Chesterton captured his own response, a spirit of unalloyed gratitude, in a short poem:

Here dies another day
During which I have had eyes, ears, hands
And the great world round me;
And with tomorrow begins another.
Why am I allowed two?

In addition to the problem of pain, G. K. Chesterton seemed equally fascinated by its opposite, the problem of pleasure. He found materialism too thin to account for the sense of wonder and delight that gives an almost magical dimension to such basic human acts as sex, childbirth, play, and artistic creation.

Why is scx fun? Reproduction surely does not require pleasure: some animals simply split in half to reproduce, and even humans use methods of artificial insemination that involve no pleasure. Why is eating enjoyable? Plants and the lower animals manage to obtain their quota of nutrients without the luxury of taste buds. Why are there colors? Some people get along fine without the ability to detect color. Why complicate vision for all the rest of us?

It struck me, after reading my umpteenth book on the problem of pain, that I have never even seen a book on "the problem of pleasure." Nor have I met a philosopher who goes around shaking his or her head in perplexity over the question of why we experience pleasure. Yet it looms as a huge question: the philosophical equivalent, for atheists, to the problem of pain for Christians. On the issue of pleasure, Christians can breathe easier. A good and loving God would naturally want his creatures to experience delight, joy, and personal fulfillment. Christians start from that assumption and then look for ways to explain the origin of suffering. But should not atheists have an equal obligation to explain the origin of pleasure in a world of randomness and meaninglessness?

After his long odyssey, Chesterton returned to faith because only Christianity provided the clues to solve the mystery of pleasure. "I felt in my bones, first that this world does not explain itself. . . . Second, I came to feel as if magic must have a meaning, and meaning must have some one to mean it. There was something personal in the world, as in a work of art. . . . Third, I thought this purpose beautiful in its old design, in spite of its defects, such as dragons. Fourth, that the proper form of thanks to it is some form of humility and restraint: we should thank God for beer and Burgundy by not drinking too much of them. . . . And last, and strangest, there had come into my mind a vague and vast impression that in some way all good was a remnant to be stored and held sacred out of some primordial ruin. Man had saved his good as [Robinson] Crusoe saved his goods: he had saved them from a wreck."

Where does pleasure come from? After searching alternatives, Chesterton settled on Christianity as the only reasonable explanation for its existence in the world. Moments of pleasure are the remnants washed ashore from a shipwreck, bits of Paradise extended through time. We must hold these relics lightly, and use them with gratitude and restraint, never seizing them as entitlements.

As Chesterton saw it, sexual promiscuity is not so much an overvaluing of sex as a devaluing. "To complain that I could only be married once was like complaining that I had only been born once. It was incommensurate with the terrible excitement of which one was talking. It showed, not an exaggerated sensibility to sex, but a curious insensibility to it . . . Polygamy is a lack of the realization of sex; it is like a man plucking five pears in a mere absence of mind."

The churches I attended had stressed the dangers of pleasure so loudly that I missed any positive message. Guided by Chesterton, I came to see sex, money, power, and sensory pleasures as God's good gifts. Every Sunday I can turn on the radio or television and hear preachers decry the drugs, sexual looseness, greed, and crime that are "running rampant" in the streets of America. Rather than merely wag our fingers at such obvious abuses of God's good gifts, perhaps we should demonstrate to the world where good gifts actually come from, and why they are good. Evil's greatest triumph may be its success in portraying religion as an enemy of pleasure when, in fact, religion accounts for its source: every good and enjoyable thing is the invention of a Creator who lavished gifts on the world.

Of course, in a world estranged from God, even good things must be handled with care, like explosives. We have lost the untainted innocence of Eden, and every good harbors risk as well, holding within it the potential for abuse. Eating becomes gluttony, love becomes lust, and along the way we lose sight of the One who gave us pleasure. The ancients turned good things into idols; we moderns call them addictions. In either case, what ceases to be a servant becomes a tyrant—a principle I had clearly seen at work in my brother and his flower children friends.

"I am ordinary in the correct sense of the term," said Chesterton, "which means the acceptance of an order; a Creator and the Creation, the common sense of gratitude for Creation, life and love as gifts permanently good, marriage and chivalry as laws rightly controlling them . . ." Under his influence I too realized the need to become more "ordinary." I had conceived of faith as a tight-lipped, grim exercise of spiritual discipline, a blending of asceticism and rationalism in which joy leaked away. Chesterton restored to me a thirst for the exuberance that flows from a link to the God who dreamed up all the things that give me pleasure.

"There are an infinity of angles at which one falls, only one at which one stands," said Chesterton, and he ultimately fell from excess, never achieving the balance he preached so convincingly. Not only did he tend to pluck five pears in a mere absence of mind—he ate them. His weight hovered between three and four hundred pounds, and that combined with general poor health to disqualify him from military service, a fact that led to a rather brusque encounter with a patriot during World War I. "Why aren't you out at the front?" demanded the indignant elderly lady when she spied Chesterton on the streets of London. He coolly replied, "My dear madam, if you will step round this way a little, you will see that I am."

That distinctive shape made Chesterton a favorite of London caricaturists. It took only a few strokes for a skilled cartoonist to capture his essence: from the side he looked like a giant capital "P." Chesterton rounded out his reputation with other eccentricities, most of which suited the stereotype of a slovenly, absentminded professor. He would show up at a wedding wearing no tie and with a price tag on his shoes. Using any available paper, even wallpaper, he would scribble notes when ideas came to him, sometimes standing, oblivious, in the middle of traffic as he did so. Once he sent his wife this telegram: "Am at Market Harborough. Where ought I to be?" She telegraphed back, "Home."

Chesterton cheerfully engaged in public debates with agnostics and skeptics of the day, most notably George Bernard Shaw—this at a time when a debate on faith could fill a lecture hall. Chesterton usually arrived late, peered through his *pince-nez* at his disorderly scraps of paper, and proceeded to entertain the crowd, making nervous gestures, fumbling through his pockets, laughing heartily in a falsetto voice at his own jokes. Typically he would charm the audience over to his side, then celebrate by hosting his chastened opponent at the nearest pub. "Shaw is like the Venus de Milo; all there is of him is admirable," he toasted his friend affectionately.

Cosmo Hamilton, one of his debating opponents, described the experience:

> To hear Chesterton's howl of joy . . . to see him double himself
> up in an agony of laughter at my personal insults, to watch the

effect of his sportsmanship on a shocked audience who were won to mirth by his intense and pea-hen-like quarks of joy was a sight and a sound for the gods . . . and I carried away from that room a respect and admiration for this tomboy among dictionaries, this philosophical Peter Pan, this humorous Dr. Johnson, this kindly and gallant cherub, this profound student and wise master which has grown steadily ever since . . . It was monstrous, gigantic, amazing, deadly, delicious. Nothing like it has ever been done before or will ever be seen, heard and felt like it again.

In Chesterton's day, sober-minded modernists were seeking a new unified theory to explain the past and give hope to the future. Shaw, seeing history as a struggle between the classes, proposed a remedy of socialist utopianism. H. G. Wells interpreted the past as an evolutionary march toward progress and enlightenment (a view the rest of the century would do much to refute). Sigmund Freud held up a vision of humanity free of repression and the bondage of the subconscious. Ironically, all three of these progressives had in common a rather stern countenance. With furrowed brows and dark, haunted eyes they would expostulate on their optimistic visions of the future. Meanwhile, puffing through his incongruously blond moustache, with a pinkly beaming face and a twinkle in his eye, Chesterton would cheerfully defend such reactionary concepts as original sin and the Last Judgment. Chesterton seemed to sense instinctively that a stern prophet will rarely break through to a society full of religion's "cultured despisers"; he preferred the role of jester.

Chesterton claimed to distrust "hard, cold, thin people," and perhaps that's why I have grown so fond of the jolly fat apologist. Nowadays in the church sober-mindedness has won the day. Evangelicals are responsible citizens whom most people appreciate as neighbors but don't want to spend much time with. Theologians with long faces lecture on "the imperatives of the faith." Television evangelists with every hair in place (often dyed) confidently name the Antichrist, predict the end of the world, and announce how to have a prosperous and healthy life in the meanwhile. The religious right calls for moral re-

generation, and ordinary Christians point to temperance, industrious-
ness, and achievement as primary proofs of their faith. Could it be that
Christians, eager to point out how good we are, neglect the basic fact
that the gospel sounds like good news only to bad people?

I have had to forgive the church, much as a person from a dysfunctional family forgives mistakes made by parents and siblings. An
irrepressible optimist, G. K. Chesterton proved helpful in that process
too. "The Christian ideal has not been tried and found wanting. It has
been found difficult; and left untried," he said. The real question is
not "Why is Christianity so bad when it claims to be so good?" but
rather "Why are all human things so bad when they claim to be so
good?" Chesterton readily admitted that the church had badly failed
the gospel. In fact, he said, one of the strongest arguments in favor of
Christianity is the failure of Christians, who thereby prove what the
Bible teaches about the fall and original sin. As the world goes wrong,
it proves that the church is right in this basic doctrine.

When the *London Times* asked a number of writers for essays on
the topic "What's Wrong with the World?" Chesterton sent in the reply shortest and most to the point:

> *Dear Sirs:*
>
> *I am.*
>
> *Sincerely yours,*
> *G. K. Chesterton*

For this reason, when people tell me their horror stories of growing up
in a repressive church environment, I feel no need to defend the actions of the church. The church of my own childhood, as well as that
of my present and my future, comprises deeply flawed human beings
struggling toward an unattainable ideal. We admit that we will never
reach our ideal in this life, a distinctive the church claims that most
other human institutions try to deny. Along with Chesterton, I've had
to take my place among those who acknowledge that *we* are what is
wrong with the world. What is my snobbishness toward my childhood

church, for instance, but an inverted form of the harsh judgment it showed me? Whenever faith seems an entitlement, or a measuring rod, we cast our lots with the Pharisees and grace softly slips away.

I n the end, I did return home as a humbled prodigal to the very institution I had fled in pain and rebellion.

> *And the end of all our exploring*
> *Will be to arrive where we started*
> *And know the place for the first time.*
> —T. S. Eliot

We could use another Chesterton today, I think. In a time when culture and faith have drifted even further apart, we could use his brilliance, his entertaining style, and above all his generous and joyful spirit. When society becomes polarized, as ours has, it is as if the two sides stand across a great divide and shout at each other. Occasionally, a prophet like Martin Luther King, Jr., arises with power and eloquence enough to address both sides at once. Chesterton had another approach: he walked to the center of a swinging bridge, roared a challenge to any single combat warriors, and then made both sides laugh aloud.

For all his personal quirkiness, he managed to propound the Christian faith with as much wit, good humor, and sheer intellectual force as anyone in recent times. With the zeal of a knight defending the last redoubt, he took on, in person and in print, anyone who dared interpret the world apart from God and Incarnation.

Chesterton himself said that the modern age is characterized by a sadness that calls for a new kind of prophet, not like prophets of old who reminded people that they were going to die, but someone who would remind them they are not dead yet. The prophet of ample girth and ample mirth filled that role splendidly. T. S. Eliot judged that "He did more, I think, than any man of his time . . . to maintain the existence of the important minority in the modern world." I know he did that for me. Whenever I feel my faith going dry again, I wander to a shelf and pick up a book by G. K. Chesterton. The adventure begins all over again.

GETTING STARTED WITH G. K. CHESTERTON:

Naturally, I suggest starting with *Orthodoxy*. If you enjoy that book, you might proceed to *The Everlasting Man*, Chesterton's summary of Jesus' life, and his biographies *St. Francis of Assisi* and *St. Thomas Aquinas: The Dumb Ox*. Various collections of his essays are in print, and for the insatiable reader Ignatius Press has for some time been engaged in the momentous task of publishing Chesterton's *Collected Works* in forty-five volumes, most of which are now available. And, of course, fiction aficionados will appreciate his *The Man Who Was Thursday* and the Father Brown stories. Several good biographies of Chesterton himself exist, but none more entertaining (or maddeningly selective) than his own *Autobiography*. For a variety of essays and reviews both by and about Chesterton, see also the informative quarterly journal *The Chesterton Review* produced out of Seton Hall University.

I spent the last four years of the 1960s as a college student. Everything in America seemed to be cracking apart then: the Vietnam war chiseled away at our national ideals, revelations about abuse of the environment challenged the industrial ethic that had built our country, and the youth counterculture exposed the hollow materialism of business and the media. The issues have since become familiar, even hackneyed, but to those of us who were forming a view of the world then, the sixties left a profound and permanent imprint.

I recall my emotions in the subsequent years as being primarily anger, loneliness, and despair. I saw bright and talented friends give up on society and seek a new path through LSD and mescaline. Others never came back from the jungles of Vietnam. I plodded through bleak existentialist novels as well as nonfiction accounts of the Holocaust and the Soviet Gulag. Looking at the church through such jaundiced eyes, I saw mainly its hypocrisy and its irrelevance to the world outside. Although people like G. K. Chesterton had led me back to God, I was still having difficulty distinguishing God from church and cultivating a stable personal faith. Questions swirled. Even while editing a Christian magazine I wrote books with titles like *Where Is God When It Hurts, Unhappy Secrets of the Christian Life,* and *Disappointment with God,* outward projections of my own struggles of faith.

I now see that my writing partnership with

Chapter 4

DR. PAUL

BRAND

DETOURS

TO

HAPPINESS

Dr. Paul Brand helped me weather that volatile period. I spent hundreds of hours interrogating him on global issues, life, and God. On trips to India and England I tracked his life, interviewing former patients and colleagues. (Operating room scrub nurses, I found, have the keenest insight into a surgeon's character.) Proud owner of one of the first "laptop" computers, a fourteen-pound monstrosity, I interviewed Brand himself on the go by keeping my fingers on the keyboard so that I could continue typing even as our Jeep bounced along the rutted roads of rural India, or as we sat in a gently rocking London subway car.

I first learned about Dr. Brand while writing *Where Is God When It Hurts?* As I was holed up in libraries reading books on the problem of pain, my wife, while cleaning out the closet of a medical-supply house, came across an intriguing essay he had written on "The Gift of Pain." Brand's approach, implied by the title itself, had about it the paradoxical quality that had so drawn me to Chesterton. He had a different conception of pleasure and pain than any I had encountered. I had interviewed scores of people who wanted desperately to get rid of pain; Brand told of spending several million dollars trying to *create* a pain system for his patients.

As I inquired further, and talked to people who knew Brand personally, I became so captivated that I called him out of the blue from Chicago and asked for an interview. "Well, they keep me pretty busy here," he replied, a bit nonplused. "But I'm sure we could carve out some time in between meetings and clinics. Come ahead if you like."

We met on the grounds of the only leprosarium in the continental United States. After flying to New Orleans and renting a car, I drove for two hours along the banks of the Mississippi River past crumbling old plantations, crawfish cafés, and gleaming new petrochemical factories. My eyes were burning from the factories' pollutants by the time I found the road that led to the backwater town of Carville, and then a smaller road that ended at the National Hansen's Disease Hospital and Research Center.

Louisiana authorities who founded the hospital situated it well away from population centers. (Due to myths about the disease, "Not in my backyard" sentiments tend to reach a feverish pitch when a leprosarium is proposed.) Laid out in sprawling, colonial style under massive live oak trees, Carville resembled a movie set of a Philippine plantation. I could see patients on crutches and in wheelchairs moving slowly along the double-decker arched walkways that connected the major buildings. Surrounding the hospital on three sides were a golf course and ball diamonds, a vegetable garden, and an enclave of staff housing. To the west lay the Mighty Mississippi, hidden from view by a twenty-foot levee. I opened the car door and stepped into a fog of delta humidity.

I knew of Brand's stature in the world medical community in advance of my visit: the offers to head up major medical centers in England and the United States, the distinguished lectureships all over the world, the hand-surgery procedures named in his honor, the prestigious Albert Lasker Award, his appointment as Commander of the Order of the British Empire by Queen Elizabeth II, his selection as the only Westerner to serve on the Mahatma Gandhi Foundation. Yet I awaited our interview in a cubbyhole of an office hardly suggestive of such renown. Stacks of medical journals, photographic slides, and unanswered correspondence covered every square inch of an ugly government-green metal desk. An antique window air-conditioner throbbed at the decibel level of an unmuffled motorcycle.

Finally, a slight man of less-than-average height and stiff posture entered the room. He had graying hair, bushy eyebrows, and a face that creased deeply when he smiled. In a British accent—a striking contrast to the bayou tones heard in hospital corridors—he apologized for the flecks of blood on his lab coat, explaining that he had just been dissecting armadillos, the only nonhuman species known to harbor leprosy bacilli.

That first visit lasted a week. I accompanied Brand on hospital rounds, hugging corridor walls to avoid the whirring electric wheelchairs and bicycles customized with sidecars. I sat in the examination room as he studied the inflamed, ulcerated feet and hands of patients, whom he quizzed like a detective in an effort to determine the injuries' cause. We grabbed bits of conversation in his office, sometimes interrupted by a call from overseas: a surgeon in Venezuela or India or Turkey shouting through the static to ask advice on a difficult procedure.

At night in their wooden bungalow on the hospital grounds, I would share a rice-and-curry meal with Brand and his wife, Margaret, a respected ophthalmologist. Then Paul Brand would prop up his bare feet (a trademark with him) and I would turn on the tape recorder for discussions that ranged from leprology and theology to world hunger and soil conservation. Every topic I brought up, he had already thought about in some depth, and his travels gave him a truly global perspective: He had spent a third of his life in England, a third in India, and now almost a third in the United States. During breaks he taught me such things as how to select a ripe fig (watch the ones butterflies light on several times, testing), how to stroke skin with a stiff hairbrush to stimulate nerve cells and relieve pain, how to make a mango milkshake.

We made an odd couple, Dr. Brand and I. I was a young punk in my mid-twenties with bushy Art Garfunkel–style hair; Brand was a dignified, silver-haired surgeon characterized by proper British reserve. In my role as a journalist I had interviewed many subjects: actors and musicians, politicians, successful business executives, Olympic and professional athletes, Nobel laureates and Pulitzer Prize winners. Something attracted me to Brand at a deeper level than I had felt with any other interview subject. For perhaps the first time, I encountered genuine humility.

Brand was still adjusting to life in the United States. He worried about the impact of television and the popular music culture on his children. Everyday luxuries made him nervous, and he longed for the simple life close to the soil in village India. When I talked him into going to a restaurant in the evening, he could hardly stand watching the waste of food scraped uneaten off diners' plates. He knew presidents, kings, and many famous people, but he rarely mentioned them, preferring instead to reminisce about individual leprosy patients. He talked openly about his failures, and always tried to deflect credit for his successes to his associates. Every day he rose early to study the

Bible and to pray. Humility and gratitude flowed from him naturally, and in our time together I sensed a desperate lack of these qualities in myself.

Most speakers and writers I knew were hitting the circuit, packaging and repackaging the same thoughts in different books and giving the same speeches to different crowds. Meanwhile Paul Brand, who had more intellectual and spiritual depth than anyone I had ever met, gave many of his speeches to a handful of leprosy patients in the hospital's Protestant chapel. At the Brands' insistence, I attended the Wednesday evening prayer service during my week at Carville. If I recall correctly, there were five of us in the choir and eight in the audience. Margaret Brand had drafted me into the choir, pleading, "We haven't had a male voice in ever so long. Paul is giving the sermon, so he's not available. You simply must sing with us." She brushed aside my mild protests. "Don't be silly. Half the people who attend are deaf because of a reaction to a drug we use in treating leprosy. But a guest chorister would be such a treat—they'll enjoy just watching you." To that motley crew, Brand proceeded to deliver an address worthy of Westminster Abbey. Obviously, he had spent hours meditating and praying over that one sermon. It mattered not that we were a tiny cluster of half-deaf nobodies in a sleepy bayou chapel. He spoke as an act of worship, as one who truly believed that God shows up when two or three are gathered together in God's name.

Later that week Brand admitted to me, somewhat shyly, that he had once tried writing a book. Some years before, when he had delivered a series of talks to a medical school in Vellore, India, other faculty members encouraged him to write them down for publication. He made the effort, but the material filled only ninety pages, not enough for a book. Twenty years had passed, and he had not touched the manuscript since. I persuaded him to dig through closets and bureau drawers until he located the badly smudged third carbon copy of those chapel talks, and that night I sat up long past midnight reading his remarkable meditations on the human body. I was staying in the hospital's antebellum guest room, and a ceiling fan periodically scattered the onionskin pages around the room. I kept gathering them up and resorting them, though, for I knew I had struck gold. The next day I asked Brand if we could collaborate, and those ninety pages eventually became two full-length books.

Sometime later we worked on a third volume, *The Gift of Pain*. In all I have spent almost ten years following the threads of Dr. Brand's life. I have often felt like James Boswell, who tailed the great man Samuel Johnson and loyally recorded every morsel of wisdom that fell from his lips. Brand's daughter Pauline once thanked me for bringing some order to "the happy jumble of my father's life and thoughts." Little did she know the role her father played in bringing some order to the unhappy jumble of my own life. True friends get their measure, over time, in their effect on you. As I compare the person I was in 1975, on our first meeting, and the person I am now, I realize that seismic changes have occurred within me, with Brand responsible for many of those tremors.

Paul Brand is both a good and a great man, and I am forever grateful for the time we spent together. At a stage when I had slight confidence to write about my own fledgling faith, I had absolute confidence writing about his. My faith grew as I observed with a journalist's critical eye a person enhanced in every way by his relationship with God. I came to know him as an actual living model whom I could watch in action: at Carville with his patients, in the villages of India, as a husband and father, as a speaker at both medical and spiritual conferences.

After retiring from medical practice, Dr. Brand moved to a small cottage overlooking Puget Sound in Seattle, the only home he has ever owned. He served a few terms as president of the International Christian Medical and Dental Society, consulted with the World Health Organization, and into his eighties has continued to lecture throughout the world. As the years passed, our roles inevitably reversed. He started calling me for advice on such matters as which word processing software to use, how to organize notes, and how to deal with publishers. He suffered a stroke on a trip to Turkey and a mild heart attack in London (a sympathetic reaction to his wife's more serious heart attack). For a time his speech slurred noticeably, and his ability to recall names and events faded. Our conversation moved to issues of aging and mortality.

As I proceed through stages of life, now approaching Brand's own age at the time of our first meeting, before me I have his slight but strong figure showing me the way. Deprived of my own father in infancy, I received as an adult from Brand much that I had missed. As much as anyone, he has helped set my course in outlook, spirit, and ideals. I look at the natural world, and environmental issues, largely through his eyes. From him I also have gained assurance that the Christian life I had heard in theory can actually work out in practice. It is indeed possible to live in modern society, achieve success without forfeiting humility, serve others sacrificially, and yet emerge with joy and contentment. To this day, whenever I doubt that, I look back on my time with Paul Brand.

Is the universe a friendly place? Einstein asked. A scientist, he searched for an answer in the vast reaches of the cosmos. Anyone who has survived the wounds of a dysfunctional family or church knows the more personal side of that question. An uncle, or perhaps a priest, sexually abuses a young child; a mother flies into an alcoholic rage; a six-year-old sibling contracts leukemia. For one who grows up in such an environment, the questions never go away. Is the world a friendly place? Can people be trusted? Can God?

I need not brood long over my own childhood to recognize these fundamental questions gnawing at my soul. In adolescence, as I read books like Sartre's *Nausea,* Camus's *The Plague,* and Wiesel's *Night,* I had little reason for optimism. And then I found myself collaborating with a man who had spent much of his life among the most mistreated human beings on the planet. Unexpectedly, instead of intensifying my questions, Dr. Brand pointed toward something of an answer.

Brand achieved fame in the medical world mainly through his pioneering research on the world's oldest and most feared disease. Before moving to the Carville hospital, he had directed a large medical college and hospital in Vellore, India, and founded a leprosy center known as

Karigiri. Leprosy disproportionately afflicts the poor. Left untreated, its victims can develop the facial disfigurement, blindness, and loss of limbs that so frightens people, who in turn respond with abuse and mistreatment. In a place like India, people with leprosy are the outcasts of society, often doubly so as members of the Untouchable caste.

In biblical times leprosy victims kept a wide berth and shouted "Unclean!" if anyone approached. In medieval times they lived outside town walls and wore warning bells. Even today in modern India, home to four million leprosy victims, a person showing signs of the disease may be kicked—literally, with a shoe—out of family and village to lead a beggar's life. Interviewing Brand's former patients, I heard stories of human cruelty almost beyond belief. If anyone has a right to bitterness or despair, it should be someone who works with these unfortunates. Instead, the single characteristic that most impressed me about Paul Brand was his bedrock sense of gratitude. For him, the universe is assuredly a friendly place.

I remember well our first conversation, for somehow I neglected to press the red "Record" button on the cassette recorder I was using. That evening, after discovering the error, I took a ferry across the Mississippi, sat in a crawfish café, and frantically tried to recall our conversation. I had a list of all my questions, and his answers had so impressed me that I found I could reconstruct them almost verbatim. As I dipped into the basket of shiny red crustaceans with one hand, I feverishly wrote down everything I remembered with the other, occasionally dripping drawn butter on my notebook pages.

How could a good God allow such a blemished world to exist? Brand had responded to my complaints one by one. Disease? Did I know that of the twenty-four thousand species of bacteria, all but a few hundred are healthful, not harmful? Plants could not produce oxygen, nor could animals digest food without the assistance of bacteria. Indeed, bacteria constitute half of all living matter. Most agents of disease, he explained, vary from these necessary organisms in only slight mutations.

What about birth defects? He launched into a description of the complex biochemistry involved in producing one healthy child. The great wonder is not that birth defects occur but that millions more do not. Could a mistake-proof world have been created so that the human genome with its billions of variables would never err in transmission? No scientist could envision such an error-free system in our world of fixed physical laws.

"I've found it helpful to try to think like the Creator," Brand told me. "My engineering team at Carville has done just that. For several years our team worked with the human hand. What engineering perfection we find there! I have a bookcase filled with surgical textbooks that describe operations people have devised for the injured hand: different ways to rearrange the tendons, muscles, and joints, ways to replace sections of bones and mechanical joints—thousands of surgical procedures. But I know of no procedure that succeeds in improving a normal hand. For example, the best materials we use in artificial joint replacements generate five times as much friction as the body's natural joints, and these replacements may last only a few years. The only joints that need to be replaced are the few that have been grossly injured or fractured or the one that has worked well, as God designed, for many years and then gradually became arthritic and worn out in old age. After operating on thousands of hands, I must agree with Isaac Newton: 'In the absence of any other proof, the thumb alone would convince me of God's existence.' "

I kept proposing exceptions, and Brand dealt with each. Even at its worst, he continued, our natural world shows evidence of careful design. Like a tour guide at an art museum, he excitedly described the beautiful way torn muscle filaments reconnect, "like the teeth of interlocking combs," after an injury. "And do you know about the *ductus arteriosus*? A bypass vessel, it routes blood directly to a developing fetus's extremities, instead of to the lungs. At the moment of birth, suddenly all blood must pass through the lungs to receive oxygen because now the baby is breathing air. In a flash, a flap descends like a curtain, deflecting the blood flow, and a muscle constricts the *ductus arteriosus*. After performing that one act, the muscle gradually dissolves and gets absorbed by the rest of the body. Without this split-second adjustment, the baby could never survive outside the womb."

Our conversation was the first of many anatomy lessons I would receive from Dr. Brand. His ability to recall what he had studied in medical school thirty years before impressed me, certainly, but something else stood out: a childlike enthusiasm, an ebullient sense of wonder at God's good creation. Listening to him, my own Chestertonian sense of wonder reawakened. I had been focusing on the apparent flaws in creation; this doctor who spent all day working with those flaws had instead an attitude of appreciation, even reverence. That attitude, I would learn, traced back to a childhood spent close to nature.

Son of missionary parents in the remote hill country of India, Brand grew up in a world of tropical fruit trees and of butterflies, birds, and other animals. His artistic mother tried to capture its beauty with her paints. His father, Jesse, a self-taught naturalist, saw everywhere in nature the fingerprint of the Creator. He would lead his son to a towering termite mound and explain the marvels of cooperative termite society: "ten thousand legs working together as if commanded by a single brain, all frantic except the queen, big and round as a sausage, who lies oblivious, pumping out eggs." He would point to the sandy funnel of an ant lion trap, or the nest of a weaver bird, or a swarm of bees hanging from a tree branch. Paul did his school lessons in a tree house high up in a jackfruit tree, and sometimes studied at night by the throbbing light of a firefly jar.

Education interrupted Paul Brand's paradise when he was sent to England at the age of nine. Five years later, a teenager far from family and home, he received a telegram announcing that his father had died of blackwater fever. A letter soon arrived, mailed by ship weeks before his father's death, which became for him a kind of final legacy. Jesse Brand described the hills around their home and concluded, "God means us to delight in his world. It isn't necessary to know botany or zoology or biology in order to enjoy the manifold life of nature. Just observe. And remember. And compare. And be always looking to God with thankfulness and worship for having placed you in such a delightful corner of the universe as the planet Earth."

Jesse Brand's son kept his advice, and keeps it to this day, whether hiking on the Olympic Peninsula or stalking birds in the swamps of Louisiana or lecturing to medical students about the wonders of the bodies they will be treating. First in the hills of India, and later through his study of the human body, he came to realize that the natural world conceals traces of God, and the God he found there was good. It was a message I needed, from a messenger I learned to trust.

Brand's career centered on perhaps the most problematic aspect of creation, the existence of pain. I was writing the book *Where Is God When It Hurts;* he invited me to consider an alternative world without pain. He insisted on pain's great value, holding up as proof the terrible results of leprosy—damaged faces, blindness, and loss of fingers, toes, and limbs—all of which occur as side-effects of painlessness. As a young doctor in India, Brand had made the groundbreaking medical discovery that leprosy does its damage merely by destroying nerve endings. People who lose pain sensation then damage themselves by such simple actions as gripping a splintered rake or wearing tight shoes. Pressure sores form, infection sets in, and no pain signals alert them to tend to the wounded area. I saw such damage firsthand in Brand's clinics.

"I thank God for pain," Brand declared with the utmost sincerity. "I cannot think of a greater gift I could give my leprosy patients." He went on to describe the intricacies of the pain system that protects the human body. It takes firm pressure on a very sharp needle for the sole of the foot to feel pain, whereas the cornea of the eye senses one-thousandth as much pressure, calling for a blink reflex when a thin eyelash or speck of dust brushes the surface. Intestines do not sense pain from being cut or burned—dangers these internal organs do not normally confront—yet they send out the urgent pain signal of colic when distended.

"We doctors experience a rude awakening after medical school," Brand continued. "After studying the marvels of the human body, suddenly I was thrust into a position much like the complaint desk of a department store. Not once did a person visit my office to express appreciation for a beautifully functioning kidney or lung. They came to complain that something was not working properly. Only later did I realize that the very things they complained about were their greatest allies. Most people view pain as an enemy. Yet, as my leprosy patients prove, it forces us to pay attention to threats against our bodies. Without it, heart attacks, strokes, ruptured appendixes, and stomach ulcers would all occur without any warning. Who would ever visit a doctor apart from pain's warnings?

"I noticed that the symptoms of illness my patients complained about were actually a display of bodily healing at work. Virtually every response of our bodies that we view with irritation or disgust—blister, callus, swelling, fever, sneeze, cough, vomiting, and especially pain—demonstrates a reflex toward health. In all these things normally considered enemies, we can find a reason to be grateful."

I had often puzzled over the Bible's dramatic scene when Job, the prototype of innocent sufferers, confronts God with his complaints about suffering. The speech God gave in reply has endured as one of the great nature passages in literature, a superb celebration of wildness. To the problem of pain itself, however, God gave no direct answer, only this challenge to Job: If I, as Creator, have produced such a marvelous world as this, which you can plainly observe, can you not trust me with those areas you cannot comprehend?

As I listened to Brand, I realized that I had been approaching God like a sick patient—as if the Creator were running a complaint desk. I anguished over the tragedies, diseases, and injustices, all the while ignoring the many good things surrounding me in this world. Was it possible, I wondered, to retain a Chestertonian enthusiasm for the marvels of the natural world despite its apparent flaws? Like the psalmists, could I learn to praise and lament at the same time, with neither intonation drowning out the other?

Brand responded to this same dilemma with a twin spirit of gratitude and trust—gratitude for those things he could see and appreciate, and trust regarding those things he could not. I remembered Chesterton's description of an "ordinary" person who accepts the world as a gift, the proper response to which is gratitude. To Brand's surprise, faith in God's trustworthiness deepened even as he worked among people least likely to feel gratitude, leprosy victims in India, because he saw transformations in the lowest of the low resulting from simple compassion and a healing touch.

As I began working with Brand and following him around the world, I met many other dedicated Christians who devote their lives to healing the wounds of humanity. In India, for example, where less than 3 percent of the population claims to be Christian, nearly a fifth of all medical work is performed by Christian doctors and nurses, many of them trained at Brand's old hospital in Vellore. I accompanied them on mobile visits to villages, where they treated tropical infections, set bones, and performed minor surgery, often outdoors under a tamarind tree. They served Hindus, Moslems, Sikhs, Jains, Parsis, and Communists alike. If you say the word "Christian" to an Indian peasant—who may never have heard of Jesus Christ—the first image to pop into his mind may well be that of a hospital, or of a medical van that stops by his village once a month to provide free, personal care.

Watching these people serve in difficult conditions with low pay and few benefits, I saw a sharp contrast between their approach and my own. I sat home in Chicago and wrote books demanding answers from God about the problems of this world. They volunteered for the front lines in a truly incarnational response. Like the Brands, they showed a level of personal fulfillment and even happiness that I had not found among many famous people I had interviewed.

I learned that part of the answer to my question, "Where is God when it hurts?" is a related question: "Where is the church when it hurts?" As the Jewish theologian Abraham Heschel wrote, "The cardinal issue, Why does the God of justice and compassion permit evil to persist? is bound up with the problem of how man should aid God so that his justice and compassion prevail." From the gentle touch of health workers like Paul and Margaret Brand, leprosy patients in India have learned that caste is not fate and disease is not destiny, and in that same touch many first sense the tactile reality of God's own love.

Although I have great respect for Dr. Brand and his service to God, I also confess relief that he is not a "saint" out of the mold of

Francis of Assisi or Mother Teresa. I needed an up-close model of someone I could relate to more naturally.

Paul Brand consulted with Mother Teresa, served on committees with Gandhi's disciples, and knew some of India's traditional "holy men." In his own life, however, he chose the middle way of balancing off the material and the mystical, the prophetic and the pragmatic. Older acquaintances at the hospital in Vellore remember him not only for his spiritual depth and sacrificial service but also for his practical jokes, love for marmalade and mangoes, and fast driving. As I emerged from the 1960s, a decade never accused of a sense of balance, I needed an example of someone who lived a well-rounded life in the midst of modern society, not off in a monastery or ashram.

Brand has struggled with the tensions facing modern civilization while not yielding to either side. On the one hand, he lived a counter-culture lifestyle long before such a phrase entered the vocabulary. In India he insisted on receiving Indian wages, not the much higher amount usually granted foreign doctors. The Brands have always eaten simply, relying mainly on homemade breads and vegetables grown in their organic garden. Dr. Brand acknowledges a few reasons for discarding clothes—unpatchable rips, for instance—but lack of stylishness is certainly not one of them. Furniture in his home and office is, to put it kindly, unpretentious. He opposes waste in all forms. Brand admits he would shed no tears personally if all advances from the industrial revolution suddenly disappeared; he prefers village life in India, close to the outdoors.

On the other hand, he has learned to use the tools made available by modern technology. Under his leadership, a hospital in the dusty town of Vellore grew into the most modern and sophisticated facility in all of southwest Asia. Later, Brand came to Carville in the United States because that research center offered the technological support needed to benefit millions of leprosy patients worldwide. And when personal computers were introduced in the 1980s, he signed up with boyish enthusiasm for one of the first IBMs. He gratefully uses electron microscopes and thermograms and jet planes, believing that technology's tools used wisely and not destructively can serve the higher goal of human compassion.

My conversations with Brand have often strayed to the question of lifestyle, for his experiences in India, England, and America have afforded him a unique perspective. He has lived in one of the poorest countries and two of the richest. Affluence in the West, he recognizes, offers a deadly temptation. The enormous gap in wealth can widen the moat separating the West from the rest of the world, dulling us to cries of need and justice.

The lifelong tension over lifestyle traces back to Brand's childhood in India. After her husband's death from blackwater fever, Paul's mother took on the style of a saint in the traditional sense. She lived on a pittance, devoting her life to bringing physical and spiritual healing to villagers in five mountain ranges. She cared nothing for her personal appearance, to the extent of banning all mirrors from her house. She continued making hazardous journeys on her pony even after suffering concussions and fractures from falls. Although tropical diseases ravaged her own body, she gave all her energies to treating the diseases and injuries of the people around her. Sometimes "Granny Brand" would embarrass Paul with an intemperate outburst; at an official dinner in Vellore, for example, she might ask in horror, "How could you possibly dine on such fine food when I have people back in the hills starving to death this very night!" She died at age ninety-five, and at her funeral thousands of villagers walked for miles to honor her in the chapel her husband had built by hand.

From his parents Paul learned the enduring lesson that love can only be applied person-to-person. They left behind few lasting institutions, only their permanent imprint on thousands of lives to whom they had taught health, sanitation, farming, and the Christian gospel. Singlehandedly, Granny Brand rid huge areas of a guinea worm infection that had persisted for centuries. She had earned such trust that villagers followed her instructions on building stone walls around the open wells where the larvae bred; no government program had been so effective.

Yet her son, Paul Brand, made his most lasting impact through rigid scientific disciplines. At Vellore he fought his wife, Margaret, for space in the icebox, preserving cadaver hands on which he could practice surgical techniques by lamplight. For years he puzzled over the physiology of leprosy symptoms: Which cells does it attack, and why? The answer, his most important medical discovery, came during an autopsy, when he concluded that the leprosy bacillus only attacked nerve tissue. Proving that theory required more years of research, in which he had to identify the precise cause of every patient's injuries. The results of such research had a dramatic effect on the treatment of leprosy and other anesthetic diseases worldwide. Fifteen million victims of leprosy gained hope that, with proper care, they could preserve their toes and fingers and eyesight. Later, he applied the same principles to the insensitive feet of diabetics, helping to prevent, by one estimate, seventy thousand amputations annually in the United States alone.

Brand told me of a comment made by Mother Teresa as he consulted with her on a leprosy clinic she was opening in Calcutta. "We have drugs for people with diseases like leprosy," she said. "But these drugs do not treat the main problem, the disease of being unwanted. That's what my sisters hope to provide."

In one of our conversations, Brand mused on why there are Christian missions devoted exclusively to leprosy. Much of his work in India was funded by the Leprosy Mission of England, sister organization to the American Leprosy Mission. "I know of no Arthritis Mission or Diabetes Mission," he said. "The answer, I think, relates to the incredible stigma that has surrounded leprosy for so many centuries. To work with leprosy required more than a natural instinct of compassion; it required a kind of supernatural calling. People such as Father Damien, who ministered to leprosy patients in Hawaii and then contracted the disease himself, believed that human beings, no matter what their affliction, should never be cast aside. It was up to the church to care for the sick, the unwanted, the unloved."

As I studied the history of leprosy in my writings with Brand, I got acquainted with the saintly few who, defying society's stigma, looked past the unsightly symptoms and ministered to leprosy's victims. As the disease ravaged Europe during the Middle Ages, orders of nuns devoted to Lazarus, the patron saint of leprosy, established homes for patients. These courageous women could do little but bind wounds and change dressings, but the homes themselves, called *lazarettos*, may have helped break the hold of the disease in Europe, by isolating leprosy patients and improving their living conditions. In the nineteenth and twentieth centuries, Christian missionaries who spread across the globe established colonies for leprosy patients, and as a result most of the major scientific advances in treating leprosy came from missionaries.

The Carville hospital itself (recently closed in a government cost-saving measure) has a history typical of leprosy work worldwide. The first seven patients, chased out of New Orleans, were smuggled by authorities up the Mississippi on a coal barge, since nineteenth-century laws forbade people with leprosy from traveling on any form of public transportation. They landed at an abandoned, rundown plantation, which the State of Louisiana had quietly procured. A few slave cabins were still standing, populated mainly by rats, bats, and snakes. The seven patients moved into the "Louisiana Leper Home," but the state had difficulty recruiting workers for the leprosarium until finally the Daughters of Charity, an order of Catholic nuns, volunteered. These women, nicknamed "the White Caps," did much of the initial labor. Rising two hours before daylight to pray, wearing starched white uniforms in bayou heat, the nuns drained swamps, leveled roads, and repaired buildings for the new leprosarium. Their successors were still serving at Carville when I visited Brand there.

In India, a melting pot of religions, Brand observed how other religions responded to the problem of pain. Buddhists taught a serene acceptance of suffering, an attitude that we in the hypochondriacal West could surely learn from. Hindus and Muslims often faced suffering with a spirit of fatalism: to the Hindu it results from sins of a former life, and is the will of Allah to the Muslim. In contrast, Christianity has traditionally responded with the paradox modeled by Jesus: we must trust the goodness of God despite the suffering and injustice we see around us, and yet do all we can to relieve it during our days on earth. Paul Brand gave me a living example of that response.

I n his twilight years, Dr. Brand has accepted many invitations from medical schools that want him to address the dehumanization of medicine. Today, high-tech medicine, HMO insurance policies, and increasing specialization conspire to squelch the very instincts that draw many of the best students into the field. Brand expresses the guiding principle of his medical career this way: "The most precious possession any human being has is his spirit—his will to live, his sense of dignity, his personality. Though technically we may be concerned with tendons, bones, and nerve endings, we must never lose sight of the person we are treating."

Although our conversations together cover a broad range of topics, inevitably they drift back to stories of individuals, Brand's former patients. Most often, these patients are the forgotten people, ostracized from family and village because of their illness. A medical staff can repair much of the physical damage. They can also provide that most basic human need, touch. But what can they do for the spirit of the patient, the corroded self-image? For hours at a time I have sat and listened to Brand tell me stories of these patients and their families, and the extraordinary treatment they got in the Karigiri leprosarium. I am amazed that an orthopedic surgeon knows so much about patients he treated decades before, and more amazed at the tears that freely flow as he tells their stories. Quite obviously, they made as great an impression on him as he made on them.

It takes a few pennies a day to arrest leprosy's progress with sulfone drugs. It takes thousands of dollars, and the painstaking care of skilled professionals, to restore to wholeness a patient in whom the disease has spread unchecked. Brand began with the rigid claw-hands, experimenting with tendon and muscle transfers until he found the very best combination to restore a full range of movement. The surgeries and rehabilitation stretched over months and sometimes years. He applied similar procedures to feet, correcting the deformities caused by years of walking without a sense of pain to guide the body in distributing weight and pressure.

Restored feet and hands gave a leprosy patient the capability to earn a living, but who would hire an employee bearing the scars of the dread disease? Brand's first patients returned to him distraught, asking him to reverse the effects of surgery so that they could return to begging, a profession that exploited obvious deformities. Paul and Margaret Brand worked together to correct that cosmetic damage. They learned to remake a human nose by entering it through the space between gum and upper lip, stretching out the skin and moist lining, then building up a new nasal structure from the inside with bone transplant. They sought to prevent blindness by restoring the ability to blink. Leprosy deadens the tiny pain cells that prompt a healthy person to blink several times a minute, and eventually the dryness leads to blindness. Margaret learned to tunnel a muscle that is normally used for chewing up under the cheek and attach it to the upper eyelid. By chewing gum all day long, her patients simultaneously moved their eyelids up and down, lubricating the eyes and thus averting blindness. Finally, the Brands replaced lost eyebrows on the faces of their patients by tunneling a piece of scalp, intact with its nerve and blood supply, under the skin of the forehead and sewing it in place above the eyes. The first patients proudly grew their new eyebrows to enormous, bushy lengths.

All this elaborate medical care went to "nobodies," victims of leprosy who had mostly made their living from begging. Many who arrived at the hospital barely looked human. Their shoulders slumped, they cringed when other people approached, and the light had faded from their eyes. Months of compassionate treatment from the staff at Karigiri could return that light to their eyes. For years people had shrunk away from them in terror; at Karigiri nurses and doctors would hold their hands and talk to them. Unrevolted, unafraid, the staff listened to the new patients' stories, and used the magic of human touch. A year or so later these patients, Lazarus-like, would walk out of the hospital and proudly head off to learn a trade.

As Brand reflects now, the process of following patients through the full rehabilitation cycle ultimately challenged his whole approach toward medicine. Somewhere, perhaps in medical school, doctors acquire an attitude that seems suspiciously like hubris: "Oh, you've come just in time. Count on me. I think I'll be able to save you." Working at Karigiri stripped away that hubris. No one could "save" leprosy patients. The staff could arrest the disease, yes, and repair some of the damage. Eventually, however, every leprosy patient had to go back and, against overwhelming odds, attempt to build a new life. Brand began to see his chief contribution as one he had not studied in medical school: to join with his patient as a partner in the task of restoring dignity to a broken spirit. "We are treating a person, not a disease," he says. "That is the true meaning of rehabilitation."

The great societies of the West have been moving away from an underlying belief in the value of a single human soul. We tend to view history in terms of groups of people: classes, political parties, races, sociological groupings. We apply labels to each other, and explain behavior and ascribe worth on the basis of those labels. After prolonged exposure to Dr. Brand, I realized that I had been seeing large human problems in a mathematical model: percentages of Gross National Product, average annual income, mortality rate, doctors-per-thousand of population. Love, however, is not mathematical; we can never precisely calculate the greatest possible good to be applied equally to the world's poor and needy. We can only seek out one person, and then another, and then another, as objects for God's love.

I had been wrestling with issues facing humanity. Yet I had not learned to love individuals—people created in the image of God. I would not predict a leprosarium in India as the most likely place to learn about the infinite worth of human beings, but a visit there makes the lesson unavoidable.

On my last trip to India with Paul Brand, in 1990, he showed me his childhood home in the Kolli Malai Mountains. Our Jeep ascended a remarkable highway featuring seventy switchbacks (each one neatly labeled: 38/70, 39/70, 40/70). A motorcycle passed us, a woman passenger clinging to the back of its driver, her sari flowing out behind her like a flag. The hairpin curves stirred Brand's memories. "There was no highway then," he said. "As a child I rode in a canvas contraption slung from porters' shoulders on bamboo poles. When I grew old enough to walk, I used to totter along at eye level with the porters' legs.

I watched for the tiny leeches that would leap from the shrub, fasten to those legs, and swell with blood."

On this trip, however, we worried more about overheating the radiator than about leeches. Finally the road leveled off and wound across a high plateau, giving us spectacular views of the verdant green rice paddies below and the pale, curvy lines across the horizon that marked other mountain ranges in the distance. Then the asphalt ended and the road dove down into a small valley. Gravel gave way to dirt, then to a pair of ruts running along a line of eucalyptus trees. We followed the ruts for half an hour without seeing a single person, and I began to wonder if our driver had lost his way.

Suddenly the Jeep crested a small hill and an amazing sight met us. A hundred and fifty people were waiting alongside the road—and had been waiting, we soon learned, for four hours. They surrounded our car, greeting us in the traditional Indian fashion, palms held together, head bowed. Women, colorful as tropical birds in their bright silk saris, draped floral leis around our necks and led us to a feast spread on banana leaves. After the meal everyone crowded into the mud-walled chapel built by Paul Brand's father and treated us to an hour-long program of hymns, tributes, and ceremonial dances.

I remember one speech especially, by a woman who spoke of Paul's mother. "The hill tribes didn't practice abortion," she said. "They disposed of unwanted children by leaving them beside the road. Granny Brand would take in these children, nurse them back to health, rear them, and try to educate them. I was one of the unwanted ones, left to die. There were several dozen of us, but she treated it more like an adoption center than an orphanage. We called her Mother of the Hills. When I did well in studies, she paid for me to go off to a proper school, and eventually I earned a master's degree. I now teach nursing at the University of Madras, and I came several hundred miles today to honor the Brands for what they did for me and many others."

After he had made a little speech and wiped away the tears, Dr. Brand led me outdoors to see the legacy his parents had left. He pointed out the hand-sawn wooden house his father had built, capping the stilts with upside-down frying pans to foil the termites. A clinic was still functioning, along with a school—his parents founded nine in the hills—and carpentry shop. Citrus orchards spread out across the hills, one of Granny Brand's pet agricultural projects. Her husband, Jesse, had set up half a dozen farms for mulberry trees, bananas, sugarcane, coffee, and tapioca. Paul kept remarking on how tall the jacaranda trees had grown since his father planted them seven decades before. Their fallen lavender blossoms carpeted the ground. When the time came to leave, he took me to the site of his parents' graves, just down the slope from the bungalow where he grew up. "Their bodies lie here, but their spirit lives on," he said. "Just look around you."

Paul chose a different course in life than his general-missionary parents, becoming an orthopedic surgeon. In order to see his legacy, I visited his former patients. One man, Namo, had a twenty-year-old photo of Brand on his wall, captioned MAY THE SPIRIT THAT IS IN HIM LIVE IN ME. When Namo told me his story, I could easily understand the affection he feels for his former surgeon.

As a youth Namo had to leave university in the middle of his final year; telltale patches of leprosy had appeared on his skin, and his hand was retracting into a claw position. Rejected by his school, his village, and finally his family, Namo made his way to the leprosarium in southern India where a young doctor was trying out some experimental hand surgery techniques. There were four million people with leprosy in India, and fifteen million worldwide, but Brand was the only orthopedic surgeon attempting to treat their deformities.

Namo recalled that dark day: "I was so angry at my condition I could hardly speak. Stuttering, I told Dr. Brand my hands were now useless to me. Soon my feet would be too. For all I cared, he could cut them off." Namo made a slashing motion with one hand across his other wrist. "Anyway, he could do anything he wanted if he thought he might learn something."

Fortunately, Namo was wrong about his prognosis. Drugs halted the spread of the disease. And after undergoing a painstaking series of surgical procedures over a five-year period, he regained the use of his hands and feet. He took training in physiotherapy, began working with other leprosy patients, and went on to become Chief of Physical Therapy at the All-India Institute.

Later that day I visited Sadan, another former patient. He looked like a miniature version of Gandhi: skinny, balding, with thick spectacles, perched cross-legged on the edge of a bed. The door to his modest apartment was open, and small birds flew in and out. A mangy dog lounged on the step. Sadan showed me his feet, which ended in smooth, rounded stumps instead of toes. "I met the Brands too late to save these," he said. "But they gave me shoes that let me walk."

In a high-pitched, singsong voice Sadan told me wrenching stories of past rejection: the classmates who made fun of him in school, the driver who forcibly threw him off a public bus, the many employers who refused to hire him despite his training and talent, the hospitals that turned him away with a brusque "We don't treat lepers here."

"When I got to Vellore, I spent the night on the Brands' veranda, because I had nowhere else to go," said Sadan. "That was unheard of for a person with leprosy back then. I can still remember when Dr. Brand took my infected, bleeding feet in his hands. I had been to many doctors. A few had examined my hands and feet from a distance, but Drs. Paul and Margaret were the first medical workers who dared to touch me. I had nearly forgotten what human touch felt like. Even more impressive, they let me stay in their house that night, and this was when even health workers were terrified of leprosy."

Sadan then recounted the elaborate sequence of medical procedures—tendon transfers, nerve strippings, toe amputations, and cataract removal—performed by the Brands. By transferring tendons to his fingers, they made it possible for him to write again, and now he kept accounts for a program that gave free leprosy care through fifty-three mobile clinics. He spoke for half an hour. His past life was a catalog of human suffering. And the stigma continues to this day: just recently he had sat in a car alone and watched his daughter's wedding from a distance, afraid his presence would disturb the guests.

As the Brands and I sipped our last cup of tea in his home, just before leaving to catch a plane to England, Sadan made this astonishing statement: "Still, I must say that I am now happy that I had this disease."

"Happy?" I asked, incredulous.

"Yes," replied Sadan. "Apart from leprosy, I would have been a normal man with a normal family, chasing wealth and a higher position in society. I would never have known such wonderful people as Dr. Paul and Dr. Margaret, and I would never have known the God who lives in them."

Two days later, our reception in England made for a striking contrast to the royal welcome we had received in India. There, too, Brand and I retraced the steps of his past. We visited the ancestral home where his missionary parents had spent their furloughs. His mother had come from wealth, and the house, located in one of London's better neighborhoods, was easily worth a million dollars. Its upper-class occupant came out to see what we were staring at, and Brand treated her to a room-by-room tour, describing how the house used to look sixty years before.

That afternoon we stood on the hospital roof where as a medical resident he had fire-watched during the German bombings. No one garlanded us with leis and no one gathered around us to sing hymns and give testimonials. To the guards and staff workers at the hospital, Brand was a confused old man interfering with their work. Offices had moved, wings had been torn down, security procedures set in place. In the setting of his early medical career Brand seemed, if anything, an anachronism. We wandered from receptionist to receptionist at University College Hospital inquiring after former faculty colleagues. "Who? Could you spell that name?" was the typical response. Finally, in a darkened hallway, we found a row of photos of some of Brand's teachers—doctors who were as famous in their day as Christian Barnard or C. Everett Koop are in ours.

I caught myself wondering how Paul Brand's career might have played itself out had he stayed in London. Even working in a remote

Indian village among outcast leprosy patients, he had achieved world renown. If he had stayed in a research capacity at a well-equipped laboratory, who knows what honors might have come his way. A Nobel Prize perhaps?

But what then? His picture would join the others in the darkened hallway, now dusty and beginning to yellow. His name, like theirs, would appear as a footnote in the medical textbooks. Fame in the annals of medicine rarely lasts long; microsurgery techniques have already outdated most of the procedures considered breakthroughs in Brand's youth. In contrast, his work as a missionary surgeon in India continues to bear fruit, in the transformed lives of Namo and Sadan and hundreds like them.

Coming so close together, the encounters in India and England became for me a kind of parable contrasting the transience of fame with the permanence of investing in service to others. Whether we live out our days in India or England or Clarkston, Georgia, the true measure of our worth will depend not on a *curriculum vitae* or the inheritance we leave, but on the spirit we pass on to others. "Whoever finds his life will lose it, and whoever loses his life for my sake will find it," said Jesus in his proverb most often repeated in the Gospels. Each career path offers its own rewards. But after sitting with Brand in the homes of Namo and Sadan, and then touring the Hall of Fame at the Royal College of Surgeons, I had no doubt which rewards truly last.

In one of our last conversations, Dr. Brand turned reflective. "Because of where I practiced medicine, I never made much money at it. But I tell you that as I look back over a lifetime of surgery, the host of friends who once were patients bring me more joy than wealth could ever bring. I first met them when they were suffering and afraid. As their doctor, I shared their pain. Now that I am old, it is their love and gratitude that illuminates the continuing pathway of my life. It's strange—those of us who involve ourselves in places where there is the most suffering, look back in surprise to find that it was there that we discovered the reality of joy." He then quoted another saying of Jesus: "Happy are they who bear their share of the world's pain: In the long run they will know more happiness than those who avoid it" (translation by J. B. Phillips).

GETTING STARTED WITH PAUL BRAND:

Dr. Brand and I have written three books together: *Fearfully and Wonderfully Made* and *In His Image,* and then, more recently, *The Gift of Pain,* which weaves together his life story and theories about pain. A more traditional missionary biography by Dorothy Clarke Wilson, *Ten Fingers for God,* focuses on his time in India, and *Granny Brand,* also by Wilson, tells the story of his mother's work. Brand has also published further thoughts in *God's Forever Feast.*

When I served as editor of *Campus Life* magazine in the 1970s, more than two hundred magazines crossed my desk on a regular basis. I would let them pile up to form tall, leaning towers, then spend an entire weekend day flipping through them in an effort to uncover my furniture.

About half the magazines represented Christian organizations, including missions, denominations, youth associations, colleges, counseling and science associations. The other half came from secular sources, the magazines you find on the rack at any newsstand. I marveled at the great gulf fixed between them. New York editors surely had heard thirty or forty million born-again Christians lived out in the heartlands somewhere, but who among them had ever met one? They might as well not exist, for all the mention they got. Meanwhile, Christians were busily constructing a counter-society—complete with schools, bookstores, television and radio stations, and even Christian businesses advertising in a "Christian Yellow Pages"—in order to protect themselves from the secular humanists bent on their destruction.

Going through the stack one afternoon, I encountered the name Robert Coles at the bottom of a brief article titled "Why Do You Still Believe in God, in the Promise of the Cross?" in, of all places, *Harper's* magazine. What kind of person could span the great divide with an article on personal faith in a prestigious New York publication? Over the years I noticed Coles's byline popping up in the

Chapter 5

DR. ROBERT

COLES

TENDER LIVES

AND THE

ASSAULTS

OF THE

UNIVERSE

most unlikely contexts: a review of the French Catholic writer George Bernanos in the *New York Times Book Review,* a discussion of Kierkegaard and Pascal in the *New England Journal of Medicine,* a tribute to Dorothy Day and her Catholic Worker movement in the *New Republic,* a review of Flannery O'Connor in the *Journal of the American Medical Association.*

While other Christians bemoaned the bias of the secular press against articles centered on faith issues, Robert Coles, a name unknown to most of them, was writing about whatever he wanted wherever he wanted from an unabashedly Christian viewpoint. I began to look on him as a bridge-builder, a thoughtful writer whom I could trust to direct me to others, many of whom became my "virtual pastors." For an entire generation of Harvard students, Professor Coles presented Christianity as a credible option in the modern world, and through his writings he did the same for me.

In a 1972 cover story *Time* called Coles "the most influential living psychiatrist in the U.S." When did he ever find time to practice psychiatry? I wondered. He taught courses at Harvard Medical School, yes, but courses in "the literature of transcendence," as he called his pet list of novels with spiritual themes. He seemed a man with a thousand interests, and whenever he discovered a new interest he wrote a book about it: a book of dialogue with the radical priest Daniel Berrigan; a book of literary criticism on novelist Walker Percy, and others on James Agee and George Eliot; biographies of Erik Erikson, Anna Freud, Simone Weil, and Dorothy Day; a book on *Flannery O'Connor's South,* collections of conversations with the poor, and other conversations with civil rights workers and rednecks and Eskimos and rich kids—more than sixty books in all, to supplement well over a thousand articles.

His most impressive work, the five-volume *Children of Crisis* series, ran to more than a million words and earned Coles a Pulitzer Prize in 1973. Later he was selected for a MacArthur Foundation "genius award," which included a tax-free grant that freed him to do more research and writing. By 1999, as he turned seventy, he was still churning out books and articles, and President Clinton acknowledged his

achievements by bestowing on him the Medal of Freedom, the nation's highest civilian honor.

As I followed Coles's career, he helped me understand one of the
peculiarities of the writing profession: the observer syndrome.
Writing is an act performed in solitude. I am tempted to call it a psy-
chotic act, for we writers construct an artificial reality that only we in-
habit and that often seems more real to us than the other world "out
there." After I have holed up for a week on an intensive writing project, I find I must go through something like reentry, having forgotten
how to have a normal conversation and conduct the subtle negotiations that comprise human contact. I have been shuffling words and
ideas around and, difficult as that may be, it is a far more controlled
and orderly process than interacting with live human beings. As a result, we writers tend to withdraw, secluding ourselves, observing life
without truly participating in it.

By journalistic background, I lead a more eventful life than many
writers. I have traveled to places like Somalia and Russia and Chile
and Myanmar—always to collect material for writing, of course—yet
the observer syndrome never goes away. I visited a refugee camp in Somalia at the height of the starvation crisis. Thirty thousand people
lived in makeshift tents in that desert camp, and forty to fifty babies
were dying each day. Never have I felt more helpless. Nurses were at-
taching IVs, doctors were administering antibiotics, and chaplains
were burying the dead—whereas I, a journalist who had flown seven
thousand miles to join them, stood alongside scribbling notes and taking pictures. Never had my role seemed more vicarious, my existence
more peripheral.

Vicariousness is, after all, a writer's business. Although not everyone
can visit a refugee camp in Somalia, if I do my job well enough, readers
will gain some sense of what it is like and may even be motivated to
help. I visit John Perkins in Mississippi, or Dr. Paul Brand in India, and
even if I enter their lives for only a few days or weeks, I open a keyhole
that allows others to peer in at a world they might otherwise miss.

In his aptly titled *Conjectures of a Guilty Bystander,* Thomas Merton tells of a trip from his monastery to a nearby city: "In Louisville, at the corner of Fourth and Walnut, in the center of the shopping district, I was suddenly overwhelmed with the realization that I loved all those people, that they were mine and I theirs, that we could not be alien to one another even though we were total strangers . . . though 'out of the world' [monks] are in the same world as everybody else, the world of the bomb, the world of race hatred, the world of technology, the world of mass media, big business, revolution and all the rest." That odd moment became an epiphany for Merton, who went on to say that the function of solitude is to realize some things—the unity of the human race, the wonder of life, the glorious irreproducibility of any one person—with a clarity that would be impossible to anyone completely immersed in the world rather than perched on the edge, observing. "There is no way of telling people that they are all walking around shining like the sun," he said.

Indeed there is not. And yet rarely, and often unconsciously, the writer of exceptional skill may, by rendering details of ordinary lives, reflect back to the reader something of that radiance. Robert Coles did that for me. In his quirky, unorthodox style, he broke down the barrier between observer and participator, entered other lives, then withdrew to a solitude that allowed him to render them for the rest of us.

Despite his Harvard roots, Coles hardly fits the mold of an ivory-tower academic. He has practiced a very unusual style of field research, following children from place to place, sitting on the floors of their homes, asking a few questions, winning their trust. He rode buses to school with such children, sitting on undersized, uncushioned bench seats and gripping the rusty bars on the seat in front of him as the bus bounced its way to school and back. He became known as "The Crayon Man," because he would pull out paper and crayons and ask the children to draw pictures. Often the pictures revealed more than the children's words: One young black girl drew white people taller than herself, and with precise features and the correct number of fingers and toes, while she pictured herself lacking an eye, an ear, or perhaps an arm.

Somehow in his life Robert Coles always managed to land in the right place. He blames the early years on luck: luck that his undergraduate classes aroused a love for literature, luck that a paper he was writing on doctor/author William Carlos Williams led him to meet Williams and as a result choose a career in medicine, luck that as a hospital intern he got to treat and converse with the physicist Enrico Fermi, luck that he started hanging around Dorothy Day and the Catholic Worker community, luck that he befriended the psychotherapists Anna Freud and Erik Erikson, that he studied under the theologians Reinhold Niebuhr and Paul Tillich, and that he got involved with Martin Luther King, Jr., and the civil rights movement.

Later decisions, though, after he gained renown, he cannot blame on luck. He made conscious choices to enter the world's hot spots, stealing into Soweto Township during the time of apartheid in South Africa, visiting irate white families during the tumultuous days of Boston school busing, listening to Protestants and Catholics curse each other in Northern Ireland, interviewing families in the *favelas* of Rio de Janeiro and in dissidents' basements in Poland.

Coles likes to quote from Flaubert's *Madame Bovary:* "Human speech is like a cracked kettle on which we tap crude rhythms for bears to dance to, while we long to make music that will melt the stars." Sometimes the speech he has gathered from the world's children taps out crude rhythms and sometimes it melts the stars. In their own way, the children deal with profound questions that have bedeviled humanity for all of history. When I first encountered Coles, I was writing books on the problem of pain, quoting mostly philosophers and theologians. I found in the psychiatrist's interviews far simpler and more poignant expressions of the problem.

"When I look at Jesus up there [in the huge statue overhanging Rio de Janeiro] I wonder what he is thinking," muses young Margarita from her *favela,* or slum. Her mother, sick with a cough and with bleeding, works in a hotel in Copacabana where the rich people play. From high up on the hill, floating above the haze, Jesus must see both the *favela* and the luxury hotels, and also the priest who drives a big car and lives in a big house. Why does he stay silent?

Or back in Massachusetts, not far from Coles's home, a nine-year-old Jewish boy wrestles with theodicy. A guest in his home, a lawyer, showed him the numbers from the concentration camp tattooed into his arm. The man said he stopped believing in God then, because Hitler almost won the war, and the nine-year-old has worried about it ever since. "I guess He never interferes; that's what our Hebrew teacher says, that God doesn't ever try to stop something or start something. I don't see how He could have sat up there and not stopped Hitler! If the Jews are His people, then He could have lost us. I asked my father, 'Then would God have cried, if all the Jews had died in those concentration camps?' Dad said he doesn't know; he doesn't know if God cries or He smiles, or what He does."

It's the same question, on broad scale, as that put forth in one of Coles's first interviews, during his residency years when he worked in a pediatric ward at the height of the polio epidemic. He asked eleven-year-old Tony if he could record their conversations. "Please record every word I speak," Tony replied with surprising passion. "I may be dead tomorrow, and this would be a chance for my words to outlive me!" In the low-tech recording, you can barely hear Tony's words over the mechanical throb of the iron lung engulfing him. "When I heard there was a polio epidemic, I said, 'Too bad, someone will get sick.' It's never you! That's how you think: *someone else!* Now it's me; I'm the 'somebody else' . . . You folks ought to climb into one of these things, and see how it feels! Like a prison—only you can't walk up and down the cell, and you can't even breathe without the machine doing it for you! That's what I ask: OK, God, I must have done something to deserve this! Tell me!"

In a museum not far from Coles's Cambridge office hangs a huge triptych painted by Gauguin toward the end of his life in Tahiti, a grand summation of his art. In actual French words, Gauguin has scrawled across the painting the meaning he wanted to convey, in three questions: "Where Do We Come From? What Are We? Where Are We Going?" Artists never express themselves so directly anymore, philosophers abandoned such questions of meaning years ago, scientists offer answers that fail to satisfy, modern universities avoid them altogether. Almost alone in the modern academy, Robert Coles the physician goes against the stream, posing both questions and answers—ironically, through the voices of children. Evidently, the hunger still exists: for years his classes have been the most popular electives at Harvard, with as many as six hundred students jammed into standing-room-only classrooms.

Through it all, Coles has forged his own path of iconoclasm and contradiction. A psychiatrist, he exposed Freud's illusions and honored the "unbalanced": martyrs, St. Francis, Simone Weil, the Hebrew prophets. An academic, he scorned jargon and won praise for his colloquial accounts of conversations with children. A Harvard professor, he rode school buses and sat cross-legged on the floor with the kids he tutored at ghetto schools. A doctor too squeamish to practice medicine, he ended up teaching courses in literature. A cultural icon honored by a pro-choice, pro-gay president, he spoke out against abortion ("an affront to the Lord") and gay liberation.

In explaining his personal dialectic of faith, Coles quotes Pascal: "Nature confutes the skeptics, and reason confutes the dogmatists." A good summary of The Crayon Man himself.

By his own admission, Robert Coles's life makes sense only when viewed in sequence. His father came from England, out of half-Jewish, half-Catholic stock. A physicist educated at the Massachusetts Institute of Technology, he viewed all matters religious with skepticism. If young Bob quoted Shakespeare on heaven his father would say, "What heaven? Show me!" If someone mentioned the Holy Ghost he would ask, for the millionth time, what the Holy Ghost was anyway. In contrast, Bob's Episcopalian mother, from Iowa, had a religious, even mystical bent. She took her two sons to church while their father waited outside in the car, reading a newspaper. She knew the Bible and the Book of Common Prayer and freely quoted them to her sons.

As an adolescent, Bob Coles felt tugged in opposite directions, toward his father's hardheaded pragmatism and also his mother's warm pietism. He never knew what to believe about God. Mother and father came together, though, in their love for literature. Both parents read George Eliot aloud to Bob and his brother, and instilled in them a love for Tolstoy and Dickens. When it came to moral issues, Bob learned to think in terms of story rather than abstract concepts. Despite their religious differences, his parents both expressed compassion in concrete ways. His mother donated time to clinics visited by the poor, to soup kitchens, to children suffering from cancer. His father paid visits to the poor and elderly in hospital beds and nursing homes.

Bob performed well enough in school to get into Harvard, where he majored in English literature. There, he fell under the spell of William Carlos Williams, who combined the dual careers of doctor and poet. The combination appealed to young Coles as a way to help people, through medicine, and then to reflect on those experiences in writing. Mainly due to Williams's influence, he decided to enter medicine.

Coles muddled through medical training, growing increasingly troubled. He spent far too much time talking with patients and too little on laboratory work. Dissecting corpses repelled him, and he could not stick needles into babies without feeling unstrung by their screams. Once, when asked to draw blood from a vein in the neck of a child, he physically recoiled. The demanding regimen pushed him toward total exhaustion, and he found himself staring blankly at stars and trees. He read Thomas Merton's poems, and retreated to Merton's Trappist monastery in Kentucky for a period of quiet contemplation. Should he return to Harvard and study literature? Should he volunteer to work at Albert Schweitzer's hospital in Africa? His teachers recommended psychoanalysis as a way to help him reconsider his future in medicine.

The analysis helped, in an unexpected way. Coles knew little about psychiatry—he had read nothing by Freud—but the idea of practicing medicine by talking to people appealed to him. He decided to become a psychiatrist. Coles came away from that residency with more questions than answers. It puzzled him that some people became "sick" while others from equally troublesome backgrounds stayed reasonably healthy. The arrogance of his own profession worried him too. His professors had a tendency to explain away behavior by slapping a label on it, whereas to Coles any one person seemed unfathomably complex and mysterious. He remembered his house calls with Williams, and the respect that physician had shown toward people who lived in a slum world utterly different from his own. To Coles, as he listened to patients spill out their stories, it seemed as important to honor their lives as to attempt a "cure."

Even while studying psychiatry he felt drawn increasingly to novelists. Paul Tillich had recommended Walker Percy, a physician-turned-novelist. Coles devoured his work and found in it a more accurate portrayal of humanity than what he was finding in his behavior textbooks. As he read more widely, it struck him that a novelist like Feodor Dostoevsky had more insight into the human psyche than any psychiatrist he had met.

Coles began to distrust the traditional psychiatric method, of an expert sitting at a desk listening to a patient and then choosing an appropriate treatment. He needed to enter into his patients' lives, to understand their extended families and homes and cultures and economic status. He needed to cross the bridge between observer and observed, between doctor and patient. He needed to, as he later expressed it, "bring alive the 'innerness' of those lives," including their dreams, their private beliefs and prejudices, their offhand jokes and casual remarks. As Dorothy Day had once told him, "I have some grand notions in my head, but they often fall by the wayside when I'm sitting at the table talking with one person, hearing all that has happened in that one life."

He learned, in short, to pay attention, actively and aggressively. Each life has its own mystery, its own tale to be told. He determined to discover that tale and attempt to "translate" it for others. His approach departed widely from tradition. Freud had said that when you begin to ask about "the meaning of life" you are already sick. Robert Coles could hardly ask about anything else.

In the early 1960s came two key moments in Coles's life that seemed mere "accidents" at the time, unscheduled interruptions of his routine. Yet they now stand out as hinge events that changed him forever.

Coles was serving in the Air Force, directing a psychiatric unit near Biloxi, Mississippi, when one Sunday afternoon he set off on a bicycle trip along the shore of the Gulf of Mexico. Rounding a corner, he heard sounds of fighting. He shook his head disgustedly, wondering why anyone would be belligerent on such a fine spring day, and stopped to watch.

A miniature race riot was under way. Some black people had attempted a "swim-in" at a beach reserved for whites only, and a crowd of white people had surrounded them. Both sides were screaming at each other. He saw a white man stomp on a black woman's glasses and smash her watch. The mood was getting ugly, and Coles feared physical violence could break out at any moment. A skinny, frightened Yankee a thousand miles from home, he squelched any moral outrage, remounted his bicycle, and rode away.

That night, working his shift at the base hospital, Coles heard two policemen talking about the incident at the beach. They were friends, gentle and courteous policemen he had grown to respect. But tonight they spoke in a threatening tone. "They'd be dead now if it weren't for all the publicity they get," said one. "They will be if they try it again," muttered the other.

Coles said nothing. But he felt irresistibly swept up in the drama being acted out in the South. What moral principle made those black people risk their lives just to be the first of their race to step into the ocean by an insignificant Mississippi beach? And what force could summon such hatred into the eyes of two mild-mannered white men? He tucked those questions away.

Meanwhile, Coles's personal life was adrift. In joining the Air Force he had hoped for an exotic place to sow his wild oats: San Francisco, maybe, or Hawaii, or Japan. Assigned instead to Mississippi, he often found himself at odds with the military style. He drank heavily, and fought off bouts of depression. Much of the time he seemed morose and withdrawn, a person who ought to be receiving analysis rather than giving it. Concerned, he found a psychiatrist in New Orleans and signed on, driving his white Porsche at high speeds weekly from the base in Mississippi to a genteel section of New Orleans.

One day, however, he had trouble getting through the lower-class industrial district of Gentilly. State troopers had cordoned off the major roads because of a racial disturbance. Coles drove over to the site of all the commotion, an elementary school. There he first saw Ruby Bridges, a tiny six-year-old black girl. Ruby was the first black child to attend the Frantz School, and all other students were boycotting the school in protest. Escorted by federal marshals (the city and state police had refused to protect her), she had to walk through the midst of a mob of white people who were screaming obscenities, yelling threats, and waving their fists at her. Inquiring, Coles learned that she ran this gauntlet every day, attending a vacant school to sit alone all day in her classroom.

As Coles watched the brave young girl, it occurred to him that she would make an ideal subject for studying the effects of stress on young children. It took some time for him to earn the trust of her family, since no white person had entered their home before. Ruby agreed to cooperate, though, and when they ran out of conversation, Coles asked her to draw pictures.

An astonishing thing happened over the next months. Dr. Robert Coles had come in as the expert, a pediatrician and psychiatrist with the full prestige of Harvard, Columbia, and the University of Chicago behind him. He had come to treat an uneducated, disadvantaged black child in the slums of New Orleans. As time went on, however, he felt a reversal of roles taking place. He was the student, not Ruby, and she was teaching him an advanced course in ethics.

At night Coles discussed with his wife, Jane, how he would respond under similar circumstances. What if a gang of angry, club-wielding men and women lined up in front of the Harvard Club to block his entrance? What would he do? He would call the police, of course. But in New Orleans federal marshals had been brought in because the police were not on Ruby's side—he remembered the policemen's conversation he had overheard at the base. He would call his lawyer and get a court order. Ruby's family knew no lawyers and couldn't afford them anyhow. At the least he would rise above the mob by explaining away their behavior in the language of psychopathology, and perhaps even write a condescending article about them. Ruby knew no such words; she was just learning to read and write.

So what did Ruby Bridges do in such daunting circumstances? She prayed: for herself, that she would be strong and unafraid, and also for her enemies, that God would forgive them. "Jesus prayed that on the cross," she told Coles, as if that settled the matter: " 'Forgive them, because they don't know what they're doing.' "

Three other six-year-old black girls were attending another school against similar opposition. Coles began meeting with them, too, twice a week. He got to know Tessie especially, and her maternal grandmother, who would greet the federal marshals at eight o'clock each morning with the expression, "Lord Almighty, another gift!" and then hand over little Tessie, who carried her lunch pail to school between the men in dark suits with revolvers on their belts. After two months of facing the abusive crowds, Tessie suggested that maybe she should stay home. Her grandmother delivered a lecture: "You see, my child, you have to help the good Lord with His world! He puts us here—and He calls us to help Him out. . . . You belong in that McDonogh School, and there will be a day when everyone knows that, even those poor folks— Lord, I pray for them!—those poor, poor folks who are out there shouting their heads off at you. You're one of the Lord's people; He's put His hand on you. He's given a call to you, a call to service—in His name!"

On Coles's academic charts of moral development, magnanimous love for enemies appeared right at the top, a level attained by people like Jesus and Gandhi and precious few saints. He had not expected to find such a philosophy being lived out daily by six-year-old girls and their "culturally deprived" families.

"He got all A's and flunked ordinary living," said novelist Walker Percy about one of his characters in *The Second Coming*. Dr. Robert Coles began to wonder if such a description applied to him too.

A voice from one of Coles's books:

> Last year we went to a little church in New Jersey . . . We had
> all our children there, the baby included. The Reverend Jackson

was there, I can't forget his name, and he told us to be quiet,
and he told us how glad we should be that we're in this country,
because it's Christian and it's not "godless." He kept on talking
about the other countries, I forget which, being "godless." Then
my husband went and lost his temper; something happened to
his nerves, I do believe. He got up and started shouting, yes sir.
He went up to the Reverend Mr. Jackson and told him to shut
up and never speak again—not to us, the migrant people. He
told him to go on back to his church, wherever it is, and leave us
alone and don't be standing up there looking like he was so nice
to be doing us a favor. Then he did the worst thing he could do:
he took the baby, Annie, and he held her right before his face,
the minister's, and he screamed and shouted and hollered at
him, that minister, like I've never before seen anyone do. I
don't remember what he said, the exact words, but he told him
that here was our little Annie, and she's never been to the doctor, and the child is sick, he knows it and so do I, because she
can't hold her food down and she gets shaking fits, and then
I'm afraid she's going to die, but thank God she'll pull out of
them, and we've got no money, not for Annie or the other ones
or ourselves.

Then he lifted Annie up, so she was higher than the reverend, and he said why doesn't he go and pray for Annie and
pray that the growers will be punished for what they're doing
to us, all the migrant people. The reverend didn't answer him,
I think because he was scared, and then my husband began
shouting some more, about God and His neglecting us while He
took such good care of the other people all over . . . and he held
our Annie as high as he could, right near the cross, and told God
He'd better stop having the ministers speaking for Him, and He
should come and see us for Himself, and not have the "preachers"—he kept calling them the "preachers"—speaking for Him.

(From *Migrants, Sharecroppers, Mountaineers*)

With his Ivy League degrees and his licenses to practice medicine
packed back home in Massachusetts, Robert Coles embarked on the

unique style of work that has not varied for forty years. A few contacts with people like Ruby and Tessie had inspired him. He began to visit the neighborhoods, house trailers, and agricultural fields of the rural South. He and his wife, Jane, a schoolteacher, got to know the children, visited their classrooms, and told both parents and children that they wanted to learn about their lives.

The first interviews proved awkward and uncomfortable, as the families viewed outsiders with suspicion. During the first few visits, not once was Robert or Jane Coles offered a glass of water. A black acquaintance explained, "No white man ever came here, except to take something away." At first Coles just listened; after a while he took some notes; when he finally believed he had earned their trust he pulled out a tape recorder. Gradually the entire family, such as the sharecropper's wife just quoted, opened up.

Coles could not always, nor did he try to, keep a distinction between observer and participator. In Atlanta, while studying the first ten black teenagers to integrate that city's public schools, he heard about the Student Nonviolent Coordinating Committee (SNCC) headed by James Foreman and Stokely Carmichael. He offered his services to them as physician and psychiatrist, and asked for permission to interview their student workers. They turned him down flat. Crushed, he asked if there was anything he might do to help the cause. Jim Foreman replied, "Yeah, you can help us keep this place clean!"

For the next weeks and months, ultimately a year, he served as the resident janitor, sweeping the floor, vacuuming, dusting, washing dishes, scrubbing down the bathroom. He realized, as he did the menial work, that half the black parents he knew did similar work as a full-time career. In the process he gained the students' grudging respect and trust, overheard their stories, and joined the movement at its lowest level. He even spent time in jail when SNCC's Freedom House in Mississippi was bombed, and by the Kafkaesque logic of the times its inhabitants were arrested for disturbing the peace. And in 1964, at the last moment he changed his plans to accompany three civil rights workers headed to register voters in Mississippi, the three who were later found murdered and buried in an earthen dam.

Out of these experiences began the flow of words that became a cascade. Coles and his wife edited the tape transcripts, reworked them into coherence, and drew conclusions about what they had learned. A book on the Southerners, *Children of Crisis: A Study of Courage and Fear*, became volume one of a series that encompassed migrants, sharecroppers, and mountaineers (volume two); Appalachians and the poor in Northern cities (volume three); Eskimos, Chicanos, and Indians (volume four); and children of the wealthy (volume five). By relying on actual conversations with children, he was attempting a unique voice, part transcriber à la Studs Terkel, and part interpreter à la Bruno Bettelheim. At last he had found a way to combine his love for literature with his scientific training.

His work with ordinary people provided a second education for Coles. He began to get to know people as individuals, not as members of a sociological group. He found in many "disadvantaged" people a reservoir of inner strength he had not encountered in middle-class suburbs or in the schools of the privileged. Where, for example, does an illiterate migrant worker, trucked from farm to farm across the South, penned up in barns and chicken coops at night, paid a dollar an hour for backbreaking labor—where does such a person get strength to endure? According to the behaviorism Coles had been taught, such poor people should have been broken by their circumstances, or permanently embittered. Instead, much like the leprosy patients Dr. Brand had treated in India, the American poor also showed moments of transcendence and grace that defied explanation.

Coles's books are filled with verbal snapshots of people who somehow rise above the misery of their lives, buoyed by grace. Because they talked to him about God so often, Coles began attending church with the poor. At first, accustomed to church as a solemn, somewhat intellectual experience that lasted exactly one hour, he found the looseness and the heavy emotionalism frightening. He sat in the services, listened to the singing, and watched the minister and the congregation with a cool, dispassionate eye, alert for telltale signs of the psychosocial forces at work in the religion of the poor.

Again and again he saw migrants and poor blacks and, yes, rednecks too, profoundly changed by what happened within their churches. Something of great power was set loose in those services, he had to admit to himself, something not easily explained by the jargon he had learned in medical school. Tired people came away renewed, oppressive pain seemed to lessen, hatred melted a little. He had no categories from his training to explain what he saw:

> I will try, though; I will try to hint at—maybe this is the way to put it—the animated spirit of the Spirit, as one like me has happened to see and hear and feel that Spirit become active, become an event. It *is* an event: something happens, something takes place; the worshiper feels taken over, feels no longer a person who only talks about the Spirit, who only uses that word, but rather, one who at last is on the way, at last is set to *do* something, I would even say *go* somewhere. In rural churches one is moved and transported, one is elevated and summoned, one uses the arms and the hands and the legs, one bends and straightens out and twists and turns, and yes, finally yes, gets there, arrives.
>
> (From *Migrants, Sharecroppers, Mountaineers*)

The poor had no answers for the unfairness of life. Had a mere accident of birth condemned them to a cycle of suffering and poverty? They had little time or leisure to contemplate such questions. But when asked about the source of strength in their lives, they often pointed to Jesus. Religion for them was no crutch but rather a source of inspiration. They found in Jesus, and in the image of the cross, a ray of hope that convinced them God knew their suffering. As Fannie Lou Hamer used to sing in the cotton fields of Mississippi, and later in jail, "Oh Lord, you know just how I feel."

One woman expressed her state this way, in almost Kierkegaardian terms:

> My will isn't what matters; it's His. If He wants me to suffer like this, I guess He has His reasons. You're here to prove your trust in Him. If someone offered me a million dollars, and said I

could have all I want to eat for myself and my children, but I'd
have to stop thinking about Him and start thinking of myself
only, then I'd know I was in real trouble. I'd start worrying about
myself. I "hope" I would. I hope I'd remember Jesus. He warned
us about thinking about ourselves and not Him. He asked a lot
of us.   (From *Migrants, Sharecroppers, Mountaineers*)

Coles reflected on the peculiar circumstances of life that God had
chosen in coming to earth: as a carpenter who associated with peasants and fishermen, his mother used to remind him, not as a doctor or
lawyer or college professor. God did, in the words of Annie's father, the
sharecropper, "come and see for Himself."

"We have the mind of Jesus Christ in our heads," a migrant farm
worker said in an interview, and at the time Coles, thinking like a
doctor, wondered if the man was drunk or crazy or delirious or slow
of thought. Only later, when Coles took time to reflect on the mind of
Jesus Christ as it was actually lived out—in exile and wandering,
in pain, in scorn, isolation, loneliness, the "mind" of *kenosis,* or
emptying—could he see the profound truth in what the man had
said. "He didn't have to come here, you know," one little girl said of Jesus.

In his work with the poor, Coles tried to avoid the trap of roman-
ticizing poverty and viewing religion as consolation to keep the poor
quiescent. He lobbied Congress and wrote in liberal journals in support of social programs and the War on Poverty. Even so, he could not
deny the reality of the life of faith among the people he had lived with.
Nonetheless, when he wrote about the effect of religion on the poor,
reviewers greeted him with polite silence. They applauded his field research and his fine portrayal of the experience of poverty. They quoted
him often. But they consistently ignored the one area—religion—that
seemed to Coles most important to the poor themselves.

Coles came to believe that what he had learned in school about religion—that as an "opiate of the people" it dulls moral and political indignation—was a myth perpetrated by irreligious social scientists who
had very little actual contact with the poor. In the poor he visited,

whether in South Africa or Brazil or Northern Ireland or the United States, religious faith usually sharpened, rather than dulled, indignation and outrage. He read again the pronouncements of the Hebrew prophets and of Jesus. And he saw firsthand the practical outworking of that message among the spiritual "base communities" of Latin America, and the blacks of South Africa, and the fiery ministers who led the civil rights movement in the American South.

As one young demonstrator from Birmingham, Alabama, told him in 1965, "I don't know why I said no to segregation. I'm just another white Southerner, and I wasn't brought up to love integration! But I was brought up to love Jesus Christ, and when I saw the police of this city use dogs on people, I asked myself what Jesus would have done—and that's all I know about how I came to be here, on the firing line."

Over the years, as I read and absorbed Robert Coles's writing, it had a peculiar effect on me. Coles lets the people he interviews speak for themselves, which leads some readers to complain that the accumulation of voices can have a numbing effect. For me, however, they were escorts leading me on a return visit to my past, this time with the blinders removed.

I grew up in some of the very places Coles worked. As he was counseling the ten black teenagers who integrated Atlanta's public schools, I attended high school in adjacent DeKalb County, in an area so Klan-infested that no black students dared to break the color barrier.

In church, I heard James Foreman, Stokely Carmichael, and the SNCC volunteers denounced as outside agitators, Communist agents sent to foment revolution. Years later, through Coles's eyes I saw them for what they really were: idealistic young people, often motivated by their faith, who included the word "nonviolent" in their organizational name as well as in their mission. They trained like soldiers, though in the tactics of nonviolent confrontation perfected by Gandhi and Dr. King. The Freedom Riders, some of them teenagers, showed incredible bravery boarding a Greyhound bus with the determination to integrate the waiting rooms of Alabama and Mississippi. At each scheduled stop, a mob of whites met them with bottles, bricks, and iron pipes. Sometimes the bus kept on rolling, speeding past the mob on to the next stop. Sometimes it stopped and the volunteers got off to face the violence unarmed. Then, with makeshift bandages over their bloody heads and broken ribs, they reboarded the bus and continued the journey—until it was destroyed by a fire bomb beside a highway.

I met not only civil rights workers in his books, but also prejudiced rednecks, like the people I grew up among. I had tried to escape them, to rise above them, to disassociate and put them out of mind; and I had succeeded, in a sense, by collecting graduate degrees and moving to Chicago. As I listened to Coles's voices, people from my childhood floated back into view, especially neighbors in the trailer parks I lived in. My friend Neal, who came to us for shelter when his drunken father went after his mother with a beer bottle, smashing the windows of a locked car as she sat on the horn and screamed for help. Gypsy Joe, the greasy-looking professional wrestler with a ponytail who had the nice trailer lot by the highway and took a dive at fake but still dangerous matches every week in downtown Atlanta. My twelve-year-old playmates who smoked cigarettes in the woods and played war games around the sewage treatment plant next door, and who broke into the trailer where a man had died of drink and lain dead for a week until the smell fouled the entire trailer park.

People just like these make their appearance in Robert Coles's books. I realized, in the recapitulation tour he led me on, that I had substituted a new kind of fundamentalism for the old, one borne of snobbery rather than ignorance. How blithely I point out the sins and failures of my childhood churches, and how rarely I dwell on the goodness I also found there. I used to look down on blacks; now I look down on racists. I used to avoid the rich; now I avoid the poor. So much of history careens along in polarity—poor vs. rich, white vs. black, Catholic vs. Protestant, Muslim vs. Hindu, Israeli vs. Arab—

with religion raising one more barrier. Coles, almost uniquely, has tried to plumb the dignity present in both sides, simply by letting them speak, and by rendering individual human beings in all their unreduced complexity.

Coles tells of an impromptu sermon Martin Luther King, Jr., gave one day to "brothers and sisters in the movement" at the SNCC office. The volunteers were growing tired of relentless opposition, and had few victories to show for all their efforts at registering voters and dismantling integration laws. King sensed the students' temptation to become bitter, and then to turn on opponents in the same spirit of hostility they had been receiving—to become the enemy, in other words. As King told them:

> A big danger for us is the temptation to follow the people we
> are opposing. They call us names, so we call them names. Our
> names may not be "redneck" or "cracker"; they may be names
> that have a sociological or psychological veneer to them, a gloss;
> but they are names, nonetheless—"ignorant," or "brainwashed,"
> or "duped" or "hysterical" or "poor-white" or "consumed by hate."
> I know you will all give me plenty of evidence in support of
> those categories. But I urge you to think of them as that—as cat-
> egories; and I remind you that in many people, in many people
> called segregationists, there are other things going on in their
> lives: *this* person or *that* person, standing *here* or *there* may also
> be other things—kind to neighbors and family, helpful and good-
> spirited at work.
>
> You all know, I think, what I'm trying to say—that we must
> try not to end up with stereotypes of those we oppose, even as
> they slip all of us into their stereotypes. And who are we? Let us
> not do to ourselves as others (as our opponents) do to us: try to
> put ourselves into one all-inclusive category—the virtuous ones
> as against the evil ones, or the decent ones as against the mali-
> cious, prejudiced ones, or the well-educated as against the igno-
> rant. You can see that I can go on and on—and there is the
> danger: the "us" or "them" mentality takes hold, and we do, actu-

ally, begin to run the risk of joining ranks with the very people
we are opposing. I worry about this a lot these days.

(From *The Call of Service*)

Reading King's words, and Coles's response, I realized that Coles
himself had, for me, turned the spotlight on that very temptation.
I had become the enlightened, right-thinking, educated cultural
observer—the perilous stance that Coles had battled all his life,
the perilous stance of the Pharisee. I needed to rediscover the leveling
truth of Jesus' gospel, which has more appeal to the prodigal son
than to his responsible and successful brother. I needed a change
in heart as much as a change in thought. Just as King sought to forgive those who had wounded him, I needed to forgive the church
that had wounded me, or I would be left with a gospel of law and not
grace, of division and not reconciliation. In his fieldwork, Coles had
unwittingly uncovered a radical Jesus who exposed my own masked
needs.

Coles recalls a road trip back to Boston after spending time among
migrant workers in Florida. For several months he had been the
paragon of sensitivity and compassion, entering the migrants' shacks,
winning their friendship, treating them with respect, coaxing words
from them, advising them medically. Yet when he crossed the state line
and stopped for a bite to eat at a roadside café in Georgia, he caught
himself snapping at the waitress who took too long to refill his coffee.
Already, so quickly, he was settling into the entitlements of privilege.
Soon he would be back home in the big yellow house in Cambridge,
with the BMW parked in the garage.

I belong, with Robert Coles, to a privileged minority. Everyone reading this sentence belongs, in fact, for only a small percentage of the
world's people has the ability and leisure to read and the resources to
buy a book. How do we, the "privileged ones," act as stewards of the
grace we have received? We can begin, Coles tells us, by ripping off the
labels we so thoughtlessly slap on others unlike ourselves. We can begin by finding a community that nourishes compassion for the weak, an
instinct that privilege tends to suppress. We can begin with humility

and gratitude and reverence, and then move on to pray without ceasing for the greater gift of love.

As Martin Luther King, Jr., told Coles in the course of a personal interview:

> I have begun to realize how hard it is for a lot of people to think of living without someone to look down upon, really look down upon. It is not just that they will feel cheated out of someone to hate; it is that they will be compelled to look more closely at themselves, at what they don't like in themselves. My heart goes out to people I hear called rednecks; they have little, if anything, and hate is a possession they can still call upon reliably, and it works for them. I have less charity in my heart for well-to-do and well-educated people—for their snide comments, cleverly rationalized ones, for the way they mobilize their political and even moral justifications to suit their own purposes. No one calls *them* into account. The Klan is their whipping boy. Someday all of us will see that when we start going after a race or a religion, a type, a region, a section of the Lord's humanity—then we're cutting into His heart, and we're bleeding badly ourselves.
>
> (From Coles's *Simone Weil: A Modern Pilgrimage*)

After four *Children of Crisis* volumes focusing on disenfranchised groups, Coles turned for his final volume to *The Privileged Ones: The Well-off and the Rich in America*. Although he followed the same style of interviewing he had perfected in his work with the poor, he found it harder to get to the rich; barriers of suspicion effectively shielded him from the inner workings of their lives.

For fifteen years Coles had heard the poor talk about "them": the privileged ones, the blessed ones, those with food on their table and doctors at their call and an education and a couple of cars and a house of their own with no landlord. Yet what had such comfort produced? Were the rich any happier? More peaceful? More grateful? Once again psychiatrist Coles encountered paradoxes in human nature that seemed to defy the neat behaviorist formulas he had been taught—the same paradoxes that novelists like Tolstoy and Dickens had explored so masterfully. Among the poor he had expected defeat and despair; he found some, yes, but he also found strength and hope and courage. Among the rich he expected satisfaction, and instead found boredom, alienation, and decadence.

Coles explained the irony of his title, *The Privileged Ones,* to one journalist:

> There is a worldview which says that anxiety, pain, and fear are part of what life is meant to be, that God himself assumed such a life, that he lived under continual anxiety, pain, and fear, and ended up as a common criminal strung up on a cross and killed. Now, if you take that kind of existence as a very important one and as a model of sorts, then you're going to have a difficult time becoming as "successful" as you may have been told you ought to be if you come from a middle-class family. You have a moral dilemma. (From *Sojourners*)

Many of the 1960s civil rights workers Coles consulted came from such middle-class families. Their parents nagged them about getting a real job and making something of themselves. One of them responded to his mother's concerned prayers over him: "I wonder what Jesus said, listening to her prayers! I felt like writing her back and asking her if Jesus ever held 'a regular job'—or ever 'found himself.' Jesus, the migrant preacher, who became so unpopular and disturbing to everyone big and important that He got crucified."

Working with the poor and oppressed, Coles marveled over how much their lives resembled the lives of the prophets and Jesus himself. Perhaps that was why they found solace in religion, and why the sophisticated reviewers so studiously ignored what they had to say about it. Middle-class churches tend to be sweet, soothing, and inoffensive, their worship services predictable and controlled. Coles, himself a product of the privileged minority, began to wonder about his own resistance to the power of a radical gospel. He could not avoid the discrepancy between the Bible's teaching on justice and fairness and the lives privileged people tend to live, marked by greed, competition, and status. What was the gospel's message to the well-off? What was its message to him? As Coles explored the mind of the privileged ones, he realized he was exploring his own mind. To his shame, he found within himself many of the same troubling tendencies.

Comfortable people, he noticed, were apt to have a stunted sense of compassion, more likely to love humanity in general but less likely to love one person in particular. Did he show compassion? As a Harvard undergraduate, he recalled with a pang, he had treated the dormitory maid as a lowly servant even while earning A's in his ethics courses.

What about arrogance? A physician, he fought the temptation every day; he was, after all, the expert, the healer who had come to help the disadvantaged. Pride? What really motivated him anyway, driving him to get the degrees, pick up the rewards, write all the books? Selfishness? He was generous, to be sure, but he had the luxury to be generous. He had never been in a situation of absolute dependence, the daily state of many poor people.

Coles reflected on these matters in that fifth volume, the book he considers the best of the series but the one most overlooked by reviewers. Ultimately, he came to believe that the most dangerous temptation of all is the temptation of plenty. In the same breath, wealth curses what it blesses. Being privileged, Coles concluded, tends to stifle compassion, curtail community, and feed ambition.

Rich kids who tried to break out of their sheltered surroundings and respond to the call of conscience presented a threat to others. Coles interviewed a child from a very wealthy Florida family who had encountered the teachings of Jesus around the age of ten. He started repeating some of Jesus' statements in school—such as how hard it is for rich people to enter heaven, and how the poor will inherit the kingdom. His questions became a thorn to his parents, his teachers, and his family doctor. Ultimately his parents stopped taking him to church and signed him up for psychotherapy to cure his "problem."

Reviewing the rich and poor people he had come to know, Coles was struck with the ironies. It was true the poor were cursed: he had treated the miners with black lung disease, and the malnourished children like little Annie whose father had held her up before the cross (she died at age three). Yet in a strange but undeniable way, the poor were also blessed, for whatever reason, with qualities such as courage and love and a willing dependence on God. The irony: Good humanists work all their lives to improve the condition of the disadvantaged, but for what? To raise them to the level of the upper classes so that they too can experience boredom, alienation, and decadence?

By the time the last of the *Children of Crisis* volumes was published, Robert Coles had arrived not in a new place, but in a very old place. He had traveled thousands of miles, recorded miles of tape, and written a million words, all of which pointed right back to the Sermon on the Mount. He had discovered that the poor are mysteriously blessed and that the rich live in peril. He had learned that what matters most comes not from without—the circumstances of life—but from within, inside the heart of an individual man or woman or child. He had begun his research with a head full of phrases such as "guilt complex," "character disorders," "response to stimuli." He had emerged with old-fashioned words like conscience and sin and free will.

What was he to make of it all? He dare not glorify poverty, for his field research had taught him the folly of that romanticism. Nor dare he glorify wealth, which he now saw as a distraction or actual impediment to what matters most. That is when he turned to a few select men and women who had made spiritual matters their entire lives' focus. Dr. Robert Coles the social scientist continued to pursue his work diligently, even as a new role also opened up: teacher of spiritual literature at Harvard.

After years of being affected indirectly by Robert Coles, I asked him for a face-to-face interview, and he graciously agreed. He told me he likes to meet visitors at a greasy-spoon restaurant around the corner from his office, away from interruptions, and so we met at Bartlee's Famous Hamburgers. Inside, the place is decorated like the Hollywood set for a Harvard hang-out: wood paneling, red plastic chairs, a menu scrawled with chalk on blackboards, a broken violin hanging on the wall. And posters, everywhere posters. "Don't criticize the coffee—you may be old and weak yourself some day," warns one. Another from forty years ago shows Ronald Reagan the actor auto-graphing boxes of Chesterfield cigarettes, recommending them as Christmas presents for all your friends.

Coles himself looks more like a student than a distinguished Har-vard professor: he enters wearing a rumpled blue cotton shirt and khaki pants, with a cranberry-colored backpack slung across his left shoulder. He is of medium height, and thin. He has a tanned, wrin-kled face, with tousled hair that looks as if he has been running his hands through it all day. He speaks in a Northeastern twang, and laughs loudly at anything slightly redolent of humor.

Traditionally, he has only a glass of iced tea for lunch before mov-ing back to his office, situated just a block away from Harvard Yard. The university provides the office for him in a spacious corner of a his-toric brick building. A plaque on the wall notes that Franklin Roosevelt used the room as a dorm room from 1900–4. Also on the wall hangs a collection of memorabilia: a poster of Simone Weil, photos of Bon-hoeffer and Walker Percy and Dorothy Day and Erik Erikson and James Agee. The office is a quiet, well-organized place of retreat, a home base from which Coles plans field research and prepares lec-tures for the various schools associated with Harvard.

Coles teaches at Duke University as well as at Harvard, but nowhere does he offer a course in his field of specialty—nothing on pediatrics, or child psychiatry, or sociology, or even interviewing tech-niques. Instead, he teaches the great novelists and Christian thinkers. His reading list includes Tolstoy and Dostoevsky, Pascal, Weil, Mer-ton, John of the Cross, Dickens, Flannery O'Connor, Emily Dickin-son, Robert Frost, Thomas à Kempis, Teresa of Avila, Kierkegaard, Bernanos, Silone, Agee, William Carlos Williams, Orwell, George Eliot, and Coles's longtime friend Walker Percy. From this list, he tailors literature courses to the needs of specialties: the course on "Literature of Christian Reflection" at the college, one on "Literature and Medicine" for the medical school, another on "Moral and Social Inquiry through Fiction" for the business school, and one on "Dickens and the Law" for the law school.

What transformed a physician and social scientist into a devotee of literature? Coles answers, "A man like Tolstoy knew more psychology than the whole twentieth-century social science scene will ever know. All this stuff about the stages of dying coming out now—why not just go back and read *The Death of Ivan Ilyich*? It said everything. And who has added any wisdom to the field of marital problems since *Anna Karenina*? And Dickens, oh my, what Dickens knew about human nature! I simply wander around from one place to the next, teaching these novels and trying to, in a way, undo the devil in the medical school, law school, and business school."

Why do they invite him in? "I don't know. For idolatrous reasons, probably. A name listed on a brochure, that sort of thing. Some of the students get the point: I hear from them, and I know they've been touched by what they've read. But it's hard here. This is the citadel of 'secular humanism,' you know!

"Yet literature has its own power that takes over. Flannery O'Connor wrote a beautiful book of essays called *Mystery and Manners,* and the title alone cuts right through all the social sciences: novels pay respect to the mystery and manners of individual human beings. Why don't we learn that instead of all this ridiculous jargon and overwrought theory—the dead language and the absurd simplifications we so often get from the experts? The novelists are not interested in theory, or in turning their brains into godlike pontifical organs. Instead they evoke and render complexity, irony, ambiguity, paradox. They discover, and acknowledge, that each person is a separate, finite mystery, not something that can be contained in one category or another."

Robert Coles is leaning back on a tan sofa, with sunlight flooding in and curtains shifting in the breeze. But he might as well be perched on the platform, behind the lectern—or pulpit, if you will—of one of his classes at Harvard. He's taking them all on now: the students with their perfect college-entrance SAT scores and their pedigrees and designer jogging outfits, faculty colleagues with their curricula vitae and committee appointments and airtight theories explaining the economy and human behavior and everything in the universe. And himself—Coles keeps coming back to himself, pointing out the idolatry and pride and self-dependence that have fueled his own life.

The students try to make him into a hero. They applaud him for the years he spent with migrant farmhands. "But what would happen at the end of the day?" he reminds them in his classes. "They'd go back to their shacks or trailers, and I'd check into the Holiday Inn. Sure I felt guilty, and I probably should. I can imagine what some of us with our phobia of guilt would say to Jesus. 'Hey, buddy, take it easy! Don't worry about those people that need some bread! Why are you visiting prisons? Do you have a hangup? There must be some shrink over in Galilee you can talk to.'"

Coles talks a lot about his own failures and inadequacies. He feels he must, to keep at bay the sins of pride and arrogance that stalk a place like Harvard. "Everyone wants to find a way to solve a problem, or silence a question," he says. "The students are demonstrating for this or that. Those same students won't walk across the city and have a conversation with people who live in similar conditions to the folks on whose behalf they're demonstrating.

"Like the Pharisees, we want to prove ourselves clean, and righteous. But Jesus and the prophets keep the questions up in the air. OK, you don't murder; do you hate? You don't commit adultery; do you lust? We like to analyze 'the problem of the poor.' But what are we doing for one poor person? I went to Mississippi at a time of crisis, expecting to learn about 'the problem of Mississippi.' I learned that there's a little bit of Mississippi in all of us—and a little bit of Massachusetts, South Africa, and Northern Ireland too."

For the students at Harvard, for the broader audience that buys his books, for the millions who read about him in magazines and newspapers, Robert Coles tries to keep the questions up in the air still. "It's quite clear," he told a reporter for the *Washington Post* in a front-page story, "that I'm a religious freak. What else do you do when you get old and stop and think about what this life is all about?" And because of his credentials, people have to pause and pay attention.

"In many ways Bob is sort of like a pastor," Coles's assistant, Phillip Pulaski, told the same reporter. "He probably is the most influential teacher at Harvard in terms of the impact on people's lives." If Coles had been in the room, he wouldn't have let Pulaski get away with such hagiography. He would have launched into a nasally diatribe on the dangers of pride and modern idolatries. But tucked away in file cabinets are letters from former students who tell him that he alone asked them to consider the most important questions of life while they were at Harvard.

Coles likes to quote Kierkegaard: "He said that Hegel explained everything in life except how to get through an ordinary day." That, more than any other reason, is why Robert Coles teaches literature to business majors rather than psychiatry to medical students. "We have systems here to explain everything—except how to live. And we have categories for every person on earth, but who can explain just one person?"

Can Robert Coles explain just one person? After a career of listening and interviewing, what has he learned about human beings? Can he distill it all into a grand summary? He thinks for a while, and then points to a Bible on his desk. "Nothing I have discovered about the makeup of human beings contradicts in any way what I learn from the Hebrew prophets such as Isaiah, Jeremiah, and Amos, and from the book of Ecclesiastes, and from Jesus and the lives of those he touched. Anything that I can say as a result of my research into human behavior is a mere footnote to those lives in the Old and New Testaments.

"I have known human beings who, in the face of unbearable daily stress, respond with resilience, even nobility. And I have known others who live in a comfortable, even luxurious environment and yet seem utterly lost. We have both sides in all of us, and that's what the Bible says, isn't it? The Bible shows us both hope and doom, the possibility and the betrayal. In its stories, sometimes the favorite becomes fatally tempted and sometimes the lowly and obscure one becomes an agent of hope if not salvation. I believe those stories are a part of each one of us. We walk a tightrope, teetering between gloom, or the loss of faith, on the one hand, and a temptation toward self-importance and self-congratulation on the other. Both extremes lead to sin.

"Some reviewers criticize me for saying the same old things about the nature of human beings: that we are a mixture of good and evil, of light and darkness, of potentiality toward destruction or redemption. They want some new theory, I suppose. But my research merely verifies what the Bible has said all along about human beings.

"If I can get some medical student who, by virtue of attending a prestigious school, is seduced by the sin of pride—if I can get that student to think of himself and his neighbor as Jesus taught us to, then I have served some kind of purpose here. I may be getting a little melodramatic, but I think maybe Jesus wouldn't mind coming to that medical student through the medium of one of Flannery O'Connor's stories. That's how I carry the biblical tradition into this university, for it belongs there and it's a privilege to call upon it as a teacher."

Each year when he begins his literature classes, Coles reads a quote from novelist James Agee. "I would as soon stand up and read from the Gospel of Luke," Coles explains, "but that probably would not work here. So I turn to the great literature that gets across that same message, such as this quotation from Agee: 'All that each person is, and experiences, and shall ever experience, in body and mind, all these things are differing expressions of himself and of one root, and are identical: and not one of these things nor one of these persons is ever quite to be duplicated, nor replaced, nor has it ever quite had precedent: but each is a new and incommunicably tender life, wounded in every breath and almost as hardly killed as easily wounded: sustaining, for a while, without defense, the enormous assaults of the universe.' "

What Robert Coles has been talking about all these years is the inherent dignity of human beings, the image of God that lives in all of us, black or white, educated or illiterate, rich or poor, healthy or sick—the spark that makes mortals immortal. He did not start out believing it. But it was what the children told him, and then the novelists, and then his own research confirmed it. And it is what he is trying to tell the rest of us now:

> Sometimes, as I sit and watch a child struggle to do just the right job of representing God's face, His features, the shape of His head, the cast of His countenance, I think back to my days of working in Dorothy Day's Catholic Worker soup kitchen. One afternoon, after several of us had struggled with a "wino," a "Bowery bum," an angry, cursing, truculent man of fifty or so, with long gray hair, a full, scraggly beard, a huge scar on his right cheek, a mouth with virtually no teeth, and bloodshot eyes, one of which had a terrible tic, she told us, "For all we know he might be God Himself come here to test us, so let us treat him as an honored guest and look at his face as if it is the most beautiful one we can imagine." (From *The Spiritual Life of Children*)

GETTING STARTED WITH ROBERT COLES:

The five-volume *Children of Crisis* series demonstrates Robert Coles's signature style—interviews, reflections, interpretations—and volumes two and three were awarded the Pulitzer Prize. Readers who find it daunting might prefer more recent summaries that he pulled together: *The Moral Life of Children, The Political Life of Children,* and *The Spiritual Life of Children. The Call of Service* and *The Call of Stories* also draw together summaries of his approach. Beyond that, browse Coles's writings as you would browse in a library. Literary reviews? Sample his works on William Carlos Williams, Walker Percy, and English Victorians. Biographies? Try his summaries of Dorothy Day and Simone Weil, or of Erik Erickson and Anna Freud. Theology? Consider *The Geography of Faith,* his book of conversations with Daniel Berrigan. Or, his 1999 book *The Secular Mind,* where Coles dares to question the most hallowed premise of modernity, that we find meaning in ourselves rather than "out there" somewhere. Children's books? He has several in print. For an intellectual biography of Coles himself, Bruce Ronda's *Intellect and Spirit* offers the best overall summary. And for someone who has no time to browse, *A Robert Coles Omnibus* brings together samples from many different writings, mostly essays on literature.

My deepest doubts about the faith can be summed up in a single question: *Why doesn't it work?* As I travel around the world, I see that Christianity brings many improvements to culture. Education, science, medicine, human rights, democracy, art, charity—all these grew most vigorously from Christian roots, and are stunted in some of the non-Christian countries I visit. Yet when I talk with devout Muslims or Hindus, they bring up the many wars that beset Europe during its most Christian era, and the crime, decadence, and family breakdown that mark the Christian West today. I have no defense against their arguments.

I have never met a serious follower of any religion who lacks appreciation for Jesus, but what about the church? As one Jewish friend said to me, "Jesus preached a beautiful gospel. We Jews are gaining in our admiration for Jesus. But show me the promised kingdom of God. Look at history, especially the Christian persecution of my race. Does this really look like a redeemed world?" The Jew looks at the world and asks why Messiah has not yet come; the Christian, who believes Messiah has come, wonders at the evil that still abounds.

In his spiritual autobiography, *A Confession,* Leo Tolstoy mentions that Christians sometimes treat each other worse than they treat people of other faiths. He grew friendly with Catholics, Protestants, Old Believers, and Anabaptist-type movements, yet the

Chapter 6

LEO

TOLSTOY

AND

FEODOR

DOSTOEVSKY

CHASING

GRACE

Russian Orthodox Church told him ". . . that these people were caught in a lie, that what gave them their vital strength was a temptation of the devil, and that we alone possessed the only possible truth. And I saw that all those who do not profess an identical faith are considered by the Orthodox to be heretics—just as the Catholics and other Churches consider the Orthodox themselves to be heretics."

As I think about individual Christians I know, I see some people made incomparably better by their faith, and some made measurably worse. For every gracious, kind-spirited, forgiving Christian, I can point to a proud, mean-spirited, judgmental one. In my own experience, those who strive the hardest and believe the most fervently are sometimes the least attractive persons. Like the Pharisees of Jesus' day, they get caught up in competition and end up self-righteous rather than righteous. Politicians tell me their nastiest letters come from people who quote the Bible and claim to speak for God—which I easily believe since my mailbox shows the same pattern. How do I resolve the tension between the ideals of the gospel and the actuality of those who profess it?

Today I see teenagers wearing WWJD bracelets to remind themselves of the disturbing question, "What would Jesus do?" That question first appeared in Charles Sheldon's novel *In His Steps,* which recounts the story of ordinary church people solemnly vowing to act as Jesus would and turning to Matthew 5–7 for guidance. As a teenager in the 1960s, long before marketers discovered the sales potential of WWJD, I read Sheldon's book and asked that question of myself every day. I nearly went crazy. If I gave to everyone who asked me, I soon ran out of money. In a flash of anger, I would call my brother "Fool!" or worse, then worry that I had put myself in danger of hellfire. If I stole a look at my neighbor's girlie magazines, should I pluck out my eye? When the kids at my bus stop jumped me after school, should I offer no defense? I tried that approach until I tired of coming home with a bloody nose.

The church I grew up in included a perfect woman. At least that's what she claimed, insisting she had not sinned in twelve years. I can remember as a child, all too aware of my own sins, marveling at her state of perfection. I never doubted her sincerity, for how could a perfect person lie? During church services I sometimes stared longingly at her, wishing I knew her secret. Now, however, I look back with pity on that woman. The apostle John could not have been more direct: "If we say that we have no sin, we deceive ourselves, and the truth is not in us." Although this woman may have managed to avoid overt and obvious sins, I doubt that she consistently obeyed what Jesus called the first and greatest commandment: to love God with all your heart, soul, and mind. And her smugly superior attitude betrayed that she had probably fallen victim to the sin of pride as well.

New Testament passages, most notably the Sermon on the Mount, spell out lofty ethical ideals—Give to everyone who asks you, Love your enemies, Never lust, Don't hate, Always forgive, Welcome persecution—which inevitably shatter against the grim reality of actual human behavior. I have felt a constant, unresolvable tension over Christian failures. As a journalist, I have observed up close both spectacular and petty defects of prominent spiritual leaders, many of which never come into public light. And when I decide to write about myself rather than others, I soon discover that I write about spiritual disciplines far better than I practice them. Are we called to strive for ideals that can never be attained?

I found no way to address the cognitive dissonance that kept me in a state of spiritual restlessness until I came upon the writings of two nineteenth-century Russian novelists. My understanding of the tension between Christian ideals and reality now consists of part Tolstoy and part Dostoevsky.

In the early 1970s Malcolm Muggeridge heard to his surprise that members of the intellectual elite in the Soviet Union, still under Communist rule, were experiencing a spiritual revival. A Russian dissident living in exile in England told him virtually every writer or artist or musician of note in the U.S.S.R. was exploring spiritual issues. Muggeridge writes, "I asked him how this could have happened, given the enormous anti-religious brainwashing job done on the citizenry, and the absence of all Christian literature, including the Gospels. His reply was memorable; the authorities, he said, forgot to suppress the

works of Tolstoy [1828–1910] and Dostoevsky [1821–81], the most perfect expositions of the Christian faith of modern times."

At the exact same time, I was living in the West surrounded by
Christians, saturated with religious literature and frankly unable to
make sense of most of it. These two Russian novelists, whom no one
would accuse of being balanced or even psychologically healthy,
helped restore to me a sense of balance. As Robert Coles had found
that novelists knew more about human behavior than all his psychology teachers, I found that they also knew more theology than most
theologians. At a crucial stage in my pilgrimage they became my spiritual guides in coming to terms with a problem that vexes every
thoughtful Christian—or follower of any religion, for that matter—
namely the huge gap between life as it should be and life as it is, between the theory of faith and its practice.

I n the long history of literature, no one has exceeded Leo Tolstoy's
ability to portray the full essence of life. As Virginia Woolf expressed it:

> Nothing seems to escape him. Nothing glances off him un-
> recorded . . . every twig, every feather sticks to his magnet. He
> notices the blue or red of a child's frock; the way a horse shifts
> its tail; the sound of a cough; the action of a man trying to put
> his hands into pockets that have been sewn up. And what his
> infallible eye reports of a cough or a trick of the hands his infal-
> lible brain refers to something hidden in the character, so that
> we know his people, not only by the way they love and their
> views on politics and the immortality of the soul, but also by the
> way they sneeze and choke. We feel that we have been set on a
> mountaintop and had a telescope put into our hands. Everything
> is astonishingly clear and absolutely sharp.

One of Tolstoy's biographers remarked that when he put down *War
and Peace* and returned to "real life" he had the sense of turning to

something paler and less true than Tolstoy's art itself. I had exactly the same experience. My world came alive in the novels of this writer separated from me by half a globe and nearly a century. When Tolstoy described spring, the wonder of tiny flowers poking up through the thawing tundra, he invested in it the same exuberance and significance that he gave to a description of religious ecstasy. In doing so, he taught me how to move beyond myself.

As I look back now on the cloister of Southern fundamentalism in which I grew up, I wonder if perhaps I suffered from a narcissistic disorder. (Perhaps all adolescents do?) I saw the world through the shuttered windows of church and family, with no ability to project out of myself and comprehend the viewpoint of, say, a sharecropper in rural Alabama or a Polish immigrant in the Bronx, much less a member of the aristocracy or a peasant in nineteenth-century Russia. Tolstoy threw open the curtains, beckoning me into a world I knew nothing about. Especially he summoned up in me a compassion for the poor.

At the time he wrote, Russia had fifty million serfs; almost half the population lived as virtual slaves, owned by their masters. Along with the ancestral estate where he would live and write, Tolstoy inherited hundreds of such peasants, a number that fluctuated wildly as he lost and regained these "souls" in bouts of gambling. Unlike most landowners, though, he moved among his peasants and got to know them. Eventually he decided that the peasants lived lives far richer and more interesting than his own life in the aristocracy:

> The life of a laboring man, with its endlessly varied forms of labor and the dangers connected with this labor on sea and underground; his migrations, the intercourse with his employers, overseers, and companions, and with men of other religions and other nationalities; his struggles with nature and with wild beasts, the associations with domestic animals, the work in the forest, on the steppe, in the field, the garden, the orchard . . . all this to us who have not these interests and possess no religious perception seems monotonous in comparison with those small enjoyments and insignificant cares of our life—a life not of labor

nor of production, but of consumption and destruction of that which others have produced for us. We think the feelings experienced by people of our day and our class are very important and varied; but in reality almost all the feelings of people of our class amount to but three very insignificant and simple feelings—the feeling of pride, the feeling of sexual desire, and the feeling of weariness of life. These three feelings, with their outgrowths, form almost the only subject matter of the art of the rich classes.

(From *What Is Art?*)

The differences between the ordinary lives of peasants and the self-indulgent lives of rich people like himself began to eat away at Tolstoy, paralyzing his ability to write. His peasants, it seemed, knew the meaning of life and work, knew how to endure suffering, and knew the place of death—all baffling mysteries to him. He studied the philosophies of Buddha, Schopenhauer, and Jesus in search of his own answers to these mysteries, and found no relief. Ultimately, he decided that the main problem was not so much that he thought incorrectly as that he lived badly. A parasite carried on the backs of his workers, he had hardly lived an authentic life at all. "My heart was oppressed with a painful feeling, which I can only describe as a search for God," he wrote. "It was a feeling of fear, orphanage, isolation in a strange land, and a hope of help from someone."

The search became so intense, in fact, that Tolstoy turned away from his artistic mission and instead sought almost exclusively to resolve the important questions of meaning. To the dismay of literary critics and readers who yearned for more great novels, he devoted the best years of his life to religious speculation. As a writer and as a pilgrim he struggled with the tension between the world as it is and as it should be. He filled hundreds of pages of notebooks with his spiritual diary, developed a highly moralistic aesthetic (*What Is Art?*), and wrote books expounding his religious beliefs.

Just as Tolstoy had the unique ability to portray the world as if he was the first person to see a plow turning up hard clods of earth or hear ice cracking apart on a frozen river, he also acted as if he was the first person truly to take the gospels seriously. He read the straightforward commands of Jesus and tried to put them into practice. "Sell everything you have and give to the poor, and you will have treasure in heaven," Jesus told the rich young ruler. After reading that, Tolstoy freed his serfs, gave away his copyrights, and began to dispose of his immense estate. To identify with the common people, he put on peasant clothes, made his own shoes, and began working in the fields.

Tolstoy's spiritual writings, unlike his fiction, stir up arguments on all sides. Mahatma Gandhi, for one, found them profoundly moving, and credited Tolstoy's *The Kingdom of God Is Within You* as the font of inspiration for his own guiding principles of nonviolence, simplicity, and intentional poverty. In Tolstoy's own day, a parade of idealists, revolutionaries, would-be saints, and anarchists made their way to his house to listen to his strong words about justice and human dignity. For every Gandhi stirred by Tolstoy's high-minded ideals, however, another reader is repelled by how miserably he failed to fulfill those ideals. What Tolstoy encountered in the gospels attracted him like a flame; his failure to attain it ultimately consumed him.

Tolstoy was tormented by the same tension all Christians feel to some degree, the tension that plagued my adolescence. When he wrote about his religious faith, or attempted to live out that faith, the antagonism between the ideal and real haunted him like a dybbuk. Novelist John Updike shows the other side in this comment about Tolstoy's thirteen-volume diary: "The sunlight of Tolstoy's art scarcely penetrates into the monk's cell of his unremitting moralism and self-scorn."

Tolstoy's attempts at honesty and reform caused endless problems in his own family. As a young Army officer he had collected a string of mistresses, frequented whorehouses, participated in drunken orgies, and several times contracted venereal disease. He dutifully recorded all these misadventures in his diary and, four days before his wedding, he insisted that his fiancée, a decorous girl of eighteen, read the lurid accounts. She never recovered.

"When he kisses me I'm always thinking, 'I'm not the first woman he has loved,' " wrote Sonya Tolstoy in her own diary. His Army flings she could forgive, but not his affair with Axinya, a peasant woman who still served on the Tolstoy estate. Every time she looked at Axinya's son, she saw her own husband's features in miniature. And when he announced his intention of giving his book royalties away, she moaned that he was giving a fortune to cranks while "black bread will do for his children and grandchildren." His inattention to the estate ruined the family income; his disposal of copyrights deprived his heirs. What Leo considered steps toward holiness, Sonya viewed as folly and family abuse.

As I read Tolstoy's diaries, I see flashbacks of my own occasional lunges toward perfectionism. The diaries record many struggles between Tolstoy and his family, but many more between Tolstoy and himself. His desire to reach perfection led him to devise ever new lists of rules. He gave up hunting, tobacco, alcohol, and meat. He determined to sell or give away everything superfluous—the piano, furniture, carriages—and to treat all people alike, from governors to beggars. He drafted rules for developing the emotional will, rules for developing lofty feelings and eliminating base ones, rules for subordinating the will to the feeling of love.

Yet he could never achieve the self-discipline necessary to abide by his own rules. He kept the piano and the furniture after all. He signed the estate over to his wife, but continued living in it, and was served his vegetarian meals by a white-gloved servant. More than once, Tolstoy took a public vow of chastity (hadn't Jesus commended it?) and asked for separate bedrooms. He could never keep that vow for long either as, much to his shame, Sonya's sixteen pregnancies broadcast to the world. He wrote in his diary that his wife was preventing his spiritual fulfillment by insisting on a "normal" way of life, and after yielding to his sexual urges he would add a comment such as "It was so loathsome as after a crime." Sonya continued to read that diary throughout his life, which inflicted on her constant pain.

Sometimes Tolstoy managed to accomplish great good. When a famine hit his area, he spent two years organizing relief, setting up makeshift hospitals, and caring for the destitute. After a long hiatus from literature he wrote one last novel, *Resurrection,* at the age of seventy-one, in support of the Dukhobors—an Anabaptist group of twelve thousand undergoing persecution by the tsar—donating all proceeds to finance their emigration to Canada. And Tolstoy's philosophy of nonviolence, lifted directly from the Sermon on the Mount, had an impact that long outlived him, in ideological descendants such as Gandhi and Martin Luther King, Jr.

Yet by any measure Tolstoy's quest for holiness ended in disappointment. In short, he failed to practice what he preached. His wife put it well (in an obviously biased account):

> There is so little genuine warmth about him; his kindness does not come from his heart, but merely from his principles. His biographies will tell of how he helped the laborers to carry buckets of water, but no one will ever know that he never gave his wife a rest and never—in all these thirty-two years—gave his child a drink of water or spent five minutes by his bedside to give me a chance to rest a little from all my labors.   (From Sonya's diary)

"Where is his love?" she demanded after one violent shouting match. "His nonresistance? His Christianity?" He never showed affection toward the children who consumed so much of her life. The one who professed such love of humanity had difficulty loving any single individuals, even the members of his own family.

Tolstoy's ardent strides toward perfection never resulted in any semblance of peace or serenity. Up to the moment of his death the diaries and letters kept circling back to the rueful theme of failure, exposing the gap between gospel ideals and the contradictions of his own life. Too honest for self-deception, he could not silence the conscience that convicted him. Some have called him a hypocrite. But a hypocrite pretends to be something he is not; Tolstoy knew above anyone how far short he fell.

Leo Tolstoy was a deeply unhappy man. He fulminated against the Russian Orthodox Church of his day and earned their excommunication.* His schemes for self-improvement all foundered. At times he

---

*In 2001 the Russian Orthodox Church refused a request by Tolstoy's great-great-grandson to review Leo Tolstoy's writings as a step toward reconsidering his excommunication.

had to hide the ropes on his estate and put away his guns in order to resist the temptation toward suicide. In the end, Tolstoy fled from his fame, his family, his estate, his identity; he died like a vagrant in a rural railroad station, surrounded by curious villagers and journalists from around the world. A poignant photo survives of Sonya peering anxiously through a dirty window to catch a glimpse of her husband, who lay dying inside; his disciples refused her entrance lest her presence upset him.

In view of such failures, what can I possibly learn from the tragic life of Leo Tolstoy? I have read many of his religious writings, and without fail I come away inspired by his reverence for God's absolute ideal. Tolstoy reminds us that, contrary to those who say the gospel solves our problems, in many areas—justice issues, money issues, race issues, personal issues of pride and ambition—the gospel actually adds to our burdens.

In modern times, it may be easy to confuse the gospel with "the American Dream" of contentment, prosperity, and a trouble-free existence. Tolstoy saw that Jesus calls us to far more than a beautiful home with pleasant neighbors. He had tasted fortune, talent, education, and worldwide fame: "I would say to myself, 'Very well; you will be more famous than Gogol or Pushkin or Shakespeare or Molière, or than all the writers in the world—and what of it?' And I could find no answer at all." Tolstoy took as dead-serious Jesus' question, "What shall it profit a man to gain the whole world and lose his soul?"

A man willing to liberate his serfs and give away his possessions in simple obedience to Jesus' command is not easy to dismiss. Other Russian nobility were buying and trading their serfs like cattle, and viciously beating those who disobeyed—this in a nation that considered itself the home of Christ's pure church. Tolstoy voluntarily set his serfs free. If others had followed Tolstoy's lead on issues of justice, the nightmare revolution of 1917 might never have happened.

If only Tolstoy could live up to all of his ideals—if only I could live up to them. Although he set many rules for himself, Tolstoy never fell for a shallow legalism. His book title *The Kingdom of God Is Within*

You says it well, for he sought to absorb the ideal moral law within himself.

Religious systems, said Tolstoy, tend to promote external rules: Judaism did so, as did Buddhism, Hinduism, and Islam. But Jesus introduced a different approach by refusing to define a set of external rules which his followers could then abide by with a sense of self-righteousness. In a pivotal passage, Tolstoy made this distinction between Christ's approach and that of all other religions:

> The test of observance of external religious teachings is whether or not our conduct conforms with their decrees [Observe the Sabbath. Get circumcised. Tithe.] Such conformity is indeed possible.
>
> The test of observance of Christ's teachings is our consciousness of our failure to attain an ideal perfection. The degree to which we draw near this perfection cannot be seen; all we can see is the extent of our deviation.
>
> A man who professes an external law is like someone standing in the light of a lantern fixed to a post. It is light all round him, but there is nowhere further for him to walk. A man who professes the teaching of Christ is like a man carrying a lantern before him on a long, or not so long, pole: the light is in front of him, always lighting up fresh ground and always encouraging him to walk further.

Despite nuggets of wisdom in individual passages, Tolstoy's religious writings in the main seem erratic and unstable. He saw the extent of his deviation and little else. As he diagnosed his own inner workings, what he saw filled him with disgust: moral failure, hypocrisy, faithlessness. Perhaps for this reason, few people today read his spiritual musings. As a counselor, he offers more discouragement than hope. If Tolstoy could hardly help himself, how could he be expected to help the rest of us?

In response to such criticism Tolstoy replied, Don't judge God's

holy ideals by my inability to meet them. Don't judge Christ by those
of us who imperfectly bear his name. One passage especially, taken
from a personal letter, shows how Tolstoy responded to such critics toward the end of his life. It stands as a summary of his spiritual pilgrimage, at once a ringing affirmation of the truth that he believed
with all his heart and a plangent appeal for grace that he never fully
realized.

> "What about you, Lev Nikolayevich, you preach very well, but
> do you carry out what you preach?" This is the most natural of
> questions and one that is always asked of me; it is usually asked
> victoriously, as though it were a way of stopping my mouth. "You
> preach, but how do you live?" And I answer that I do not preach,
> that I am not able to preach, although I passionately wish to. I
> can preach only through my actions, and my actions are vile. . . .
> And I answer that I am guilty, and vile, and worthy of contempt
> for my failure to carry them out.
>
> At the same time, not in order to justify, but simply in order
> to explain my lack of consistency, I say: "Look at my present life
> and then at my former life, and you will see that I do attempt to
> carry them out. It is true that I have not fulfilled one thousandth
> part of them [Christian precepts], and I am ashamed of this, but
> I have failed to fulfil them not because I did not wish to, but be-
> cause I was unable to. Teach me how to escape from the net of
> temptations that surrounds me, help me and I will fulfil them;
> even without help I wish and hope to fulfil them.
>
> "Attack me, I do this myself, but attack *me* rather than the
> path I follow and which I point out to anyone who asks me
> where I think it lies. If I know the way home and am walking
> along it drunkenly, is it any less the right way because I am stag-
> gering from side to side! If it is not the right way, then show me
> another way; but if I stagger and lose the way, you must help me,
> you must keep me on the true path, just as I am ready to sup-
> port you. Do not mislead me, do not be glad that I have got lost,
> do not shout out joyfully: 'Look at him! He said he was going

home, but there he is crawling into a bog!' No, do not gloat, but give me your help and support."

I feel sad as I read Tolstoy's religious writings. The X-ray vision into the human heart that made him a great novelist also made him a tortured Christian. Like a spawning salmon, he fought upstream all his life, in the end collapsing from moral exhaustion. As a child, he had believed in a magical "green stick" on which words were carved that would destroy all evil in the hearts of man and bring them good. He never found that green stick, never truly came to terms with the fallenness of humanity, including himself. He thought that his own will would suffice to chase away evil, and it failed him. In his last novel, *Resurrection*, one of his own characters realizes "quite clearly that the only sure means of salvation from the terrible wrongs which mankind endures is for every man to acknowledge himself a sinner before God and therefore unfitted either to punish or reform others."

Yet I also feel grateful to Tolstoy, for his relentless pursuit of authentic faith has made an indelible impression upon me. I first came across his novels during a period when I was suffering the delayed effects of "church abuse." The churches I grew up in contained too many frauds, or at least that is how I saw it in the arrogance of youth. When I noted the rift between the ideals of the gospel and the flaws of its followers, I was sorely tempted to abandon those ideals as hopelessly unattainable. Then I discovered Tolstoy. He was the first author who, for me, accomplished that most difficult of tasks: to make good as believable and appealing as evil. I found in his novels, fables, and short stories a source of moral power.

Many modern novels explore depravity and little else. Tolstoy, who had drunk of that depravity, kept reaching higher, toward a vision of what we could be and should be, toward a rule of love that he always yearned for and never realized. His futile striving helped convince me that my failures fully to realize the truth do not devalue the truth itself but instead point out my continuing need to cast myself on God's mercy. An idea cannot be held responsible for those who profess to believe it. With Tolstoy, I learned to say to critics, ". . . attack *me* rather than the path I follow." Thanks to his profligate past, Tolstoy knew that other paths led even further from the truth.

"I am not an orphan on earth as long as that man lives," said Maxim Gorky, one of Tolstoy's most talented contemporaries. He raised the sights of an entire nation, and still today his writings bear that message to the world. A few years ago a friend of mine, a literature professor, received a frantic cry for help from a former student then serving in a shabby refugee camp in Thailand. Every day she was interviewing people who had escaped Cambodia and Vietnam, listening to their stories of human brutality and evil. She could hardly believe in human goodness anymore, she said. She could hardly believe in God. Could he send her a few books that might help resuscitate her faith? My friend chose five books, and first among them was Tolstoy's *Resurrection.* That final novel, which tells of the relentless, unquenchable love of an abused former prostitute, and the guilt of a man who abused her, may represent the closest Tolstoy ever came to comprehending grace.

One of Tolstoy's finest novels, *Anna Karenina,* ends with two paragraphs that chronicle the spiritual awakening of Levin, a major character. Levin says, "Knowledge unattainable by reasoning has been revealed to me personally, to my heart, openly and beyond a doubt, and I am obstinately trying to express that knowledge in words and by my reason." As I read Levin's final words, I cannot help seeing in them the projection of Tolstoy himself, both his desperate hope and his unrealized dreams:

> "This new feeling has not changed me, has not made me happy
> and enlightened me all of a sudden as I had dreamed it would—
> just the same as with my feeling for my son. There was no sur-
> prise about it either. But whether it is faith or not—I don't know
> what it is—but that feeling has entered just as imperceptibly
> into my soul through suffering and has lodged itself there firmly.
>   "I shall still get angry with my coachman Ivan, I shall still ar-
> gue and express my thoughts inopportunely; there will still be a
> wall between the holy of holies of my soul and other people,
> even my wife, and I shall still blame her for my own fears and

shall regret it; I shall still be unable to understand with my reason why I am praying, and I shall continue to pray—but my life, my whole life, independently of anything that may happen to me, every moment of it, is no longer meaningless but has an incontestable meaning of goodness, with which I have the power to invest it."

That credo, recognizing at once stubborn imperfectibility and incontestable goodness, I could accept for myself.

Reading Tolstoy and Dostoevsky transformed my view of what can be conveyed in words. I had read many books of theology and apologetics, with some profit but much frustration. Some of the arguments from atheistic philosophers, after all, seemed equally compelling on a rational level. Yet as I read the two Russians, the core of Christian truth penetrated me more deeply. I learned the power of story, of truth being expressed in an embodied form, inarguably, incontestably. Concepts like grace and forgiveness, which constitute the core of the gospel, get little play in many theology books. I began to grasp why Jesus relied so strongly on story: The Prodigal Son says most of what we need to know about redemption, the Good Samaritan most of what we need for ethics. Jesus contrasted a Pharisee who had a finely tuned theology with a sinner who could only cry for help—and it was the sinner's cry, of course, that God heard.

Tolstoy's own writings bear out the same principle as they cross from one genre to another. His religious writings contradict each other and rely on blatant rationalization. In his best stories, though, the scent of propaganda evaporates. The novels present doctrine and ethics not as abstract ideals, rather as life forces incarnated within real characters. His fictional portrayal of life, the truth about men and women that he had learned by observing them with his photographic eye, contained within it the heart of the gospel that had always eluded his rational search. Tolstoy was far better at painting a picture of redemption than explaining it.

Sadly, Tolstoy never allowed that gospel to bring comfort to his own life. A. N. Wilson, a biographer of Tolstoy, remarks that his "religion was ultimately a thing of Law rather than of Grace, a scheme for human betterment rather than a vision of God penetrating a fallen world." With crystalline clarity Tolstoy could see his own inadequacy in the light of God's ideal. But he could not take the further step of trusting God's grace to overcome the inadequacy.

Shortly after reading Tolstoy I discovered his countryman Feodor Dostoevsky. These two, the most famous and accomplished of all Russian writers, lived and worked during the same period of history. Though they read each other's work with admiration, they never met. Like revolving planets they circled around the same cities, attracting attention and exerting a powerful force, but with their orbits never intersecting. Perhaps it was just as well—they were opposites in every way.

Where Tolstoy wrote bright, sunny novels, Dostoevsky wrote brooding, interior ones. Where Tolstoy worked out ascetic schemes for self-improvement, Dostoevsky periodically squandered his health and fortune on affairs, alcohol, and gambling. Tolstoy kept a disciplined work schedule; Dostoevsky usually worked all night, churning out stories at a frantic pace in order to pay off gambling debts. Thousands of pilgrims made their way to Tolstoy's home, seeking wisdom; no one would think of going to the disheveled Dostoevsky for wisdom. He was socially awkward. He managed money so poorly that sometimes he could not afford the postage to send in a completed novel to the publisher. He suffered from epilepsy, and a grand mal seizure might drive him into despair for days afterward.

Dostoevsky made many mistakes in life, but achieved an amazing feat in art. His novels communicate grace and forgiveness, the heart of the Christian gospel, with a Tolstoyan force. Dostoevsky taught me the remedy for the relentless failures exposed by Tolstoy.

Early in his life, Dostoevsky underwent a virtual resurrection. He had been arrested for belonging to a group judged treasonous by Tsar Nicholas I, who, to impress upon the young parlor radicals the gravity of their errors, staged a mock execution. After spending eight months in jail awaiting sentence, suddenly on a frigid morning three days before Christmas the conspirators were ordered out of their cells and carted to a public square where to their horror an official read the sentence condemning them to death. They had no time to absorb the news, and no possibility of appeal. A firing squad stood at the ready. Bareheaded, robed in white burial shrouds, hands bound tightly behind them, they were paraded through the snow before a gawking crowd.

A clerk pronounced the words, "The wages of sin is death" to each prisoner, and held out a cross to be kissed. The first three were selected to die, and then tied to posts. At the very last instant, as the order, "Ready, aim!" was heard, as drums rumbled and rifles were cocked and lifted to shoulders, a horseman galloped up with a prearranged message from the tsar: he would mercifully commute their sentences to hard labor. Dostoevsky, a member of the nobility, had a sword broken over his head as a sign of shame. One of the prisoners fell to his knees crying, "The good tsar! Long live our tsar!" Another had a mental collapse from which he never recovered.

In a very different way, Dostoevsky never recovered from this experience either. He had peered into the maw of death, and from that moment life became for him precious beyond all calculation. Back in the prison, he walked up and down the cell, singing in sheer joy of having life restored. He wrote his brother, "Never has there seethed in me such an abundant and healthy kind of spiritual life as now . . . Now my life will change, I shall be born again in a new form." He folded away the burial shroud to keep as a memento.

His next ordeal involved transport to Siberia. At the stroke of midnight on Christmas Day, guards pounded ten-pound shackles on his legs and marched him to an open sledge. For eighteen days, in freezing cold that caused him frostbite, he endured this horse-drawn journey. The convoy paused for a few days in Siberia before final dispersal of the prisoners, and the commandant allowed a visit by three women, wives of other political prisoners, who had settled there to be near their husbands. The three had made it their mission to welcome new prisoners and try to bring them comfort. One of these, a devout woman who had studied German philosophy and knew the Bible almost by heart, handed Dostoevsky a New Testament, the only book allowed in prison. She whispered that he should search it carefully, and inside he found ten rubles.

Believing that God had given him a second chance to fulfill his calling, Dostoevsky pored over the New Testament during his confinement. "He studied the precious volume from cover to cover, pondered every word; learned much of it by heart; and never forgot it," wrote his daughter Aimee years later. "All his works are saturated with it, and it is this which gives them their power." Even after his release, Dostoevsky took that New Testament with him on his travels and at home kept it in a drawer in his writing table, always within reach.

Dostoevsky spent the next four years in hard labor and then another six in exile. At the end of that decade he emerged with unshakable Christian convictions, as expressed in a letter he wrote to the woman who had given him the New Testament: "This *Credo* is very simple, here it is: to believe that nothing is more beautiful, profound, sympathetic, reasonable, manly, and more perfect than Christ . . . Even more, if someone proved to me that Christ is outside the truth, then I would prefer to remain with Christ rather than with the truth."

D ostoevsky suffered terribly while in prison. His disordered nerves gave him epilepsy so severe that the seizures would send him to the ground shrieking, foaming at the mouth, his limbs convulsing. He often lay ill in the prison hospital, treated for rheumatism as well as the epilepsy. He sorely missed having literature to read, cringed at the constant fighting and general uproar, chafed at the shackles, and yearned for just a moment of solitude away from the din—a need, he decided, as urgent as eating and drinking. In the years in prison, he never received a single letter from his family.

Some of his fellow prisoners responded to their punishment with hatred and a thirst for revenge. Remarkably, Dostoevsky returned to civilization with a renewed joy in life and optimism about human nature. He tucked away memories of standing for hours at a gap in the fence, his head resting on the palings, watching the green grass and the deepening blue of the sky; one particular work site was "the only place where we saw God's world—a pure and bright horizon, the free desert steppes whose bareness always made a strange impression on me."

He remembered the kindness of the woman who had given him the New Testament and of a little girl who had come running up to him as he walked in the street with a guard, crying, "There, poor unfortunate, take a kopek in the name of Christ!" He kept the kopek coin, like the New Testament and the burial shroud, as a memento. He remembered a period in solitary confinement when each evening a shutter in the cell door opened, and an anonymous voice whispered: "Courage, brother, we also suffer." These small notes of grace interposed in the midst of suffering would find a place in his later novels.

Above all, Dostoevsky reveled in the sheer generosity of life. "Life is a gift," he wrote several hours after the fake execution. "Life is happiness, every minute can be an eternity of happiness . . . Life is everywhere, life is in ourselves, not in the exterior." Once he had returned to freedom, he wrote:

> *Love every leaf, every ray of light.*
> *Love the animals, love the plants, love each separate thing.*
> *Loving all, you will perceive the mystery of God in all.*

I had not expected this surge of joy in Dostoevsky. I read his novels during a dark period of my own, after immersing myself in existentialist novels. I lived in an emotional flatland. I stood back from other people and judged them, approaching new acquaintances with suspicion. People could win me over, yes, but it was exactly that, a winning over. I found my numbed character type in Dostoevsky's *Underground Man*, and then went on to meet his other characters, whose overflowing goodness made them stand out in sharp contrast. I could not help noting the paradox: Tolstoy, who had everything, ended up irascible and embittered while Dostoevsky, who lost everything, ended up grateful and exuberant.

Prison offered Dostoevsky a unique opportunity, which at first seemed a curse: it forced him to live at close quarters with thieves, murderers, and drunken peasants. Indeed, he later reflected that the worst pain he had endured in prison was the sheer hatred he confronted in peasant prisoners, who viewed him as one of the despised upper class. This revelation came as a great shock, for his aristocratic friends had been leading the reform movement to bring rights to the very people whom he now found despised them. His shared life with these prisoners later led to unmatched characterizations in his novels, such as that of the murderer Raskolnikov in *Crime and Punishment*.

Dostoevsky's liberal view of the inherent goodness in humanity could not account for the pure evil he found in his cell mates, and his theology had to adjust to this new reality. Over time, though, he also glimpsed the image of God in the lowest of these prisoners. Like Tolstoy, he discovered that remnants of traditional Christianity survived in the peasants, which he began to see as their only hope for a new beginning. He came to believe that only through being loved is a person made capable of love. Dostoevsky saw part of his task as "raising up the lowly." In the brilliant and complex novels he would go on to write, he did just that, redeeming in the eyes of educated Russians a class of peasants and criminal outcasts.

Himself, he began to see as the prodigal son in exile, living in a far country among the husks and the swine. Every convict, he concluded, feels with the prodigal that he is *not at home*, but on a visit. Hope, "this strange impatient and intense hope," that something awaits outside the prison walls keeps the prisoner alive, literally. For Dostoevsky, the hope behind bars became a symbol of the eternal hope he had felt in a flash when he heard the death sentence in the public square. "We shall be with Christ," he had whispered instinctively to a friend beside him. ("A bit of dust," his atheist friend laconically replied.) Dostoevsky came to believe it, to believe in immortality, in fact, as the only way to conceive of this life as anything but meaningless.

At the time, Russian intellectuals were toying with the exciting new philosophy of nihilism, the belief that nothing matters, that all morality is arbitrary, that no benevolent God rules over the world, that all actions are predetermined by our biology, that love is a physical sensation inseparable from sexual desire. After his release from exile, Dostoevsky countered each of these claims, one by one, in his writings. He did not so much argue against them as show the consequences of the ideas lived out. His novel *The Possessed,* for example, recounts the story (based on a true incident) of committed revolutionaries who kill one of their own group as the most convenient way to resolve differences with him. *Crime and Punishment* shows the end result of a Nietzschean "extraordinary man" who lives above standard conventions of morality and commits two murders simply for the experience.

Always, though, a poignant note of grace sounds. It was in Dostoevsky's novels, in fact, that I first began to understand grace, not as a theological concept but a living reality worked out in a world of ungrace. Although *Crime and Punishment* portrays a despicable human being who commits a despicable crime, the soothing balm of grace enters Raskolnikov's life through the person of the converted prostitute Sonia, who follows him all the way to Siberia and leads him to redemption. "Love resurrected them," writes Dostoevsky; "the heart of one contained infinite sources of life for the heart of the other." In *The Idiot,* Dostoevsky presents a Christ figure in the form of a strange and unpredictable epileptic prince. Quietly, mysteriously, Prince Myshkin moves among the circles of Russia's upper class, exposing their hypocrisy while also illuminating their lives with goodness and truth. *The Idiot*'s final scene presents perhaps the most moving depiction of grace in all of literature: the "idiot" prince compassionately embracing the man who has just killed the woman he loved.

In a world ruled by law, grace stands as a sign of contradiction. We want fairness; the gospel gives us an innocent man nailed to a cross who cries out, "Father, forgive them." We want respectability; the gospel elevates tax collectors, prodigals, and Samaritans. We want success; the gospel reverses the terms, moving the poor and downtrodden to the head of the line and the wealthy and famous to the rear. Having embraced Christ in the hellhole of a Siberian prison, among cell mates who mocked his infirmities and despised his advantages, Dostoevsky understood grace at its most contradictory. In his novels it enters stealthily, without warning, silencing the skeptics and disarming the cynics. They think they have life figured out until suddenly an encounter with pure grace leaves them breathless.

It had happened to Dostoevsky himself. Racked with debts from gambling and a failed magazine venture, he had fallen for the scheme of an unscrupulous publisher, who would obtain copyrights to all his past work if he did not produce a new novel by a certain date. Dostoevsky procrastinated, suffering from writer's block until only three weeks remained before the deadline. The task seemed impossible and he despaired of life until Anna, a nineteen-year-old stenographer, showed up to help him. Having suffered an epileptic seizure a few days before, he was in a foul mood. He treated her harshly at first, scolded her, and complained about her speed. She wrote down his every word, working through the night, then went home to copy it over and returned with an edited manuscript in hand the next day. With such superhuman efforts, she won him over and coaxed out of him a novel, *The Gambler,* which was delivered two hours before the deadline.

By then, Dostoevsky had fully recognized his stenographer's charms, and proposed marriage. Anna felt no physical attraction toward him, an unkempt widower twenty-five years her senior with a notorious weakness for alcohol and gambling. Yet she pitied him, and knew he needed her. At considerable personal sacrifice, she agreed to the match, moved in to organize his career and household, and gave him fifteen years of happiness—"The Miraculous Years," his biographer calls them, for in that period Dostoevsky produced all his masterpieces.

Dostoevsky's last work, *The Brothers Karamazov,* one of the greatest novels ever written, draws a contrast between Ivan the brilliant agnostic and his devout brother Alyosha. Ivan can analyze the failures of humankind and critique every political system designed to deal with those failures, but he can offer no solutions. Alyosha has no answers to the intellectual problems Ivan raises, but he has a solution for humanity: love. "I do not know the answer to the problem of evil," said Alyosha, "but I do know love." Ivan articulates the case against God as powerfully as anyone has since Job. Alyosha, speechless and filled with compassion, rises and softly kisses him on the lips—just as Christ had done to his tormenter in Ivan's great poem "The Grand Inquisitor."

The Brothers Karamazov contains every important element in Dostoevsky's own tragic life: his father's brutal murder at the hands of his serfs, the experience of being a jilted darling of the literary establishment, the arrest and mock execution, years in a prison camp, extramarital affairs, the torture of unrequited love, epilepsy, emphysema, a difficult marriage, the deaths of children from disease, the burden of heavy debts, gambling. He had been studying the book of Job as he wrote the book, and he left out none of his personal agony. Two months after completing the novel, as if he had nothing more to say, he died, virtually penniless. On his lap as he died lay the New Testament given him on his way to Siberia so many years before.

Author Frederick Buechner sums up *Karamazov* as a "great seething bouillabaisse of a book. It's digressive and sprawling, many too many characters in it, much too long, and yet it's a book which, just because Dostoevsky leaves room in it for whatever comes up to enter, is entered here and there by maybe nothing less than the Holy Spirit itself, thereby becoming, as far as I'm concerned . . . a novel less *about* the religious experience than a novel the reading of which is a religious experience: of God, both in his subterranean presence and in his appalling absence."

When I first read *The Brothers Karamazov*, I realized that I was standing with Ivan. I had a long list of complaints about the world. I had sound arguments against God's injustice and unfairness. I felt anger and resentment against God. To quote Dostoevsky, "Can't I simply be devoured without being expected to praise what devours me?" Tortured by the lack of love in the world, I was nevertheless doing nothing about it. I lacked Alyosha's instinct for common goodness, for a compassionate response.

It was then I began to see what Dostoevsky had learned in prison: the gospel of grace infiltrates this world not primarily through words and rational arguments but through deeds, through love. The people I was learning to admire most, such as Paul Brand and Robert Coles, were expressing their faith through action, incarnationally. As I traveled to other countries—Brazil, Nepal, the Philippines, Kenya—I found humble people who each day faced human problems more extreme than I could imagine, and yet who responded not with paralysis or resentment but with compassion and love. Dostoevsky showed me the logical consequences of a life based on nihilism and doubt; living Christian servants showed me the logical consequences of a life based on faith and love. To follow Jesus, I learned, does not mean to solve every human problem—Christ himself did not attempt that—but rather to respond as he did, against all reason to dispense grace and love to those who deserve it least.

By and large, the intellectuals in Dostoevsky's day did not find him convincing. His faith in the latent Christianity in the lower classes, his appeal to charity and compassion, his distrust of the latest theories of social engineering—these exposed him as an old-fashioned moralist, wholly unable to address the problems of modern Russia. They chose another path, the path of a morality based on utilitarianism, cut loose from transcendence. "Without God, everything is permitted," Dostoevsky warned in *The Brothers Karamazov*. The twentieth century would demonstrate just how prescient Dostoevsky had been. "Man must bow down to something," Dostoevsky also wrote. In the case of twentieth-century Russia, human beings chose to bow down to each other, enshrining Lenin in a mausoleum and treating Marx and Stalin like prophets. Atheists, they worshiped man-Gods rather than a God-man, with results more tragic than any our planet had before seen.

In his 1983 Templeton Address, 102 years after Dostoevsky's death, Alexander Solzhenitsyn reviewed the tragic history of Russia in the twentieth century. It was through reading Dostoevsky, Solzhenitsyn reports elsewhere, that he first began to understand the primacy of the spiritual over the material. That led the way to a conversion experience, also in a prison camp, which changed the course of his life and ultimately affected the course of his nation. This is what he said in the Templeton Address:

> Over half a century ago, while I was still a child, I recall hearing
> a number of older people offer the following explanation for the
> great disasters that had befallen Russia: "Men have forgotten

God; that's why all this has happened." Since then I have spent well-nigh fifty years working on the history of our revolution; in the process I have read hundreds of books, collected hundreds of personal testimonies, and have already contributed eight volumes of my own toward the effort of clearing away the rubble left by that upheaval. But if I were asked today to formulate as concisely as possible the main cause of the ruinous revolution that swallowed up some sixty million of our people, I could not put it more accurately than to repeat: "Men have forgotten God; that's why all this has happened."

Why doesn't it work? I began with this question about the Christian church, the source of many of my underlying doubts. Christian ideals attract admiration even from unbelievers, yet what good are those ideals if I cannot put them into practice? Two great Russian thinkers came up with different answers to this stumbling block of faith. Tolstoy founded his philosophy on a belief in the perfectibility of human nature. It doesn't work because we don't try hard enough, he concluded, though he tried harder than anyone and never managed to resolve the contradictions within himself, let alone anyone else. Ten years in Siberia purged Dostoevsky of any such delusion: "In every man, of course, a demon lies hidden," said his character Ivan Karamazov. He had no quarrel with Tolstoy on the ideal for which Russia should strive, but many differences on the path to get there.

While exiled in Siberia, and before his marriage to Anna, Dostoevsky had impulsively married a widow with a young son. They returned to St. Petersburg together, but it was a marriage no happier than Tolstoy's. Feodor's epilepsy and general slovenliness repulsed Marya. She fell into bouts of hysterical rage, which only made his epilepsy worse. He took long trips to Europe partly in search of a cure for his ailment, but partly to get away from her. The two had made a bad match.

After seven years of marriage, Marya Dostoevsky died of tuberculosis. All too characteristically, her husband had spent much of the time during her illness touring Europe with a twenty-year-old mistress.

Now, having returned for her death, he sat in the room beside her corpse, overcome with nostalgia over their happier times together, grief over her death, and remorse over his own behavior. All night he kept a vigil beside her bier, making jottings by candlelight. "Masha is lying on the table," he began writing. "Will I ever see Masha again?"

His melancholy reflections that night led to an odd discussion of immortality. In answering the question of whether he will ever see his wife again, Dostoevsky ignores traditional arguments—from the resurrection of Jesus, say, or the need to balance the scales of justice—and turns the document into a kind of personal confession. No one lives up to the ideal, he admits. No one can perfectly love his neighbor as himself. No one can fulfill the law of Christ. God cannot ask so much and be satisfied with so little. We are made for that which is too big for us. It is for this very reason, he concludes, that he must believe in an afterlife. Without such a belief, our futile struggle to fulfill the law of Christ would have no point. It is our very longing, our failure, our sense of incompleteness that forces us to throw ourselves on God's mercy. Our imperfection in this life calls for another, more complete realization of that ideal.

Thus Dostoevsky adds a note of wistful longing, of grace, to the Christian ideals he shared with Tolstoy. Today, I claim these two Russians as my spiritual guides because they help answer my underlying doubts by throwing light on a central paradox of the Christian life. From Tolstoy I learn the need to look inside, to the kingdom of God that is within me. In that glance, I see how miserably I fall short of the high ideals of the gospel. But from Dostoevsky I learn the full extent of grace. Not only the kingdom of God is within me; God himself dwells there. "Where sin increased, grace increased all the more," is how the apostle Paul expressed it in Romans.

There is only one way for any of us to resolve the tension between the high ideals of the gospel and the grim reality of ourselves: to accept that we will never measure up, but that we do not have to. Tolstoy got it halfway right: anything that makes me feel comfort with God's moral standard, anything that makes me feel, "At last I have arrived," is a cruel deception. Dostoevsky got the other half right: anything that makes me feel discomfort with God's forgiving love is also a cruel deception. "There is now no condemnation to those who are in Christ Jesus," Paul insisted: that message, Leo Tolstoy never fully grasped.

Absolute ideals and absolute grace: after learning that contrapuntal message from Russian novelists, I returned to Jesus and found that it suffuses his teaching. In his response to the rich young ruler, in the parable of the Good Samaritan, in his comments about divorce, money, or any other moral issue, Jesus never lowered God's ideal. "Be perfect, as your heavenly Father is perfect," he said. "Love the Lord your God with all your heart and with all your soul and with all your mind." Not Tolstoy, not Francis of Assisi or Mother Teresa, not anyone has completely complied with those commands.

Yet the same Jesus tenderly offered absolute grace, perhaps the greatest distinctive of the Christian faith. God loves us not because of who we are and what we have done, but because of who God is. Grace flows to all who accept it. Jesus forgave an adulteress, a thief on a cross, a disciple who had denied ever knowing him. Grace is absolute, all-encompassing. It extends even to the people who nailed Jesus to the cross: "Father, forgive them, for they do not know what they are doing" were among the last words he spoke on earth.

I read the New Testament, especially passages such as the Sermon on the Mount, with a different spirit now than in my adolescence. Jesus did not proclaim these exalted words so that we would, Tolstoy-like, furrow our brows in despair over our failure to achieve perfection. He proclaimed them to impart to us God's ideal toward which we should never stop striving, and also to show that none of us will ever reach that ideal. The Sermon on the Mount forces us to recognize the great distance between God and us, and any attempt to reduce that distance by somehow moderating its demands misses the point altogether. We are all desperate, and that is in fact the only state appropriate to a human being who wants to know God. Having fallen from the absolute ideal, as Tolstoy did, we have nowhere to land but with Dostoevsky, in the safety net of absolute grace.

GETTING STARTED WITH
LEO TOLSTOY AND FEODOR DOSTOEVSKY:

Tolstoy's greatest novels are *War and Peace* and *Anna Karenina.* Both are very long, however, and newcomers may prefer starting with his shorter works, which can be quite charming. I recommend *The Death of Ivan Ilyich,* "Master and Man," and "The Kreutzer Sonata," as well as some of his fables. Of the many biographies of Tolstoy, Henri Troyat's is considered a classic while A. N. Wilson's recent effort is breezier and more subjective. (William L. Shirer's aptly titled *Love and Hatred* focuses on the Tolstoys' torturous marriage, telling more than you may want to know.) Wilson also compiled selections from Tolstoy's religious writings in a slim volume, *The Lion and the Honeycomb,* from which I drew several excerpts for this chapter.

Dostoevsky had a larger output of full-length novels, most notably *The Brothers Karamazov, The Idiot, Crime and Punishment,* and *The Possessed. The House of the Dead* gives insight into his prison days; *Notes from the Underground* had a major impact on later existentialist literature. Joseph Frank has published four volumes of a projected five-volume biography of Dostoevsky, a magisterial account of his life that gives much historical and cultural background and thus sheds light on what subsequently happened in Russia. A book published by the Plough Publishing House, *The Gospel in Dostoevsky,* extracts explicitly religious passages from the novels.

What if a young man encountered the stark words of Jesus in the writings of Leo Tolstoy and ever after took seriously the question "What would Jesus do?" What if he determined to treat every person he met—the homeless beggar on the street, the millionaire, the mayor, the woman who cleaned his toilet—with care and dignity and respect. What if he gave away all his possessions except necessities so few that he could tote them all in a backpack. What if he insisted on long periods of daily meditation, never letting a hectic schedule interfere with his time of silence and solitude. What if he shunned modern conveniences, stayed immune to styles and fashions, and devoted his life to cultivating inner, spiritual strength.

Moreover, what if this solitary figure became, despite his eccentricities, one of the most famous people in the world, the moral leader of the second most populous nation. And to complicate matters, what if this man who modeled his life after Jesus decided, as an adult, deliberately to stay outside the Christian fold. Such is the life of Mohandas K. Gandhi (1869–1948), a man who lived in italics. There has been no one like him: no one more disciplined or stubborn or inconsistent or creative or baffling or lovable or infuriating. Many of the political principles we take for granted today originated in the mind of this man who led a fifth of humanity to independence. He broke every rule in the political manual, and in the

Chapter 7

MAHATMA

GANDHI

ECHOES

IN A

STRANGE

LAND

process helped found the largest democracy in the history of the world.

Fifty years after his death, we can at least begin to assess Gandhi by asking what relevance he has in our speeded-up world of Internet sites and cruise missiles. In my trips to India with Dr. Brand, I was surprised to find how little Gandhi's modern compatriots know about this remarkable man. And because he was called a saint—a Hindu saint, certainly, but one strategically informed by Christianity—we in the West should pause to ponder what message he has for us. He sits like a superego on the shoulder of the Western church, asking all of us the question Tolstoy asked himself: Why don't we practice what we preach?

Gandhi died three years after the United States dropped the atomic bomb on Japan, an event further convincing him that, for the planet to survive, the world must look to the East for solutions. Gandhi believed the West had forfeited its ability to lead the human race, and represented a future of decadence, materialism, and armed conflict.* He looked for a new way based on spiritual, not material, strength. Few, very few, are heeding that call today. The United States stands as the world's sole superpower, and its sex-and-money culture continues to spread around the world. Modern India honors, but hardly follows Gandhi. Giant textile mills have supplanted the wooden spinning wheels. High-tech office complexes churn out software that runs the world's computers. And, three bloody wars after Gandhi, his nation brandishes the ring of power that had appalled him: nuclear weaponry. Even so, India cannot get the strange little man out of her consciousness.

If someone staged a beauty contest to select the least likely world leader, Gandhi would win easily. Barely five feet tall, he weighed a mere 114 pounds, and his skinny arms and legs stuck out from his body

---

*Dr. Robert Coles recalls a scene from his medical school days, when he was volunteering with the Catholic Worker movement. A fellow worker had painted this wry graffito on the side of the building that housed the poor:

"Mr. Gandhi, what do you think of Western civilization?"

Gandhi: "I think it would be a great idea."

like the limbs of a malnourished child. His ears flared straight out from his shaved head; his squat, oversized nose looked fake, like one of the rubber noses attached to glasses that people wear to costume parties. Steel-rimmed spectacles kept slipping from that nose, tilting down toward his mouth, itself oddly shaped due to his habit of wearing dentures only while eating. His lips curled over nearly toothless gums. "He's rather like a little bird," said Lord Mountbatten, the last British viceroy of India, "a kind of sweet, sad sparrow perched on my armchair."

As Gandhi walked, he leaned either on a bamboo stave or on the shoulders of his "crutches," as he called his two young grandnieces. He wore the same clothes every day: a loose Indian loincloth and sometimes a cotton shawl, both made of coarse material he had spun at his own wheel. He carried all his belongings in a small sack, except for one, an Ingersoll pocket watch, which he proudly wore on a string. Gandhi followed a strict schedule and no one, not the king of the British Empire nor the leaders of India nor his closest friends, could alter it. He would arise daily at 2 A.M. to read from the Hindu or Christian scriptures and say prayers, spend the next quiet hours answering correspondence, then do his ritual ablutions, complete with a salt-and-water enema. At noon he paused for another health regimen, placing a porous cotton sack packed with oozing mud on his abdomen and forehead.

Modern historians, who tend to pick at the scabs of the famous, tell of Gandhi's petty demands on associates, his bizarre personal habits, his cranky stubbornness. He tested his vow of chastity by sleeping with nude young women. The man who could galvanize millions failed as a leader of his own family, mistreating his wife and raising a son who rebelled to become an embezzler, gambler, and penniless alcoholic. And when his wife lay dying from acute bronchitis and the British flew in a vial of rare penicillin that could save her life, Gandhi refused the doctor permission to give it to her intravenously lest the violence of the needle violate her body. As a result, she died.

Nevertheless, after the gossip is heard, and Gandhi's image corrodes, and his own nation continues to forsake much of what he lived and died for—even after all that, Gandhi still radiates a unique quality, one that never failed to affect those who knew him. Mountbatten, a seasoned military commander, summed up his moral power with a simple strategic formula, at a time when civil war was breaking out across India: "On my Western front I have 100,000 crack troops and unstoppable bloodshed. On my East I have one old man, and no bloodshed."

Somehow Gandhi mobilized his followers, millions of them, into joining a crusade like none the world had seen. "Those who are in my company," he warned his followers, "must be ready to sleep upon the bare floor, wear coarse clothes, get up at unearthly hours, subsist on uninviting, simple food, even clean their own toilets." They fought with the weapons of prayer, fasting, prison terms, and bodies bruised from beatings, and in the end their unorthodox methods helped liberate half a billion people.

The methods Gandhi taught, Martin Luther King, Jr., adapted to similar effect in the American South. They surfaced again in South Africa, and in Eastern Europe, where one night thousands of marchers holding candles and singing hymns brought down an Iron Curtain that had stood for forty years. And when Benigno Aquino stepped off an airplane in Manila to face an assassin's bullet, he had a speech in his hand quoting Gandhi: "The willing sacrifice of the innocent is the most powerful answer to insolent tyranny that has yet been conceived by God or man." People power in the Philippines soon substantiated Gandhi yet again; the army's fifty-ton tanks lurched to a halt before unarmed figures kneeling in the street.

I have been fascinated by Gandhi ever since my visits to India. From Christians there, and Christians back in the West, I heard radically different opinions of the little man. I learned that even if you dismiss him you cannot easily get him out of mind. His brush stroke on history was too broad simply to ignore. I do not write about Gandhi because he had the answers for our planet. To the contrary, I turn to him because he asked the questions most provocatively. We may reject his answers, surely, but can we do so before first considering his questions?

Though not a Christian by belief or practice, Gandhi attempted to an impressive degree to live out some of Jesus' principles. The Christian church, birthed in the East but fashioned in the West, shares many of the crises of Western civilization as a whole. Although some Christian leaders have addressed these issues, we have grown so accustomed to our own prophets that we no longer hear their message clearly. When a sound is too loud, sometimes we can discern it better in its echo.

Gandhi's most famous contribution, the technique of civil disobedience, evolved gradually. Indian-born, he trained as a lawyer in London, then moved to South Africa. He led marches, took his share of beatings, spent a few hundred days in jail, and learned the discouraging results of protest under an oppressive regime. Upon return to India he confronted a very different situation: not a minority community of Indians living in a strange land, but a majority, five hundred million citizens strong, in a subcontinent ruled by the British. Indians had expected the British to reward their loyal service in World War I with more independence, but instead the colonial power clamped down with a series of harsh laws not unlike the discriminatory laws in the American South.

As the British Empire tightened the screws, Gandhi mediated long hours about the appropriate response. It came to him early one morning, in the dawning moments between sleep and consciousness. He decided to call for a day with no activity at all. India would respond to its masters by simply refusing to cooperate. Shops would close, traffic would cease, the country would shut down for one day. We who live in its wake, after dozens of adaptations around the world, can easily miss the extraordinary nature of that move. Nothing like it had been attempted before.

Next, Gandhi tackled the colonial economic system. Britain was growing raw cotton in India, transporting it to England for milling and manufacture, then shipping the finished product back to India for sale at high prices. To break that chain, Gandhi urged every Indian, villager or city dweller, to spend at least an hour a day spinning cotton. He set the example himself, digging up an old wooden spinning wheel that he would use the rest of his life.

In response to Britain's monopoly control over salt, a staple required by everyone, Gandhi countered with his famous Salt March, a 240-mile, painstakingly slow march to the sea. As officials back in London anxiously followed every step, a million peasants joined his entourage along the way. Arriving at the coast, Gandhi waded into the shallow salt-gathering pools and scooped up a fistful of salt, holding it in the air like a scepter as a symbol of defiance to the empire. Let India boycott the British and gather her own salt.

To appreciate Gandhi's mark on history, contrast the Salt March with the American colonists' reaction to Britain's stamp tax: We fought a war over it. And as Gandhi surveyed the history of Europe, *Christian* Europe, he saw a series of wars fought over racial differences, fine points of religious doctrine, land borders, and acts of colonial aggression. Yet Jesus himself had preached love for enemies and showed a spirit of sacrifice, not violence. Gandhi sought a new way of change, something closer to the spirit of Jesus.

Gandhi stuck like a thorn in the side of the British because the standard means of control had no effect against his unorthodox protests. When policemen tried to stop demonstrators by hitting them with clubs, the protestors lined up in orderly rows to receive the blows. Indians soon flooded the nation's prisons beyond capacity, which was exactly their intent. When authorities hauled Gandhi himself into court and threatened him with prison, he calmly asked for the maximum sentence. Far from being a punishment, prison provided more luxury than he allowed himself when free, and gave him extended periods of time for reflection and writing. In all, Gandhi spent 2,338 days in British jails.

When the British tried more brutal methods of oppression, such as opening fire on the demonstrators, they created martyrs and unwittingly united the nation against them. In one notorious incident at Amritsar, British-led troops trained rifles on a peaceful but illegal gathering of unarmed men, women, and children, shooting 1,650 rounds in ten minutes and causing 1,516 casualties. The crusade for independence only gathered more steam.

Later in his life, Gandhi devised a form of protest that proved the most potent of all: he simply refused to eat. He planned his fasts as carefully as a general plans military strategy, sometimes setting them for specified lengths of time and sometimes declaring a fast unto death unless certain demands were met. The ironies defy comprehension: voluntary starvation within a nation of hungry masses, one man's self-sacrifice opposing the most widespread empire in history.

Against all odds, the tactics worked. Churchill fumed at "the nauseating and humiliating spectacle of this one-time Inner Temple lawyer, now seditious fakir, striding half-naked up the steps of the Viceroy's palace, there to negotiate and parley on equal terms with the representative of the King Emperor." Meanwhile, Gandhi gained the reputation within his own nation as "Mahatma—the Great Soul." When he publicly staked his own life on the outcome of negotiations, no one was willing to risk being responsible for letting the Great Soul die. One by one, the generals, viceroys, prime ministers, and finally the king emperor yielded to that fasting, half-naked fakir.

Gandhi's commitment to nonviolence developed while he was working as a lawyer in South Africa. Demonstrating for civil rights, he was tossed off trains, ejected from hotels and restaurants, charged by mounted police, and jailed. His protests seemed to be having little effect on the people who made and enforced the laws. Only after reading Tolstoy's *The Kingdom of God Is Within You* and corresponding with its Russian author did Gandhi decide to accept the literal principles of the Sermon on the Mount, especially its words on peacemaking and loving one's enemies.

Richard Attenborough's movie *Gandhi* contains a fine scene in which Gandhi tries to explain his new philosophy to the Presbyterian missionary Charlie Andrews. Walking together in a South African city, the two suddenly find their way blocked by young thugs. Reverend Andrews takes one look at the menacing gangsters and decides to run for it. Gandhi stops him. "Doesn't the New Testament say if an enemy strikes you on the right cheek you should offer him the left?" Andrews mumbles that he thought the phrase was used metaphorically. "I'm not so sure," Gandhi replies. "I suspect he meant you must show courage—be willing to take a blow, several blows, to show you will not strike back nor will you be turned aside. And when you do that it calls on something in human nature, something that makes his hatred decrease and his respect increase. I think Christ grasped that and I have seen it work."

Gandhi's deeply felt sensibility gradually took shape as a firm doctrine. Violence against another human being—even against a soldier firing into an unarmed crowd—contradicted everything he believed about universal human dignity. You cannot change a person's conviction through violence, he believed. Violence brutalizes and divides; it does not reconcile. If his supporters ever turned violent during one of his campaigns, Gandhi would call it off. No cause, no matter how just, merited bloodshed. "I would die for the cause," he concluded, "but there is no cause I'm prepared to kill for."*

Since Gandhi, other political leaders have adopted his tactics. Martin Luther King, Jr., who considered himself a spiritual successor, visited India and imported the methods to the United States. He and others proved that nonviolence can move mountains in relatively open societies, but what about in places like Nazi Germany, or modern China and Myanmar/Burma, where military regimes quash all protest? (Ironically, some Hindu leaders, Gandhi's own religious heirs, suggest that this principle grew out of his Christian influences and has no place in Hinduism.) Ethicists, politicians, and theologians will continue to disagree on whether and when armed force is justified. But after Gandhi, no one can deny the power of nonviolence in effecting change. It did, after all, bring freedom to the second most populous nation on earth.

---

*In later years, Gandhi became absolutely inflexible on this issue. During World War II he counseled first the Ethiopians invaded by Nazi armies, then the Jews, then Great Britain, to invite their enemies in and stand before the slaughter with serenity and a clear conscience. He told his followers if an atom bomb were dropped on India they should look up, "watching without fear, praying for the pilot."

When Gandhi lived in India, one sixth of its population seemed more animal than human. They lived in squalid slums amid open sewers in which swarmed rats and every other disease-bearing agent. The Hindu doctrine of *karma* gave a theological basis for the elaborate system of five thousand subcastes that kept people in their place. Caste, a grouping of human beings that went deeper than tribe or race, had been accepted for five millennia, and few questioned it. The lowest caste of all, Untouchables, provided a valuable service to society, sweeping the streets and cleaning the latrines and sewers—acts a higher-caste Hindu would never perform.

You could tell Untouchables by their dark color and by their posture, for they cringed like beaten animals. The name defined them: if a caste Hindu so much as touched one, or touched a drop of water one had polluted, he would recoil and begin an elaborate purification process. An Untouchable had to shrink from the path of caste Hindus to avoid casting a shadow and thus defiling their superiors. In the 1930s the British discovered a new subcaste, the Invisibles, whom they had not encountered in three centuries of presence there: assigned the role of washing clothes for the Untouchables, these poor creatures believed they would pollute higher castes by sight, so they emerged only at night and avoided all contact with other people.

With little to gain but rejection from his peers, Mahatma Gandhi took up the cause of the Untouchables. First, he bestowed on them a new name; they were no longer to be called *Untouchables,* but rather *Harijans,* the Children of God. At his first ashram, a spiritual commune, in South Africa, Gandhi stirred up a storm of protest by inviting an Untouchable to move in. When the chief financial backer of the commune experiment withdrew his support, Gandhi made plans to move to the Harijan's own quarters. Finally he committed the most defiling act possible for a Hindu, cleaning the latrines of the Untouchables. When he returned to India, he called them his brothers and stayed in their homes whenever possible.

Years later, after independence, when other leaders in India were pressing Lord Mountbatten to accept the honorary post of governor-general, Gandhi proposed an alternative candidate, an Untouchable

sweeper girl "of stout heart, incorruptible and crystallike in her purity."
Although his candidate did not get the nomination, by such symbolic
actions Gandhi helped change the perception of Untouchables all
across India. Laws were modified and strictures removed. Today in India, the caste system continues in a milder, less repressive form. But
one hundred million people now call themselves not by a curse—Untouchable—but by a blessing: they are the Children of God.

Gandhi strove to recognize the inherent dignity in every person. In
his ashram in India, he adopted a leprosy patient, another of India's
outcasts. Each day he changed the man's bandages and bathed him.
He wanted, he said, to devote the same care in making a mud pack for
a leprosy victim as in conducting an interview with the viceroy of India. He also helped elevate the status of women in the country by surrounding himself with highly competent women followers.

Gandhi summarized his beliefs in three points, which he credited
to the Victorian author John Ruskin: (1) That the good of the individual is contained in the good of all; (2) That a lawyer's work has the
same value as a barber's inasmuch as all persons have the same right
of earning their livelihood from their work; (3) That a life of labor, such
as that of the tiller of the soil and the handicraftsman, is the life worth
living. Gandhi sought ways to put those principles into practice. In
cities like Bombay and Calcutta, he preferred staying in a hovel of the
Sweepers' Colony to a hotel. He used a pencil until it was reduced to
an ungrippable stub, out of respect for the human being who made the
pencil.

John Ruskin was a Christian writer, and Gandhi acknowledged
that in some ways the Christian church has led the way in respecting
human dignity. A visitor to India finds hospitals, orphanages, leprosar-
iums, and schools operated by missionaries for the downtrodden. But
we in the West are still learning the difference between acts of charity and the more difficult task of changing a person's self-perception.
Too often our motives smack of paternalism (as do the words: *downtrodden, underclass*). I, the educated, wealthy American, reach out in
compassion to help you improve yourself. We see ourselves as on the
side of Christ by giving to the needy. The New Testament makes plain,

however, that Jesus is on the side of the poor, and we serve best by elevating the downtrodden to the place of Jesus.

"I see the face of Jesus in disguise," said Mother Teresa about the dying beggars she would invite into her home in Calcutta—"sometimes a most distressing disguise." She, like Gandhi, understood that the direction of charity is not condescending, but rather ascending: in serving the weak and the poor, we are privileged to serve God himself.

Gandhi worked hard at identifying with the poor, by removing any barriers that might distance him. To anyone who has been to India, I need cite only one instance of Gandhi's outreach: his insistence on traveling third-class on trains. He would sit on hard benches crammed together with the unwashed peasants and their farm animals, an experience of crowdedness, noise, filth, and smells unimaginable to most Westerners. Why? he was once asked. He replied, "Because there is no fourth class." (I contrast that attitude to my own excitement when I collect enough mileage points to earn an upgrade to an airline's business class.)

Gandhi had no innate love of suffering, and had been assertive in early battles for personal rights in South Africa after he was thrown out of a first-class compartment because of his skin color. Yet as he immersed himself in the sacred scriptures of Hinduism, Islam, Buddhism, and Christianity, he became convinced that the humility of a servant is the one posture required by God. Only then did he strip off his European clothes, dispossess himself of material things, and seek companionship with the poor and suffering. "A leader," he said, "is only a reflection of the people he leads."

Gandhi allowed no VIPs to interfere with his preferred style. When Lord Mountbatten offered to fly him to an important meeting on his private plane, Gandhi chose instead his normal third-class rail passage. He caused something of a scandal on a visit to England to meet with Parliament and King George. He arrived amid great fanfare and press coverage, and the nation gasped as he tottered down the steamship gangplank wearing only a cotton loincloth and leading a goat, his milk supply, by a rope. Declining offers from the best hotels, he chose instead to stay in an East End slum. When reporters asked him to explain why he dared meet with a king in a "half-naked" state, Gandhi replied with a smile, "The king was wearing enough clothes for both of us."

Gandhi never insisted that political leaders follow his strict path; his was a moral and religious crusade, not just a political one. But he did ask, after independence, that each government minister live in a simple home with no servants and no car, practice one hour of manual labor daily, and clean his or her own toilet box. Long after his death, Congress leaders continued to wear the homespun cotton uniform he espoused, and conducted party meetings while spinning cotton threads.

Today, Gandhi's philosophy seems quaint and archaic. Whereas he proposed an Untouchable sweeper for a national office and spent time in slums and leprosy clinics, we in the West elevate dot-com billionaires and gorgeous supermodels. For chasing a ball around a field, we reward our professional athletes with more money than it would take to run dozens of hospitals in a country like India. Meanwhile many slum dwellers in the West, who have electricity, running water, and other luxuries beyond the reach of village India, live in a state of greed, resentment, and unrest. By elevating the rich, the beautiful, the powerful, what have we done to the dignity of those who do not measure up? And what can we learn from a Gandhi, who chose another way?

The Christian message that gets widest exposure in the Western world today follows the cultural mainstream. It offers the appeal, "God has something good in store for you," and holds out the promise of self-fulfillment. Jesus' statements about finding oneself by losing one's self are conveniently overlooked. In the United States a success-based theology may work out plausibly well, if only because the resources of the nation are so large. But such a theology has little to say to Christians in China or Indonesia or Iran, where Christian faith compounds suffering.

In his own study of the New Testament, Gandhi found the counsel to seek truth with the whole heart, expecting nothing, regardless of results. He used to sing an Indian poem as he walked among the rice paddies at a time when his own people were persecuting him: "If they answer not your call, walk alone, walk alone." In countries like the United States, that message, frankly, does not sell.

Recent times have demonstrated the moral power of a single individual. Nelson Mandela calmly stepped into the leadership of a nation that nearly every observer expected to erupt into a civil war, and the tone of conciliation he set ultimately proved the prophets wrong. Alexander Solzhenitsyn, Lech Walesa, Cory Aquino, and Vaclav Havel all stood up courageously and with their moral authority helped to change history. In other nations—Sudan, Rwanda, Yugoslavia, Congo—where no one had the moral leadership to restrain violence, slaughter ensued.

In 1947, as the momentum for independence swept across India, centuries-old animosities began to boil to the surface. Hindus and Muslims turned against each other with ferocity. Muslims burned the huts of their Hindu neighbors, forced them to eat sacred cows, raped the Hindu women and butchered their husbands. Hindus fought back in kind, and thousands of Muslims also died in the months leading up to independence. Increasingly it appeared the whole country would burst into flames.

While politicians sat in elegant palace rooms in New Delhi and bartered for power and land, Gandhi went on an "ointment" crusade. Let them argue, he said; he was going to the people, to the angry hordes who were assailing each other so viciously. At the age of seventy-seven he headed to the region where the most violence had occurred. He led his ragtag group of Hindu disciples into charred Muslim villages to face taunts and rocks and bottles. If turned away, he would look for a tree to sleep under. If accepted, he would read from the Bhagavad Gita and Koran and New Testament, teach basic principles of health and hygiene, then trudge on to the next village. In all he visited forty-seven villages, walking 116 miles barefoot.

In each village Gandhi tried to persuade one Hindu and one Muslim leader to move into the same house together and serve as guarantors of peace. He asked them to pledge themselves to fast unto death if one from their own religion attacked an enemy. Incredibly, the method worked. While debates continued in the Delhi palaces, Gandhi's personal ointment began to salve the wounds across the region. For a while the killing stopped.

When the politicians decided to carve the separate nation of Pakistan out of India, however, the country needed more than ointment; it needed huge swaths of bandages to stanch the flow of blood that quite literally turned rivers scarlet and filled the skies with vultures. As Gandhi had predicted in his appeals against it, partition provoked a reaction with no historical precedent. When boundary lines were finally announced, Hindus found themselves caught within the borders of a newly created and hostile Pakistan, and Muslims found themselves in Hindu India. Thus began the greatest mass migration ever as ten million people left their homes and attempted a frantic march across mountains and desert plains to a new home.

Lord Mountbatten, the British viceroy who oversaw independence, knew that two areas were potential conflagrations. On the west where India bordered West Pakistan, hostilities would undoubtedly break out. But the eastern territory, along the gerrymandered border of East Pakistan (now Bangladesh), posed a greater threat. Sitting along that border was Calcutta, the most violent city in Asia. No city in the world matched its poverty—more than four hundred thousand beggars—its religious bigotry, its unrestrained passions. Calcutta brazenly worshiped the Hindu goddess of destruction, who wore a garland of skulls around her waist. In a one-day preview of what was to come, violence had flared in Calcutta and six thousand bodies were tossed in the river, stuffed in gutters, or left to rot in the streets. Most had been beaten or trampled to death.

As reports of atrocities flooded in, Mountbatten sent his crack Boundary Force to the western frontier to check the escalating violence (it would ultimately claim half a million victims). That left him no reserves for the eastern front. Desperate, Mountbatten pleaded with Gandhi to go to Calcutta and there, among the Untouchables he had embraced as brothers, somehow to work a miracle. Gandhi consented only after a Muslim leader, one of the most corrupt politicians in Calcutta, agreed to live with him, unarmed, in one of Calcutta's worst slums. If a single Hindu died at Muslim hands, Gandhi pledged, he would fast to death.

So it was that two days before India's independence Mohandas Gandhi arrived in Kipling's "City of Dreadful Night." A large crowd awaited him as usual, but this one greeted him not with cheers but with shouts of anger. They were Hindus out for revenge, and to them Gandhi represented a capitulation to Muslim injustices. Hadn't they seen relatives butchered and wives and daughters defiled by Muslim mobs? Gandhi got out of his car amid a shower of rocks and bottles. Raising one hand in a frail gesture of peace, the old man walked alone into the crowd. "You wish to do me ill," he called, "and so I am coming to you." The crowd fell silent. "I have come here to serve Hindus and Muslims alike. I am going to place myself under your protection. You are welcome to turn against me if you wish. I have nearly reached the end of life's journey. I have not much further to go. But if you again go mad, I will not be a living witness to it."

Peace reigned in Calcutta that day, and then on the formal day of India's independence, and the next, and the next, for sixteen days in all. In the alley outside Gandhi's slum home, people gathered each night to attend his prayer meetings—a thousand at first, then ten thousand, and finally a million people jamming the streets of the slum to hear him lecture over loudspeakers on peace and love and brotherhood. Once again Gandhi was confronting a political crisis with what he called "soul force," the innate power of human spirituality. While whole states in India were going up in flames, with millions of people fleeing their homes and hundreds of thousands dying, not one act of violence occurred in that most violent city. "The miracle of Calcutta" it was called worldwide. A relieved Lord Mountbatten dubbed Gandhi, "My One-Man Boundary Force."

The miracle did not endure. On the seventeenth day two Muslims were murdered, a rumor about a Hindu victim spread, and then, a few hundred yards from Gandhi's house, someone lobbed a grenade into a bus full of Muslims. The people had broken their pledge, and Gandhi began a fast unto death, directed not against the British but against his own countrymen. He would not eat food again unless all those who had committed violence repented and solemnly vowed to stop.

At first no one cared. What was the life of one shriveled old man in the face of an assault on one's religion and family and honor? Revenge seemed far more appropriate than forgiveness. Gunfire echoed through the streets of Calcutta during the first day of Gandhi's fast. Within twenty-four hours his already weak heart started missing one beat in four, and his blood pressure dropped precipitously. The next day, as his vital signs plummeted, rioters paused and listened to broadcast reports of the old man's blood pressure and heart rate. Soon the attention of every citizen of Calcutta was riveted on the straw pallet where he lay, too weak to speak. The violence stopped. No one was willing to take an action that might cause the Great Soul to die.

One day more and the gang responsible for the murders came to confess to Gandhi, to ask forgiveness, and to lay their arms at his feet. A truck arrived at his house filled with guns, grenades, and other weapons that people had surrendered voluntarily. The leaders of every religious group in the city signed a declaration guaranteeing that no more killing would take place. Persuaded by their actions, Gandhi took his first few sips of orange juice and said his prayers. This time the miracle held. Calcutta was safe.

As for Gandhi, he made plans to head west, as soon as he regained strength, into the heart of the violence that had killed half a million people.

When I read the history of Mahatma Gandhi alongside the history of the Christian church, I cannot help wondering what went wrong. Why did it take a Hindu to embrace the principles of reconciliation, humility, and vicarious sacrifice so clearly modeled by Jesus himself? Gandhi credited Jesus as his source for these life principles, and he worked like a disciplined soldier to put them into practice. What has kept Christians from following Jesus with the same abandon?

Yes, we have the examples of St. Francis of Assisi trying to halt the

Crusades, of monks who outdo Gandhi's asceticism, of missionaries who serve the suffering, of Quakers and Anabaptists who oppose all violence. But by and large the history of European Christianity is the record of a church that relies on wealth, power, prestige, and even coercion and war to advance its cause.

The world has changed, of course. Now, just over a third of Christians worldwide live in Europe and North America, and the center of the church is moving to Africa and Asia. After two millennia of Western domination, is it time to look East for wisdom about the faith we have practiced so erratically?

When I turn to Gandhi's autobiography, a chill wind blows in my soul, for he shifts the spotlight away from movements and leaders of history and focuses it instead on himself. The crucial question for him was not how other Christians, Hindus, or Muslims had acted in the past, but how he was acting in the present. Confronting Gandhi, I am forced to turn from an armchair review of Christian history to a much more painful look at myself as an individual follower of Jesus. Historians may dwell on the outer results of Gandhi's actions; he bores in on the inner life.

The autobiography presents events in a strange proportion. *The Story of My Experiments with Truth* he titled it, portraying external events as merely the stage on which the internal drama of his own character development was playing out. One paragraph will mention the Great Salt March, a turning point in Gandhi's career and India's history, but four consecutive chapters will explore his internal agony over whether or not to include goat's milk in his vegetarian diet. Gandhi cast his life as the gradual refining of a soul.

In the autobiography, Gandhi traces the evolution of his simple lifestyle. He had tried Western ways as a law student in London, outfitting himself in an evening suit, silk top hat, patent leather boots, white gloves, and a silver-tipped walking stick. He remained something of a dandy when he returned to India, and did not begin to change until he went to South Africa. First he ironed his own shirts, much to the ridicule of his law colleagues. Then he practiced cutting his own hair, leaving patches of unevenness that drew even more laughter. While drawing a good salary, he experimented by halving household expenses, then halving them again. At the end of every day he made a meticulous accounting of every penny spent.

From these experiments, Gandhi found that the process of spending less money and acquiring fewer possessions simplified his life and gave him inner peace. In addition, it allowed him to identify more closely with the poor people he often represented in court. Over time, he winnowed his material possessions down to these: eyeglasses, a watch, sandals, a book of songs, a bowl. To answer correspondence he used pads made from the cut-up envelopes of the letters he was answering. He ate with a spoon that had been broken off and repaired with a piece of bamboo lashed to it with string.

Reading his account, I recall with a pang that when I moved from Chicago to Colorado the movers calculated my household belongings to weigh twelve thousand pounds. Even subtracting the six thousand pounds of books, that leaves three tons of material accumulation! And with all this baggage, do I have a life measurably richer than Mahatma Gandhi's?

Yesterday, I interrupted this chapter to spend an hour scrambling on the roof of my car trying to repair a garage door opener. I had another frustrating interruption tinkering with the software that runs my fax machine. The battery for my portable phone ran down. I realized with a start how much of my life is ruled by material things. I can justify, or at least rationalize, some of these possessions, especially those that help me in my work. Yet how carefully do I attend to Jesus' warning against the danger of gaining the whole world and losing one's soul? Jesus' lifestyle, I must admit, had much more in common with Gandhi's than with mine.

Voices in the West today are calling for a return to simplicity. Some Christians uphold the virtues of a simple lifestyle and raise questions about the morality of Western standards in the light of world inequities (though, in fairness, the level of simplicity they recommend more closely resembles what Gandhi started with than what he later attained). I will leave the issue of lifestyle morality to others more confident than I. What I learn from Gandhi is the reason for simplicity, not its level. Gandhi pursued simplicity not out of guilt but rather out of necessity, for the sake of his own spiritual health.

Gandhi had dined with great leaders. He had seen the seduction of power, the reliance on servants to carry out every whim, the endless spiral staircase of luxury, the absorbing anxiety over investments, the deluge of letters and speaking invitations and endorsements and phone calls. Knowing well the burden of fame, he also knew the only way to combat it was to seek simplicity with all his heart. If he did not, his soul force, the inner strength from which he got the stamina and courage for moral confrontations, would leak away.

Gandhi had suspicions about modern technology. He believed people who owned cars, radios, and well-stocked refrigerators and clothes closets would become psychologically insecure and morally corrupt. He knew enough about soil conservation to realize that India's land could not tolerate even a few decades of the soil abuse caused by high-technology farming. (In 150 years, Iowa has lost more of its topsoil than India has lost in five thousand years.) He had questions about how long energy sources would last. And besides, Gandhi said, he would continue to recommend cows until a tractor was invented that could produce milk, yogurt, and fertilizer. Ironically, the stimulus for Gandhi's drive toward simplicity came from the writings of Westerners—Tolstoy, Ruskin, and Thoreau—who convinced him that riches were a burden, and that only the life of labor was worth living. Gandhi named his first commune Tolstoy Farm in the novelist's honor.

The West, and India too for that matter, has ignored Gandhi. Capitalism rules worldwide, and a society whose economic fabric depends on constant growth requires that its citizens have ever-expanding needs and wants. If ten million Gandhians in Europe, with the highest of motives, suddenly decided to simplify by forgoing new cars, wearing unfashionable clothes, raising their own food, and eliminating appliances, economic chaos would result and thousands of people would lose their jobs. That dilemma is exactly what Gandhi wanted to avoid in India. In the West, it will take one with soul force equal to Gandhi's to change the prevailing dogma of ever-increasing GNP. We may be forced to change our profligate ways some day, when the soil is depleted, the aquifers drained, the icecaps melted, and all the oil wells pumped dry. But the crisis will wait another fifty years or so; we'll leave those problems to a generation yet unborn.

Every month I read about a new invention that allows me to connect to the rest of the world. Three stations on my cable television now offer round-the-clock news. I could, if I wanted, send e-mail via the Internet over a wireless cell phone. I can get news, sports, and stockmarket reports on a text-messaging pager. Whenever I yield and purchase such a device, I feel important and self-validated. I have a busy life, in the communication industry no less. These devices allow me to reach more people more efficiently.

Somehow, though, Mahatma Gandhi managed to be fairly effective without even a hand-crank telephone. "Our inventions are wont to be pretty toys, which distract our attention from serious things," said Thoreau, his mentor. "They are but improved means to an unimproved end, an end which it was already but too easy to arrive at . . . We are in great haste to construct a magnetic telegraph from Maine to Texas; but Maine and Texas, it may be, have nothing important to communicate." (A century and a half later, one need only click on to virtual "chat rooms" to grasp his point.) Gandhi also observed every Monday as a day of silence, both to rest his vocal cords and to promote harmony in his inner being. He held to that silence even when summoned to meetings in the heat of negotiations over India's future.

From the inside, as a journalist, I have watched a disturbing pattern in what we do to religious leaders today. We reward them with applause, fame, enticing new contracts, and a flurry of requests for speaking engagements and media appearances. We push our pastors to function as psychotherapists, orators, priests, and chief executive officers. When a leader shows unusual acumen, we dangle the temptation of a radio show or TV program, complete with a fund-raising machine to float the organization. In short, we in the church slavishly copy the secular model of media hype and corporate growth. I wonder how much more effective our spiritual leaders would be if we encouraged them to take Monday as a day of silence for reflection, meditation, and personal study.

I n his personal habits Gandhi moved far beyond self-discipline into renunciation. He allowed no room for sensuous pleasures, and in his autobiography you read nothing of a pleasant experience with music or with nature or the delights of taste or smell. A typical meal consisted of two segments of grapefruit, some goat's curds, and lemon soup. He also waged a lifelong struggle against lust. At the age of thirty-seven, though married, he took a solemn vow of celibacy. He spent much energy investigating what foods might have the slightest aphrodisiacal quality, then eliminated salt, spices, tea, and most exotic vegetables and fruits from his diet.

Such strictness seems strange to modern Westerners, though of course Christian history has seen its share of ascetics. The East has a continuing rich legacy of "holy men" who seek to control human passions. "It is for my sake," explained Gandhi to his critics, "that I insist on such spartan practices. I am the one who will suffer if I give in to my carnal nature."

At a conference in South Carolina, I heard Arun Gandhi, grandson of Mahatma, tell the story of traveling from South Africa to India at the age of twelve in order to meet his grandfather. Arun's father, a leader of the civil rights movement in South Africa, arranged the trip out of fear that Arun was growing up as a spoiled brat. The first meeting with the famous grandfather did not go well.

Mahatma was trying to teach the young boy to keep an anger diary. "It is normal for you to feel anger," he said. "What matters is how you channel that anger." He asked Arun to pause each time he had angry feelings, and in the heat of the moment to write down all his thoughts and feelings. Then, the next day, after the emotions had cooled, he should go back and read the diary, and reflect on how to channel that power for good. "Go ahead and try it," said his grandfather. "Write down whatever makes you angry."

The twelve-year-old Arun soon felt so much rage against having to waste time recording his anger that he broke his pencil in two and threw it over his shoulder. Gently but firmly, his grandfather sat him down and gave him a lecture. "That pencil was just a stub," he said. "But imagine if twenty million boys around the world threw away a pencil. Think of the trees that would have to be cut down. Think of the workers who put the graphite inside the pencil. Think of the needless waste." He borrowed a flashlight, and the old man and young boy spent the next hour searching on hands and knees for the pencil stub.

For the next several weeks, Mahatma coached his grandson on controlling his expression of emotions. "He taught me to master myself," Arun recalled. "It took many more months of practice after I returned home. But in time I saw that it set me free. I had been a helpless victim of my own passions. Now I was learning to be the master." Back in South Africa, Arun followed in his father's footsteps as a civil rights leader, and eventually emigrated to the United States, where he heads the Mohandas K. Gandhi Institute of Nonviolence. "I could never have taken the abuse and even physical violence involved in the campaign for civil rights in South Africa had I not learned that lesson as a twelve-year-old."

The next day, at the same conference, I sat on a panel discussing the cultural trend toward obscenity and rage as seen in rap music by performers like Eminem and in television programs like "South Park" and "Beavis and Butthead." I listened as parents voiced concern over lyrics describing wife-murder, cop-killing, and racial hatred, and then teenagers vigorously defended their right to express whatever emotions they felt. "Shows like that, and rap music, they're our ways of getting out the hostility we feel," said one eighteen-year-old. "Take them away, and kids'll probably turn to violence." The difference between two approaches to human passion, the way of the East and the way of the West, had never seemed so stark.

Mahatma Gandhi knew that his only moral power for others came from what he had already mastered himself. Once, a woman in his village brought her son and asked him to tell the child to stop eating sugar because it was bad for him. She said the child would not listen to her, but he would listen to Gandhi. "Bring the boy back in a week, and I will tell him," said Gandhi. A week later the woman returned with her son. Gandhi took the boy in his arms and told him not to eat any sugar, then bid them both good-bye. The mother lingered behind and asked, "Bapu, why did you have to wait a week? Could you not have told him last week?" "No," he replied. "Last week I myself was eating sugar."

It was this principle, of moral persuasion through example, through vicarious suffering, that Gandhi would hone to perfection in his practice of fasting. Early in his career, two of the young people under his tutelage lapsed into immorality, and Gandhi agonized for days over a fitting response. Most members of the ashram called for strict punishment of the offenders, but it seemed to Gandhi that a guardian or teacher was at least partly responsible for the failures of his ward or pupil. He doubted the other students would realize the depth of his distress and the seriousness of sin unless he did some penance. And so, in response to the students' transgression, he went on a total fast for seven days and took only one meal a day for four-and-a-half months. "My penance pained everybody," he concluded, "but it cleared the atmosphere. Everyone came to realize what a terrible thing it was to be sinful, and the bond that bound me to the boys and girls became stronger and truer."

Eventually, fasting became Gandhi's most powerful weapon. I have already mentioned his fast against violence in Calcutta. After that, Gandhi announced one more fast, in New Delhi, the capital of the brand-new country, a city that in early 1948 lay under a pall of smoke. Five million refugees had fled across the Punjab from Pakistan toward the capital, and many of them were now living in Delhi's makeshift refugee camps. After being preyed upon, raped, and brutalized by Muslims, these Hindus thirsted for revenge.

When Gandhi arrived and sensed the atmosphere of hatred, he announced a fast unto death. His doctors argued against it, for he had not yet recovered from the near-fatal fast in Calcutta. The crowds had had their fill of the old man and his hallucinations of peace and brotherhood. For the first two days, they mocked the crumpled figure on a straw pallet, marching past with a new chant on their lips: "Let

Gandhi die! Let Gandhi die!" Then on the third day his kidneys stopped functioning, his heart missed beats, and he began to breathe with great difficulty. All India Radio began broadcasting hourly bulletins on his condition.

On the fourth day, in desperation, the most powerful leaders in India—fascists, Communists, and all parties in between—came to Gandhi and took a solemn vow to protect Muslims and renounce violence. Truckloads of arms were collected and destroyed. Civic leaders guaranteed the return of homes, shops, and mosques to their rightful Muslim owners. The Indian parliament voted to pay the archenemy Pakistan fifty-five million pounds. At last, after every one of Gandhi's strict conditions had been met and the country was again at peace, Gandhi agreed to break his fast. It had lasted 121 hours.

Two weeks later, his wasted body lay again on that straw pallet, killed not by a fast but by three bullets from a Hindu fanatic who resented what he saw as Gandhi's betrayal of his nation. In that last act of death, Gandhi accomplished more than the thousands of policemen and soldiers who were vainly patrolling villages in the Punjab. At Gandhi's death, all India paused; communal killing stopped; the young nation was shocked to its senses. A holy man in Bombay walked through the city crying, "The Mahatma is dead. When comes another such as he?"

Many of Gandhi's accomplishments died with him. His beloved nation took a different path than the one he had advocated, and so has the world, growing since his death more belligerent and less receptive to his core beliefs. But for a time this strange, baffling man somehow managed to raise other men and women above the level of their usual selves. He held no office, and any who obeyed him did so voluntarily. His only claim to leadership was the force of his own soul. "The commonplace deed is a great step and a beautiful compromise," said Gandhi. "The beauty of it consists in today's compromise being less impure than yesterday's; it consists in our eyes being carried in a straight line towards something beautiful when we look, not at the deeds, but at the direction in which they are set."

In 1983, after I had just returned from India and Richard Attenborough's film *Gandhi* was released, I wrote a profile of the man for *Christianity Today* magazine. Although I have received plenty of venomous letters over the years, I was not prepared for the volume of hate mail the article generated. Readers informed me that Gandhi is now roasting in hell, and that even the devil believes in God and quotes the Bible. "So it's Gandhi on the cover this month," wrote one reader. "Who will it be next month, the Ayatollah?" Another called him "a heathen agitator who did more than any other person to undermine the influence of western civilization." A prominent Christian spokesman railed against the magazine for "replacing Jesus on the cover with Mahatma Gandhi!"

Most of the complaints boiled down to one question: Do Christians have anything to learn from someone who rejected our faith? I had concluded yes. Although Gandhi never accepted the claims of Christian theology, he based his life philosophy on principles learned from Jesus. In an odd sort of way, the impact of his life helped convince me of the truth of the Christian faith. I began to see that Jesus unleashed on earth a new kind of power, a reversal that turned upside-down history's basic assumptions. "So the last will be first, and the first will be last," he said, and proceeded to live out that principle by reaching out to the outcast, the poor, the suffering. The most influential person who has ever lived, Jesus held no office, had an attitude approaching contempt toward political power, and left no material possessions other than the robe on his back.

Jesus offered forgiveness to sinners, love to enemies, prophetic compassion to those with whom he disagreed. Today, every marginalized group in the world—minorities, women, the disabled, prisoners, the sick—can look to Jesus as a source of moral inspiration and a model for effective action, whether or not they follow his teaching. Through Gandhi, I saw that besides founding a church, Jesus set loose a stream of moral authority that releases captives, liberates the oppressed, and undermines a violent, competitive world. That stream flows on whether the church joins it or chooses instead to stand on the banks. Due to my own background, I had been quick to accuse the church of standing still while the stream flowed on. Gandhi taught me that the gospel has a life of its own, and does its slow, steady work regardless. Although he never accepted Jesus in the way Christians urged him to, he proved the truth of Jesus' teaching by channeling that stream of truth into a nation marked by passion and violence.

Gandhi had intimate Christian friends, such as the missionaries Charlie Andrews and E. Stanley Jones. As his writings demonstrate, he understood the details of Christian doctrine better than most Christians. Why, then, did he ultimately reject it?

Growing up in India, Gandhi had little contact with Christians as a youngster. Rumors spread in his town that if a Hindu converted to Christianity he would be forced to eat meat, drink hard liquor, and wear European clothes. Gandhi also recalls one very unpleasant memory of a Christian missionary on a street corner of his town deriding Hindus and their gods.

As a law student in London, Gandhi had a more prolonged exposure to Christianity. At a friend's request, he read through the entire Bible. He confesses that the Old Testament was uninspiring and put him to sleep, but the New Testament produced a profound impression. Throughout his life, Gandhi found himself going back to the teachings of Jesus, his model for nonviolence and simple living. He also read Pearson's *Many Infallible Proofs* (which "had no effect on me") and Butler's *The Analogy of Religion* among a host of other Christian books and commentaries. Still, he could not reconcile the disparity he saw between Christ and Christians.

Gandhi lived in South Africa during the most formative period of his life, and a few nasty incidents there did little to disabuse him of his notions of Christianity. He encountered blatant discrimination in that ostensibly Christian society, being thrown off trains, excluded from hotels and restaurants, and barred from some Christian gatherings.

One white woman who used to invite Gandhi for Sunday meals made it clear that he was unwelcome after she observed the influence

Gandhi's vegetarianism was having on her five-year-old son. Before then, he had been attending the Wesleyan church with her family every Sunday. "The church did not make a favorable impression on me," he remembers, citing dull sermons and a congregation who "appeared rather to be worldly-minded, people going to church for recreation and in conformity to custom."

In his autobiography, Gandhi recounts several episodes of Christians attempting to convert him. One kindly man took him to a revival to hear the Reverend Andrew Murray. Gandhi was quite impressed by stories Murray told about the faith of George Müller, founder of an English orphanage. This is how Gandhi recalls the experience:

> Mr. Baker was hard put to it in having a "coloured man" like me for his companion. He had to suffer inconveniences on many occasions entirely on account of me. We had to break the journey on the way, as one of the days happened to be a Sunday, and Mr. Baker and his party would not travel on the sabbath. . . .
>
> This convention was an assemblage of devout Christians. I was delighted at their faith. I met Mr. Murray. I saw that many were praying for me. I liked some of their hymns, they were very sweet.
>
> The Convention lasted for three days. I could understand and appreciate the devoutness of those who attended it. But I saw no reason for changing my belief—my religion. It was impossible for me to believe that I could go to heaven or attain salvation only by becoming a Christian. When I frankly said so to some of the good Christian friends, they were shocked. But there was no help for it.
>
> My difficulties lay deeper. It was more than I could believe that Jesus was the only incarnate son of God, and that only he who believed in him would have everlasting life. If God could have sons, all of us were His sons. If Jesus was like God, or God Himself, then all men were like God and could be God Himself. My reason was not ready to believe literally that Jesus by his death and by his blood redeemed the sins of the world.

Metaphorically there might be some truth in it. Again, according to Christianity only human beings had souls, and not other living beings, for whom death meant complete extinction; while I held a contrary belief. I could accept Jesus as a martyr, an embodiment of sacrifice, and a divine teacher, but not as the most perfect man ever born. His death on the Cross was a great example to the world, but that there was anything like a mysterious or miraculous virtue in it my heart could not accept. The pious lives of Christians did not give me anything that the lives of men of other faiths had failed to give. I had seen in other lives just the same reformation that I had heard of among Christians. Philosophically there was nothing extraordinary in Christian principles. From the point of view of sacrifice, it seemed to me that the Hindus greatly surpassed the Christians. It was impossible for me to regard Christianity as a perfect religion or the greatest of all religions.

I shared this mental churning with my Christian friends whenever there was an opportunity, but their answers could not satisfy me.   (From *Gandhi: An Autobiography*)

He summarized his position. "I cannot concede to Christ a solitary throne."

Sadly, the concepts of grace and forgiveness from God do not appear in Gandhi's works. Hinduism stumbles at grace. "If one is to find salvation," said Gandhi, "he must have as much patience as a man who sits by the seaside and with a straw picks up a single drop of water, transfers it, and thus empties the ocean." At the end of his autobiography, he is still lamenting that he is not passion-free in thought, speech, and action. "I must reduce myself to zero," he concludes.

Gandhi graciously omits from his autobiography one other painful memory from South Africa. The Indian community especially admired the missionary C. F. Andrews, whom they themselves nicknamed "Christ's Faithful Apostle." Having heard so much about Andrews, Gandhi wanted to meet him. But at his first chance to hear Andrews,

Gandhi was turned away from the church meeting because his skin color was not white. Later Gandhi and Charlie Andrews became fast friends, but Gandhi never forgot the sting of that incident.

Commenting on Gandhi's experiences in South Africa, E. Stanley Jones concludes, "Racialism has many sins to bear, but perhaps its worst sin was the obscuring of Christ in an hour when one of the greatest souls born of a woman was making his decision."

On one visit to India I found myself in a Christian community in New Delhi, a kind of ashram composed of young Indians who are trying to work out corporately Jesus' radical call to his followers. For some time we discussed parallels between Gandhi and Jesus Christ. As I have said, Gandhi freely credited Jesus' teaching for his most important principles. Yet while Gandhi had a profound impact on the whole country, Christianity has barely made a dent in India: less than 3 percent of the population call themselves Christian. Together, we explored the notion that its representatives had presented Christianity to India, but not the true Christ.

We talked about the perception of Christianity by the average educated Indian. Those who have been to America come back impressed with all the churches. They tell stories about the television ministers and how much money they collect from supporters. They tell of Christian leaders meeting with the president and of politicians themselves claiming to be born-again. Western spiritual leaders tend to be middle class and well groomed, not the austere holy men they are accustomed to in India. No one is called "the Great Soul" in the United States. Reflecting on Christianity, these Indians speak of its power and success. They rarely talk about Jesus' life or the principles he laid down.

Wanting to encourage my fellow Christians in New Delhi, I reminded them of Gandhi's statement that insight into the world's problems must come from the East and not the West. "We must be the change we wish to see," Gandhi said. I urged them to take the best of what their continent has produced, some of the same ideals that appealed to Gandhi, and trace their Christian roots. They could challenge my nation in a way that I as an American could not, as shown by the fact that young Americans will sometimes listen to a Gandhi before they will listen to Jesus. The world may be receptive to this message, I said.

One thoughtful young Indian who had sat quietly through the discussion spoke up at this. "I don't understand," he said. "You seem to say that the West in general is receptive to a saint, someone like Gandhi who stands apart from culture. But is the *church* receptive? You have said that American Christianity has never produced a saint who follows along the lines of a Gandhi. All the Christian leaders are so different from Gandhi. You seem to imply that if a Gandhi rose up in the American church today, he would not be taken seriously, would perhaps be laughed at and rejected. And yet those same Christians say they worship Jesus Christ. Why don't they reject him? He lived a simple life, preached love and nonviolence, refused to compromise with the powers of this world. He called on his followers to 'take up a cross' and bear the sufferings of the world. Why don't American Christians reject him?"

It was a good question. One I still cannot answer.

Stoning prophets and erecting churches to their memory afterwards has been the way of the world through the ages. Today we worship Christ, but the Christ in the flesh we crucified.
                                        —Mahatma Gandhi

GETTING STARTED WITH MAHATMA GANDHI:

Authors have attempted biographies of Gandhi from various political, psychological, and sociological points of view. Erik Erikson's *Gandhi's Truth* is one of the most rewarding. *Freedom at Midnight* by popular authors Larry Collins and Dominique Lapierre captures the spirit of the time of Indian independence in magazine-style prose. Gandhi's own *Autobiography* gives a glimpse of the complex man, and E. Stanley Jones's *Gandhi* describes Mahatma's unlikely friendship with the Methodist missionary Jones. Also, consider the Internet: Arun Gandhi runs a comprehensive Web site in the United States (*www.gandhi institute.org*) that incorporates much material about his grandfather, and a good search engine can quickly locate a host of other such Web sites based in India.

When I grew up, politics was a dirty word. We Christians saw ourselves as a beleaguered minority—grateful for our nation's religious freedom, yes, but resigned to live as a puny counterculture in a society dominated by worldly secular humanists. In Sunday School we pledged allegiance to the Christian flag as well as the American flag, and we never doubted which allegiance took priority. Certainly no one looked to Washington for moral leadership, and few in my church took an active role in political campaigns.

John F. Kennedy helped rouse us from lethargy in 1960. An alarmist deacon passed out copies of a scary book, *If America Elects a Catholic President,* and the pastor hinted darkly that a Catholic president would be obliged to take orders from the pope, not the people. Kennedy got elected and none of the doomsday prophecies came true. In 1964 I served as a state officer in the Young Republicans for Barry Goldwater campaign, and my candidate got trounced. The next election, the first in which I could vote, my political leanings had swung all the way over to the liberal Democratic candidate, Hubert Humphrey—I really preferred the senator-poet Eugene McCarthy—but my state voted overwhelmingly for George Wallace. Richard Nixon won nationwide, however, and Christians perked up when Billy Graham started hanging out with him (Graham would live to regret that coziness after he learned the true character of the man by reading Watergate tape transcript).

Chapter 8

DR. C.

EVERETT

KOOP

SERPENTS

AND DOVES

IN THE

PUBLIC

SQUARE

Next, Georgia's native son Jimmy Carter won election, attracting widespread attention for his born-again religion. *Time* declared "The Year of the Evangelical," and some Washington politicians assigned aides to find out anything they could about this large constituency that seemed to pop up overnight. Not many evangelicals appreciated the pious Jimmy Carter, transferring their support instead to Ronald Reagan four years later. It seemed an unlikely choice: Reagan rarely went to church, gave almost nothing to charity, and despite his "family values" ticket was the first divorced president and had gay and estranged children. Reagan acknowledged his debt to evangelicals by promoting a conservative social platform and by appointing some of them to key positions.

Reagan's successor, George Bush, got a lukewarm reception and lasted only one term. The next occupant of the White House, a Southern Baptist, attended church faithfully, knew the Bible better than any president since Woodrow Wilson, and counted such evangelicals as Tony Campolo, Bill Hybels, and Gordon MacDonald among his closest advisers. Yet no president in recent times stirred up as much scorn and outright loathing from the Christian community as Bill Clinton, even before his moral failures became public. Politics and religion do make strange bedfellows.

In other countries, the scene gets stranger. Evangelicals in places like Europe, Australia, and New Zealand tilt well to the left in their politics, as do Catholic leaders in Latin America. To complicate matters, history shows that when Christians control the reins of power they pass restrictive laws, launch crusades against the infidels, and persecute their own heretics. Yet when secular governments take control and begin to oppress Christians, very often the church flourishes. In my own lifetime China has seen the greatest numerical increase of Christians in the history of the world, a revival occurring under a government that restricts worship and imprisons pastors.

In the United States, issues of faith and politics have continued to attract a spotlight in recent years. A Jewish vice presidential candidate, Joseph Lieberman, spoke openly about God and attracted criticism from Jewish political groups. A Pentecostal attorney general, John Ashcroft, came under scrutiny for his convictions about abortion and homosexuality. President Bush shifted grants toward faith-based charities and promoted the use of vouchers in religious schools.

Can a person of faith get involved in politics without making crucial compromises? I have cited renowned religious figures—Tolstoy, Gandhi, King—who helped transform the political landscape. Though I learn from these giants, I have more curiosity about the role of the ordinary citizen. Can a person effectively serve both "the city of God" and "the city of man," to use Augustine's terms? Will not one inevitably crowd out the other?

I have observed one example up close of an ordinary citizen, a physician with no political experience, who tried his best to strike a balance and who provides a fascinating case study. I have known him since 1971, when my wife worked on a committee that he chaired, supervising international assignments for medical residents. During Reagan's administration he became perhaps the most famous evangelical in high office. He had deep convictions on some of the most important moral issues of our time, and spoke out with unprecedented bluntness. The results surprised everyone, most of all himself.

I n three decades of surgery at Philadelphia's Children's Hospital, Dr. C. Everett Koop pioneered ways to save and repair premature and damaged babies. Meanwhile, in another part of the same hospital an abortion clinic sprang up, capable of eliminating ten or fifteen lives in the time it took him to save one or two. To Koop, abortion seemed a black-and-white moral issue, and so he spoke passionately against the practice, calling the *Roe v. Wade* ruling that legalized abortion "the most important event in American history since the Civil War." For a time Koop even suspended his brilliant career in pediatric surgery to go on the stump with evangelical author Francis Schaeffer and warn the American public about human life issues. In a dramatic scene from the Schaeffer-produced film series *Whatever Happened to the Human Race?*, Koop looks out over a thousand naked dolls strewn across the salt wastes of the Dead Sea and proclaims, "I am standing on the site of Sodom, the place of evil and death."

Koop tends to see theology, too, in shades of black and white. He became a committed Christian as an adult while attending a Presbyterian church, and his faith centers on the doctrine of the sovereignty of God. A confident surgeon who respects chain-of-command authority, who is used to giving orders and making split-second decisions about life and death, Koop seems virtually immune to Kierkegaardian bouts of angst. If God is all-powerful, then naturally everything that happens—*everything*—falls under his complete control at all times.

That serene faith was tested in 1968 when Koop suffered the most painful tragedy of his life, an event that profoundly changed his emotional makeup. Before then, Koop thought it a sign of weakness for a doctor to cry with grieving parents; afterward, he found it hard not to. His son David, a twenty-year-old Dartmouth College student, fell to his death in a mountain climbing accident. David's body lay on the rocks for fifty-two hours before rescuers could reach it, an excruciating ordeal for the Koop family. Yet Koop's personal journal of the time, published as the book *Sometimes Mountains Move,* contains no hint of any wrestling with God. It ends with a quotation from the New Testament Book of Jude, "And now unto him who is able to keep you from falling . . ." followed by Koop's own declaration of faith: "God was able, but in His sovereignty He chose not to."

The aftermath of a momentous telephone call in August 1980 put to a very different kind of test this core belief in God's sovereignty. Ronald Reagan, who had read two of Koop's books and admired his pro-life convictions, wanted him to serve as the nation's surgeon general. The appointment would help cement Reagan's support among pro-life constituents and especially among evangelicals, the group who knew Koop best. Shortly after his inauguration, Reagan named him Deputy Assistant Secretary for Health and nominated him as surgeon general. That appointment, however, needed congressional action because, at sixty-four, Koop exceeded the age limit for the office by a hundred days. What he, Reagan, and nearly everyone in the administration thought would be a *pro forma* legislative procedure set off a political firestorm.

Koop's outspokenness came back to haunt him, especially after a well-meaning Pentecostal group aired the Schaeffer film series on a

Washington, D.C., television station. Planned Parenthood, NOW, and other pro-choice groups led the cavalry charge, brandishing every extreme statement Koop had ever made on abortion, women's rights, and homosexuality. In a case of reverse McCarthyism, they questioned not only his beliefs but also his competence as a physician, his emotional stability, and even his sanity. The staid *New York Times* ran an editorial entitled "Dr. Unqualified," and the Washington press coined the even more unflattering nickname Dr. Kook. Congressman Henry Waxman branded him as scary and intolerant. Others called him a right-wing crank, a mean-spirited nut, a religious zealot. For the first time in its hundred-year history the American Public Health Association went on record against a nominee; "We'd be better off with no surgeon general than with Koop," said their executive director.

The Koops arrived in Washington like innocent tourists who had accidentally stumbled into a war zone. In Philadelphia, Dr. Koop's surgical triumphs—separating Siamese twins, repairing facial deformities, repositioning a child's external heart—had attracted generous publicity. The recipient of many awards, including France's *Légion d'honneur,* he was often identified in the newspapers as Philadelphia's "best-known favorite son." Now the hometown press joined the chorus against him, printing a cruel cartoon of Koop as a two-headed monster. Each morning Koop's son, working in another city, would find a newspaper under his office door with the defamatory articles about his father circled in red grease pencil.

Koop and his wife Betty were living in temporary quarters, surrounded by boxes still unpacked. Each day Koop would report to a spacious office from which, if he leaned back in his chair, he could view the dome of the Capitol and its huge American flag. Though near the seat of power, he had none; he had only the city's scorn. After four decades of twelve-hour, frenetic workdays, he now faced an empty inbox, a silent telephone, and a blank calendar—a setting that seemed to him like solitary confinement. Dr. Paul Brand, who visited him then, told me, "For years this fine surgeon had been making medical news. He was a dynamo, a man with a mission. Now, though, I had the impression of a caged lion, full of enormous power; he paced the room with literally nothing to do. And I also had the impression of a wounded man, a man in need of comfort."

Koop himself reflects: "I couldn't understand why God would disrupt such a peaceful, productive life. I had never sought public office, so I believed that God plucked me out of Philadelphia and dumped me in Washington. I used to ask God a lot of questions about it! During those agonizing nine months of the nomination process, I would stare at the Bible on my desk, trying to understand what had happened. The worst day was when I went home one afternoon—the sun was coming in through the half-drawn Venetian blinds in our little one-room apartment in Georgetown—and I opened the door with my key and saw Betty standing there reading the *Washington Post* with tears falling down her cheeks."

"I don't need this!" Koop fumed. "I've never been treated this way before, and it's wrong to put my family through it." This time it was Betty who reminded him that a sovereign God must somehow have a purpose behind the disruption of their lives. "If you quit now," she said, "you'd always wonder." She added with a wry smile, "And don't forget—you no longer have a job in Philadelphia."

A s everyone knows—everyone who watched a television, read a newspaper, or listened to a radio in the 1980s—C. Everett Koop finally got the job of surgeon general, and against all odds emerged as one of the most visible, colorful, and admired public servants in the nation. When he announced his resignation in 1989, his former critics fell over one another heaping praise on the man they had once vilified. News broadcaster Dan Rather pronounced him "the best surgeon general in history." Congressman Waxman, converted into one of Koop's biggest fans, readily agreed: "He's a man of tremendous integrity. He's done everything a surgeon general can do, and more." The American Public Health Association, the same group that had fought his nomination, honored him with their highest award for excellence. Nearly everyone except, oddly, Koop's original allies, the evangelicals, joined in the applause.

What caused the dramatic turnabout in Koop's image? The answer lies partly in the media's fundamental misconception of Koop, partly in Koop's skillful molding of an office to fit his strengths, and partly in the hellish nine months when he sat in a vacuous office with nothing to do. As for his evangelical critics, Koop believes they misunderstood just about everything he did as surgeon general. He tried to serve like the wily prophet Daniel in a secular administration; they were expecting something closer to an Amos or a Jeremiah.

If Koop's secular critics had looked closer at his background, they would have seen he was no cardboard-cutout ideologue. Human compassion not only tempered but in fact formed his firm beliefs. Even in his hectic first years as a surgeon, he had carved out time to treat the homeless at a downtown rescue mission. One of his closest aides explained, "What people didn't understand about Dr. Koop is that he is pro-life in the purest sense of the word: not *anti-death*, but *pro-life*. I have seen him with thousands of people—malnourished children, Washington socialites, dying AIDS patients, abused wives, abortion rights activists—and he treats every one of them as if he truly believes, which he does, that they are created in the image of God. He'll interrupt his busy schedule to meet with some disturbed person who insists on talking to 'the top doc.' He truly does respect the value of all human life."

Koop had taken such a strong stand on abortion, after all, because of his experience with over a hundred thousand pediatric patients, many of them small enough to hold in one hand, many so deformed that no other surgeon would touch them. Over the years Koop had seen these babies grow into fully functioning adults with names, personalities, and individual histories: Paul, the recipient of thirty-seven facial and abdominal surgeries, now a graduate of West Chester University; Chris, who required fifteen operations to get his external heart in place and his lungs functioning adequately; Maria, for whom Koop fashioned an esophagus out of a section of colon and who went on to earn a Ph.D. and become a pediatric surgeon herself. Koop knew that every baby lost to abortion or neglect was a potential Paul, Chris, or Maria.

Something about the helplessness of tiny human beings had attracted Koop to the field of pediatric surgery at a time when there were only a handful of such specialists in the entire country. He had a soft spot for the weak and disenfranchised. And as he sat in his Washington office during the nomination hearings, for the first time ever he too felt weak and disenfranchised. A proud man accustomed to success, suddenly he was both humbled and isolated. As the weeks dragged by, one by one the various special interest groups paid a call in order to probe the nominee with whom they might have to deal. Most knew little about him other than the overwrought reports they had read in the newspapers. They found that the prospective surgeon general with no power and little hope had one commodity in plentiful supply: time—time to listen to their concerns.

During that nine-month period, Koop heard diverse voices from across the country. Some, such as the gay rights advocates and the pro-choicers, fiercely opposed his positions. Yet they too were part of the nation whose medical needs he would oversee. Koop now looks back on that period as a wonderful gift: "I had a chance to look at the health problems of the nation and wonder what I could do about them when I was finally let loose. I decided I would use the office to espouse the cause of the disenfranchised: handicapped children, the elderly, people in need of organ transplantation, women and children who were being battered and abused. During that nine months I developed a detailed agenda, something no surgeon general has ever had before. In the end, that period of acute frustration made possible every single thing I was able to accomplish in office. Now that's the sovereignty of God at work!"

In short, Koop used the time to dream about what difference a surgeon general could make. And his very notoriety ensured that after his installation—which finally came after a rancorous Senate hearing—everything he said or wrote attracted a swarm of media attention. His detractors, who meant to do him harm, paradoxically helped deliver to him the public platform he would need to accomplish his goals.

After his installation, Koop found that he had the rank of three-star admiral but no ship to command. The office of surgeon general, vaguely defined to begin with, had been sorely neglected (President Nixon never even got around to appointing one). Koop had little decision-making power, no budget authority, and a minuscule staff. Morale among the Public Health Service's Commissioned Corps had sunk to an all-time low. In an attempt to bolster that morale, Koop urged the corps to wear the uniform that had long since fallen out of vogue. He set a personal example, dressing in a starched uniform bedecked with bars, epaulets, ribbons, and gold braiding. The practice took a while to catch on. More than once airplane passengers mistook Koop for a steward and asked for help with their luggage. And political cartoonists now had a visual focus for their derision. Who was this strange M.D. with a Captain Ahab beard and a cruise-ship uniform, this man who in a city of designer briefcases carried a canvas tote bag?

The very distinctiveness of Koop's style, however, held the media's attention. At six foot one and two hundred ten pounds, he made an imposing uniformed figure, and as he began delivering pronouncements on the nation's health in his strong Brooklyn voice, fascination soon replaced derision. As one reporter put it, "On television, the steely beard and gold shoulderboards of the PHS uniform project a stern Dutch uncle inveighing against the evils of indulgence." In person, those same reporters came away impressed with the cordiality and openness of the new surgeon general. Before long, he was the hottest interview in town. Magazines put his stern visage on their covers, Johnny Carson wrote him into monologues; Elizabeth Taylor blew him on-air kisses; television's "The Golden Girls" proposed a cameo appearance.

"Where there's Koop, there's controversy," became a Washington slogan. He lashed out against drunk drivers, convened task forces on child abuse and spouse abuse, criticized American eating habits. Koop's superiors didn't know what to think, especially when he broke ranks to challenge their policies. For example, Ronald Reagan had promised Southern senators such as Jesse Helms that he would not use a bully pulpit against smoking. Here was Reagan's surgeon general calling the tobacco lobbyists "sleazy" and "flat-footed liars," and accusing them of exporting death to the third world. Over White House objections, Koop declared nicotine to be as addictive as heroin, proposed a ban on all cigarette advertising, urged the creation of smoke-free workplaces, and even called for a smokeless society. The administration was embarrassed; North Carolina's Senator Jesse Helms, once Koop's strongest supporter, was appalled.

Despite enormous pressure, Koop would not back down. One thousand Americans a day were dying of tobacco-related illnesses, and as the nation's top doctor he felt obligated to speak out. (He now points to the decline in cigarette smoking—almost twenty million Americans quit during his term—as his greatest accomplishment.) On cigarette smoking, sex education, free needle distribution for addicts, and many other issues, Koop traveled his own path.

To a public starved for integrity in their leaders, Koop became a genuine folk hero. What had looked like a cul-de-sac job gradually developed into a central arena for what Koop calls "moral suasion." "I have a sense of right and wrong," he said. "A lot of other people in this town don't have that." In essence, Koop managed to satisfy Americans' expectations of a family doctor. Your doctor may deliver grim news, and may in fact lecture you about your bad habits, but still you want a doctor who will tell it to you straight and not mince words, who makes your personal health the overriding issue. That image, Koop fulfilled on a grand scale.

As former critics learned to respect his independence and integrity, and the public at large came to revere him as an avuncular folk hero, Koop's original constituency looked on in dismay at what they saw as a betrayal of their cause. Here is Koop's report card as graded by the conservatives:

- "Koop has been one of the major disappointments of the Reagan Administration." *National Review*

- "Koop should have kept his lip buttoned."
  Phyllis Schlafly, conservative spokeswoman

- "I think the guy's a disgrace. . . . He sold out to the very principles that made him Surgeon General."
  Michael Schwartz, Free Congress Foundation

- "If he couldn't act on what he believed to be correct, he should have resigned. He has revealed himself to be a man who prized the public spotlight rather than his conscience."
  Howard Phillips, Conservative Caucus

Some evangelicals, who had once looked upon Koop as their great white political hope, shared the sense of dismay. "Longtime support- ers of Dr. Koop are bitter and depressed," groused commentator Cal Thomas, adding ". . . an atheist would have performed just as effec- tively for the left." Koop told me at the time, "That kind of criticism affects me in a strange way. I don't like to go to church anymore—af- ter all, Cal happens to go to the same church as I do."

Theologian Harold O. J. Brown typified the concern of evangeli- cals. It was he who, more than a decade before, had convinced Koop that abortion was always wrong, even in the difficult cases. In 1975, at Billy Graham's home in Minneapolis, he and Koop had helped found the Protestant pro-life lobby. He had openly admired Koop: "Not since Williams Jennings Bryan has another evangelical Christian of Dr. Koop's degree of clarity, forthrightness, and determination to bring spiritual values into play in public life been appointed to similarly high office." Soon Brown, too, began to wonder aloud whether Koop was undermining the pro-life cause.

Conservatives' complaints centered around three major crises: Baby Doe, AIDS, and the effects-of-abortion letter. The Baby Doe controversy came early on (1982–83), and involved a case in which a doctor and family agreed to withhold nourishment from a birth-defec- tive child. No issue was closer to Dr. Koop's heart. He had performed 475 surgeries to correct precisely the problem from which Baby Doe suffered, and withholding treatment from her seemed to him infanti- cide, plain and simple. After six days without proper food and care, Baby Doe died. After Baby Doe died, and Koop's stiff regulations to prevent future occurrences were overturned in court, Koop met with both sides (the medical establishment vigorously opposed the regula- tions) and came up with a compromise based on "patient-care review committees" within local hospitals.

The Supreme Court eventually struck down this agreement as

well, mooting the entire issue. But the process of compromise had opened a crack between the surgeon general and doctrinaire pro-lifers, who viewed Koop's acceptance of the review committees as caving in to the medical establishment. If the pro-life lobbyists came away slightly disillusioned with Koop, he came away frustrated by their all-or-nothing mentality. Despite his ironclad personal views on the issues, he could see the occasion, even the necessity, for legislative compromise.

As soon as heat from the Baby Doe issue dissipated, a new crisis fell into Koop's lap, like a live grenade. As early as 1981 administration officials had detected the rumblings of a major health epidemic concentrated in groups practicing "high-risk behaviors," notably, homosexuals and intravenous drug users. Ignoring outcries from the gay community, the president avoided all mention of the disease that became known as AIDS. For five years Koop was kept out of the flow of information and forbidden to speak on AIDS. Not until 1986, with ten thousand cases confirmed, did the administration ask the surgeon general to prepare a report on the topic.

We forget now the climate of hysteria that once surrounded the AIDS crisis, much of it coming from the religious right. Prominent evangelicals hosted people on their radio programs who claimed AIDS could be contracted via mosquito bites and toilet seats. According to one staff worker at the time, five thousand letters a week were pouring into the Department of Health and Human Services from conservatives pleading against research and education funds: "God's judgment," they argued, should be allowed to run its course. Given the prevailing political climate, nearly everyone expected a reproachful, moralistic report from the evangelical surgeon general. Gay rights leaders were openly cynical.

But Koop took his assignment seriously. He scheduled two-hour interviews, off-the-record, with twenty-five different groups, ranging from the National Gay and Lesbian Task Force to the Southern Baptists. He asked for authority to prepare the report himself, avoiding the normal bureaucratic channels that might weaken it. Working at home at a stand-up desk, he went through twenty-seven drafts. These words set the tone of the report: "At the beginning of the AIDS epidemic many Americans had little sympathy for people with AIDS. The feeling was that somehow people from certain groups 'deserved' their illness. Let us put those feelings behind us. We are fighting a disease, not people."

The AIDS report was remarkably candid, spelling out the dangers in anatomical detail, and calling for sex education "beginning at the lowest grade possible." Although prescribing abstinence and sex within monogamous marriage as the safest course, it also recommended condoms for anyone who had multiple sex partners or engaged in homosexual acts. "The silence must end," Koop declared.

The silence did end. Voices within the Reagan administration denounced Koop's stance against compulsory AIDS testing and for early sex education. Liberal politicians such as Ted Kennedy and Henry Waxman commended the report for its candor and its emphasis on the health aspects of the disease. Gay rights activists declared Koop a "certifiable AIDS hero." Congress stood behind Koop, mandating something unprecedented: that an educational booklet on the disease be mailed to every household in America, 107 million in all, the largest mass mailing in American history.

Some political conservatives were outraged. Paul Weyrich, a founder of the religious right, and conservative spokeswoman Phyllis Schlafly mobilized against Koop, organizing a boycott of a Washington dinner scheduled in his honor. Their letter read, in part, "Not only has Koop publicly departed from pro-life principles, but many believe that his statements about AIDS are a cover for the homosexual community. His report on AIDS issued last November reads as though it were edited by the National Gay Task Force. . . . Dr. Koop's proposals for stopping AIDS represent the homosexuals' views, not those of the pro-family movement." Buckling to the pressure, three Republican candidates for the presidency withdrew their sponsorship of the dinner.

As a further complication, in the midst of the furor over the AIDS report, Koop awoke from a nap one afternoon to find himself essentially quadriplegic; he could move neither hands nor feet. Years of bending over to operate on infants had aggravated an old ski injury, and when his head slipped from an orthopedic pillow during the nap, the pressure pinched off an artery. Though surgeons repaired most of the damage, recuperation kept him in bed for the next several weeks.

Koop now looks back on that time of enforced inactivity, much like the nine-month nomination process, as a providential gift. He began to see that AIDS was one disease in which the moralist and the scientist could work hand in hand—indeed, *needed* to work hand in hand—to contain the epidemic. "For seven weeks I watched the impact of what had been done as reported in the press. I made up my mind that I had an obligation and a chore, and so I decided to do something that probably nobody else ever has done in public office. For the first seven weeks in 1987 I addressed only religious groups. I started with Jerry Falwell's church and the chapel at Liberty University, went to the National Religious Broadcasters' convention, talked to conservative people in Judaism, and to Roman Catholics, and ended up with a series of radio shows for Moody Broadcasting Network."

In those addresses, delivered in full uniform and a neck brace, Koop affirmed the need for abstinence and monogamous marriage. But he added, "Total abstinence for everyone is not realistic, and I'm not ready to give up on the human race quite yet . . . I am the Surgeon General of the heterosexuals and the homosexuals, of the young and the old, of the moral and the immoral." Speaking in familiar language, he admonished fellow Christians, "You may hate the sin, but you are to love the sinner." While Koop expressed his personal abhorrence of sexual promiscuity—consistently he used the word "sodomy" when referring to homosexual acts—he also insisted, "I'm the Surgeon General, not the Chaplain General."

To explain his position, he often used the analogy of an emergency room physician. If an ambulance pulls up and unloads two wounded men, a bank robber who shot a guard and the bank guard who returned fire, which man does the doctor treat first? He must go to the man with the most urgent wounds, not the most moral one. Koop had seen enough AIDS patients, their bodies gaunt, emaciated, and covered with purplish sores, to know who needed the most urgent treatment. He had vowed to look out for the weak and disenfranchised, and clearly there was no more weak or disenfranchised group in the nation. Regardless of the political cost, he would defend their right to treatment and the need to educate them on ways to prevent this deadly disease.

The surgeon general lost much support among political conservatives over the AIDS issue. Yet Koop now looks back with pride on the attitude of the grassroots church. "I really think we turned people around on this issue," he says. "I must have gotten twenty supportive letters from Southern Baptist ministers alone. That denomination was one of the groups I interviewed before writing the AIDS report. They had never heard of the kinds of sexual practices I was talking about. One day in my office I very gently tried to explain what the problems were, to tell them what bathhouse sex was like, for example. They didn't know whether to scream and run, or to cry, or to bury their faces. But they came around, and proved very supportive. I said, 'If you are so worried about your kids getting sex education—and I understand why you would be—why can't you, a denomination of twenty-six million people, write your own curriculum?' Nine months later they invited me down to help launch that very curriculum."

Those conservatives who had stood by Koop during the Baby Doe and AIDS controversies were rocked yet again in early 1989 when the press reported on a letter from Koop to President Reagan regarding abortion. The previous fall, one of Reagan's pro-life advisers had convinced him that the surgeon general should research the health effects of abortion on women. "The findings would be so devastating that they would reverse *Roe v. Wade,*" he predicted. Pro-choice activists, knowing Koop's absolute views opposing abortion, braced for the worst. In January 1989, Koop submitted his findings to the president in a letter which concluded, "I regret, Mr. President, in spite of a diligent review on the part of many in the PHS and in the private sector, the scientific studies do not provide conclusive data about the health effects of abortion on women." Leaders of the pro-choice movement trumpeted the message, slightly distorted: "Koop says abortion does not harm women."

KOOP'S STAND ON ABORTION'S EFFECT SURPRISES FRIENDS AND FOES ALIKE, read a *New York Times* headline the next day, a headline that could win a Pulitzer Prize for understatement. For some evangelicals, Koop's letter was the last straw, for it appeared that Koop had abandoned the very principles that had got him nominated. The controversy left a permanent stain on Koop's career, and may have contributed to his retirement from public service.

Koop himself feels personally betrayed over the issue. He had reviewed 255 reports on the health effects of abortion. Some "proved" abortion was harmful, some "proved" it was harmless. Taken together, they all seemed flawed methodologically. Moreover, only half the women who have had an abortion ever admit to it on a survey, and the existing studies did not account for that group at all. Although Koop had much anecdotal evidence of the harmful psychological effects of abortion, he had no rigorous scientific data to back it up. In fact, his letter to the president recommended such a study—it would take five years and cost one hundred million dollars, he later estimated, and would likely prove what the president wanted proved—but for the present he had to acknowledge insufficient statistical data. He was asked to make a scientific judgment, not give a personal opinion.

Koop delivered his letter in person to the White House, extracting a promise that no one would disclose its contents until the president had a chance to respond. When Koop reached his home a short time later, however, his wife met him in the driveway in a panic. She had just heard newscasters Peter Jennings, Tom Brokaw, and Dan Rather quoting from the "confidential" letter. More, they were reporting flatly that "The Surgeon General could find no evidence that abortion is psychologically harmful." Koop stayed on the phone until one o'clock in the morning trying to clarify his position, and appeared the next morning on "Good Morning America" to correct wrong impressions. The damage had been done. Pro-choice activists continued to misquote his findings; pro-lifers still felt double-crossed.

"There was so much misunderstanding on that issue," Koop now reflects. "I remember a woman who came running up to me and said, 'Oh, Dr. Koop, I'm so pleased that you've turned your position on abortion. And I said, 'Madam, you have misunderstood me completely. I have not turned my position on abortion; I just refuse to be dishonest with statistics, that's all.' In view of all I'd said and written on the subject, how could anyone question my views on abortion? There are certain conversations I expect to take place wherever I go. Someone will come up to me and tell me I operated on them when they were three days old. Someone else will come up and say, 'I owe you a debt of gratitude—I was never concerned about human life issues until I heard you speak with Francis Schaeffer.' At the time I told pro-life people, You have been magnificent in the fight against abortion by making it a moral issue, with the life of the fetus as the primary concern. Don't shift the grounds of the argument to the health of the mother. If the other side perceives that you've had to shift your base, you've lost."

Koop's next few months in Washington were almost as unpleasant as the first ones. A new administration led by the senior George Bush took office, naming someone else for the cabinet position Koop wanted. No one asked him to leave, but neither did they offer to reappoint him as surgeon general. And through a series of petty pressure tactics, Koop was made to feel unwelcome. He was denied access to the executive dining room. He was excluded from a departmental retreat for senior executives. His top aide was dismissed. White House staffers no longer returned his phone calls.

Once a reporter asked Dr. Koop how he earned the medals on his uniform: "The top row is for what liberals did to me, the bottom row is for what conservatives did to me," he replied. In the end, the man who had, in the face of ceaseless opposition, overcome an enormous media bias and transformed his office into one of the most respected posts in government, quietly resigned.

Public life did not end for Koop when he took off his uniform. If anything, the spotlight brightened. He continued to testify before Congress on such matters as tobacco policies and partial-birth abortions. He won an Emmy award for a television series, "C. Everett Koop, M.D." A new president, Bill Clinton, called to solicit his help. Hillary Clinton would be conducting meetings across the country to gather facts about the health care crisis; would Koop introduce her to the medical establishment? He agreed, and sat beside her at many of those meetings, again enraging some conservatives. Then he lobbied strenuously before Congress in favor of the government's settlement with big tobacco companies. Both of these initiatives fell victim to political infighting.

Disgusted, Koop and his wife moved back to Dartmouth, his alma mater, which had founded a C. Everett Koop Institute for training health care professionals. Though he still traveled the world delivering lectures, the pace of life gradually slowed to something more appropriate to his age. Until the Internet revolution caught up with him at age eighty-one, that is. A new startup company, Drkoop.com, went public in 1998 as a portal to advice on health care, and co-owner Koop suddenly found himself a millionaire fifty times over. Like most dot-com wealth, his stock in the company evaporated, ultimately losing 99 percent of its value, yet the site still attracts five million visitors a month. Much of America continues to get its advice from the family doctor who used to be surgeon general. And Koop continues in the thick of controversy, fending off criticism that his Web site taints medical opinion with commercial interests.

Having known Chick Koop for thirty years, I have followed his career closely, as a case study of a Christian citizen thrust into the political arena. No one could accuse the man nominated to be surgeon general in 1981 of waffling on moral issues. He opposed all abortion, even after rape, even in the case of a severely defective fetus. He opposed all sex outside of marriage, and all homosexual acts. His nomination prompted a chorus of opposition from liberals and loud cheers of support from conservatives, especially evangelicals. Yet in the end, it was the evangelicals who felt betrayed and the liberals who were left cheering.

What went wrong, and what went right, in this zigzag saga of a believer who sought to serve God equally well in two conflicting arenas at once? I have discussed these matters at length with Dr. Koop and have learned much from his experience. I had seen few effective models of Christians penetrating the wider society, especially in the field of politics. Partisan politics runs on power and antagonism, forces that directly counter the gospel principles of love and reconciliation. Is it even possible, I wondered, to wield power in a loving way, or to oppose behavior without opposing the one who behaves? And what good is a faith that has little relevance to the broader culture? "Be wise as serpents, and harmless as doves," Jesus cautioned his disciples as he sent them out into the world. All too often, Christians in politics demonstrate instead the wisdom of doves and the harmlessness of serpents.

In the first place, Koop managed to convince a skeptical public of his basic integrity. Even those who disagreed with him came to accept his sincerity and trustworthiness. Koop tells stories of other Christians in the administration who were willing to stretch the truth to serve their political ends. When he wrote the AIDS report, for example, a White House staffer tried to change Koop's words from "Most Americans are opposed to homosexuality, promiscuity of any kind, and prostitution" to *"All* Americans . . ." The fact that such a statement was patently untrue bothered the staffer not at all. Similarly, when Koop concluded that the effects-of-abortion research was flawed, conservatives reacted angrily because he would not certify that the facts supported their position, regardless of the statistical flaws he had uncovered. As Koop saw it, their agenda took precedence over the truth.

I asked Koop what advice he could give concerned citizens, like myself, who want to affect the laws of this country. How could we do so more effectively? He replied, "What bothered me most, as I reflect, was the lack of scholarship by Christians—as if they felt that by leaning on a theological principle they didn't have to be very accurate with the facts. People talk about knee-jerk liberals. The liberals have no corner on that market; I've learned there are also knee-jerk conservatives. Christians should be involved in politics, and use their Christian principles, morality, and ethics in that process. But they shouldn't jump over the process and voice their beliefs as the only possible outcome."

Koop insists that his basic moral views did not change in office, that his underlying beliefs provided the foundation for all his major actions. Yet after stepping down, he received an astonishing outpouring of support and acclaim: honorary degrees from universities, standing ovations at farewell banquets, public apologies in newspaper editorials, and the nation's highest civilian award, the Presidential Medal of Freedom. Some simply liked the fact that his decisions, regardless of the motives behind them, served their own political ends. But to many Washington cynics, Koop offered a refreshing new model of integrity from an evangelical Christian—and this in a time when other well-known evangelicals were attracting attention for their *lack* of integrity. In the words of *Time* magazine, "The city that worships at the gray altar of ambiguity found there was room for a man of black and white."

Koop has always insisted that in health matters, the moralist and the scientist walk together. The church opposed tobacco and alcohol abuse long before scientists verified their suspicions. And in the battle against sexually transmitted diseases, Koop admits, a morality based on religious commitment—not more sex education—offers our best chance to change the behavior of promiscuous adolescents. Now that he is out of office, he feels freer to speak out about marital fidelity and sexual abstinence. People listen to him because of the trust he accrued while serving as surgeon general.

Koop's experience may, in fact, offer a model for Christians concerned about cultural trends. It does no good to quote Bible verses to people who do not revere the Bible, or threaten God's judgment on people who do not believe in God. There is a better way to communicate, as Koop showed. Many of the leading health concerns in this country relate to behavioral choices: heart disease and hypertension exacerbated by stress, emphysema and lung cancer caused by cigarette smoking, fetal damage stemming from maternal alcohol and drug abuse, diabetes and other diet-related disorders, violent crime, AIDS, sexually transmitted diseases, automobile accidents involving alcohol. These are the endemic, even epidemic concerns for health experts in our society.

After valiantly conquering most infectious diseases, we have now substituted new health problems for old, many of which stem from moral choices. Christians believe that the commands God gave were not arbitrary, but for our own good, and the health results in modern society bear out that principle. If we can communicate more of the spirit of a concerned family doctor, and less of the spirit of a nagging moralist, we may catch the attention of a society headed down a path of self-destruction.

Although most people will remember his term in office mainly by the major controversies, Koop sees it differently. Wherever he goes, ordinary citizens come up to him with a heartfelt word of thanks. "I'm in a spouse-abuse support group now." "I kept my baby because of you." "My son has AIDS—God bless you for all you did." "You gave me the courage to quit smoking." Because of them, Koop looks back on his eight years in public service, for all their turbulence, with few regrets and much satisfaction. People listened to him because they learned to trust him, and then many took a further step of changing behavior.

Nowadays, in his new role as America's Internet family physician, that integrity is being questioned. Reporters found that a list of recommended hospitals on his Web site had paid a forty-thousand-dollar fee for the privilege, and that Koop was testifying as a scientist on behalf of chemical manufacturers that had paid him as a consultant. Koop defends his actions vigorously, but the controversy merely underscores the point that moralists and scientists both have only one platform from which to speak, that of integrity.

When he assumed public office, Koop also had to learn to distinguish the *immoral* from the *illegal*. Not everything he believed to be immoral could be made illegal, a distinction many other conservatives failed to make. "Thou shalt not covet" is a moral issue so serious that it ranks as one of the Ten Commandments. What municipality or national government could enforce a law against coveting? Pride is a moral sin, perhaps the worst sin, but can we make pride illegal? Jesus summed up the Old Testament law in the command, "Love the Lord your God with all your heart and with all your soul and with all your mind"; what human authority could police such a commandment? Though Christians have the obligation to obey God's commands, it does not automatically follow that we should enact those moral commands into laws enforced by the state. Not even John Calvin's Geneva would dare adopt the legal code of the Sermon on the Mount.

As an example, Christians are now debating the pros and cons of gay rights—a moral issue, as both sides would agree. If we believe homosexual practice to be immoral, should we make it illegal? Not so long ago the Church of England debated an issue with close parallels: divorce. The Bible has far more to say about the sanctity of marriage and the wrongness of divorce than it says about homosexuality. C. S. Lewis shocked many people in his day when he came out in favor of making divorce legal, on the grounds that we Christians have no right to impose our morality on society at large. Although he would preach against it, and oppose it on moral grounds, he recognized the distinction between morality and legality.

Of course, we will have to exercise the skill of ethical surgeons in deciding which moral principles apply to society at large. If we fail to exercise that skill, once again we will risk confusing the two kingdoms, the kingdom of God and that of this world. Old Testament prophets used a double standard in their pronouncements. Their own nation of Israel, they held accountable for keeping every part of God's covenant, including Sabbath-keeping and the rituals of Temple sacrifice. Secular nations around them, they critiqued on more "common law" grounds, such as war crimes, injustice, and decadence. And in the New Testament, Paul asks, "What business is it of mine to judge those outside the church? Are you not to judge those inside? God will judge those outside."

While he was in office, Koop attracted much opposition from conservatives who had an all-or-nothing approach to morality. They attacked him for agreeing to a compromise on the Baby Doe issue even though courts had overthrown his initial strict guidelines. They opposed any compromise on abortion. Koop says, "One of the problems with the pro-life movement is that they are one-hundred-percenters. Historically it is true that if the pro-life movement had sat down in, say, 1970 or 1972 with the pro-choice people, we might have ended up with an agreement on abortion for the life of the mother, defective child, rape and incest, and nothing more. That would have saved ninety-seven percent of the abortions since then. Ninety-seven percent of twenty-five million is a lot of babies."

An absolutist on issues like abortion and homosexuality, Koop nonetheless learned as surgeon general that Christian absolutes cannot always be imposed on those who do not share Christian beliefs. He learned instead compassion and mercy for the downtrodden, and love for the enemy. The world took notice. *Mademoiselle* magazine, for example, began an article on him by saying, "Identifiable goodness is encountered rarely enough in ordinary life—it's as rare as a gold ostrich egg in politics." The article went on to praise Koop for his example of intellectual, moral, and ethical honesty, concluding, "Koop, by exercising an agonized compassion for the poor, the wounded and the disenfranchised, has successfully and spectacularly integrated his religious and professional life: He is Christian, but he is not sectarian."

Koop proved to me that it is indeed possible to separate the sin from the sinner, opposing the one while embracing the other. In our conversations after his resignation, he kept circling back to the AIDS crisis and the disturbing response of many in the church. "When the AIDS example came along, my obligation seemed pretty clear. I viewed the lifestyle with a certain revulsion, but as a health officer I had to look upon AIDS patients primarily as sick people. On the same principle, if a fat lady enters the hospital with a gall bladder attack, you can't refuse her treatment on the basis of her lack of discipline in eating. I sit at the bedside of patients dying of AIDS. They remind me of kittens, so sick and so weak that they open their mouths to cry and no sound comes out. How can you not put your arm around that kind of person and offer support? Instead, to say, 'God is punishing them and I support God's punishment'—that attitude is what makes me so mad.

"As I've often said, the large part of this nation considers sodomy to be legally and spiritually wrong. So do I. Yet I know that some of the people who persist in leading their flocks astray on the AIDS issue do so out of homophobia. Really, we need a new word. 'Homophobia' is not at all like, say, 'Francophobia.' These people combine fear with an unbelievable hatred for homosexuals. I've had conversations with people who, if they could, would push a button and get rid of homosexuals by any means whatsoever."

As surgeon general, Koop continued to label homosexual acts as "sodomy" and to warn against their health dangers. Yet when he spoke to twelve thousand gay people in Boston, they chanted enthusiastically, "Koop! Koop! Koop!" The gay community, who disagreed strongly with his personal beliefs, had learned to trust him when he said he was surgeon general of all the people, even those whose lifestyle he opposed. He had won them over by calling for compassion for the sick among them, and for volunteers to care for them. Koop was, as he said, simply following the heritage of Christians in health care. Early hospitals were church-supported, he reminds his critics, as were hospices and orphanages.

The gospel presents both high ideals and all-encompassing grace. Very often, however, the church tilts one direction or the other. Either it lowers the ideals, adjusting moral standards downward, softening Jesus' strong commands, rationalizing behavior; or else it pulls in the boundaries of grace, declaring some sins worse than others, some sinners beyond the pale. Few churches stay faithful both to the high ideals of gospel and its bottomless grace. Dr. C. Everett Koop's life in the spotlight shows how difficult a balancing act that is. Nevertheless, I am convinced that unless we embrace both messages we will betray the good news that Jesus brought to earth.

"I've noticed that Christians tend to get very angry toward others who sin differently than they do," one man said to me, a man who directs an organization ministering to people with AIDS. I've noticed exactly the same pattern. After I wrote in a book about my friendship with Mel White, formerly a ghost writer for famous Christians and now a prominent gay activist, I received a number of letters condemning me for continuing the friendship. "How can you possibly remain friends with such a sinner!" the letter writers demanded. I've thought long and hard about that question, and come up with several answers which I believe to be biblical. The most succinct answer, though, is another question: "How can Mel White possibly remain friends with a sinner like me?" The only hope for any of us, regardless of our particular sins, lies in a ruthless trust in a God who inexplicably loves sinners, including those who sin differently than we do.

GETTING STARTED WITH C. EVERETT KOOP:

Dr. Koop told his own story in the memoir *Koop*. Concentrating on his time in public office, he defends each of the decisions that made him such a controversial figure and offers rich insights on the ethical issues he dealt with. A much briefer book, *Sometimes Mountains Move*, tells of the personal agony surrounding his son's death. His Web site, *www.drkoop.com*, offers much medical advice and information. For those readers interested in the intersection of faith and politics, I recommend books by H. Richard Niebuhr, Stephen Carter, James Davison Hunter, and Richard John Neuhaus.

In the late 1980s, as the AIDS epidemic was decimating the gay community and Surgeon General Koop was attracting criticism for his compassionate attitude, a friend of mine contracted the disease. I came to know David first through classical music. A board member of the Chicago Symphony, he invited Janet and me to several concerts, and introduced us to musicians in the orchestra.

As we got acquainted, David told us about his pilgrimage. He had grown up in a Christian home and attended a conservative Christian college. It was there, in fact, that he had made his first homosexual contacts. Later, he had "come out" in the gay community and chosen a life partner. "I still consider myself an evangelical Christian," he said. "I believe everything in the Bible—almost. Those two or three verses on same-sex contact, I don't know what to do with. Maybe I'm sinning in my lifestyle. Maybe those verses are talking about something different. I don't know how to put all that together. But I do love Jesus, and I want to serve him."

I didn't know how to put it together either. David witnessed of his faith to others and gave large sums of money to Christian causes, including the urban outreach programs of our church, which he used to attend. He now attended Moody Memorial Church, keeping a low profile and wincing whenever the pastor condemned homosexuality from the pulpit. But he liked the music, and of all the churches he had tried, Moody most closely reflected his own theology. "Most gay Chris-

Chapter 9

JOHN

DONNE

❧

AS HE

LAY

DYING

tians are quite conservative theologically," he explained. "We get so much abuse in church that we wouldn't bother going unless we really believed it was true."

Janet and I tried to be faithful friends to David despite our differences. The disease took a slow and terrible toll on his body. He spent his last several weeks in the hospital, and we visited him as often as we could. Sometimes we found him lucid and reflective. Sometimes, hallucinating, he imagined us as relatives or people from his past. Near the end his body broke out in purplish sores and, his tongue swollen and his mouth full of thrush, he could not speak.

When David finally died, his distraught partner asked me to speak at the funeral. "You can say anything you want," he told me. "But I have one request—please, don't preach judgment. Most of the people who will come haven't been to church in years. They've heard nothing but judgment from the church. They need to hear about a God of grace and mercy—the God that David worshiped. They need hope."

Over the next two days I got little work done. I composed and tore up several drafts of what I would say. The day before the funeral, in a sudden moment of inspiration, I reached up on my bookshelf and pulled down a small book I had not looked at in several years: *Devotions Upon Emergent Occasions* by John Donne. It was dog-eared and highlighted, with many notes in the margin, and as I went through it yet again I realized I could find no more "modern" and appropriate message than that written by an Elizabethan poet almost four centuries before.

I looked out over the audience as I stood in the pulpit the evening of David's funeral. He ran with a sophisticated, fun-loving crowd, and many had gathered to honor his life. Some musicians in the Chicago Symphony had left the evening's concert early and rushed to the church to perform a musical tribute. I had watched as we sang a few hymns, and many seemed uncomfortable even using a hymn book, much less singing. Indeed this was not a church crowd. It was a grieving crowd, though: they seemed like small, helpless birds, hungry for words of comfort and hope. Most of them had lost other close friends to AIDS in the past few years. They felt guilt and confusion as well as grief. Sorrow clung to us like a fog in the sanctuary.

I began by telling the story of John Donne (1572–1631), a man well acquainted with grief. During his term as dean of St. Paul's Cathedral, London's largest church, three waves of the Great Plague swept through the city, the last epidemic alone killing forty thousand people. In all, a third of London died, and a third more fled to the countryside, transforming whole neighborhoods into ghost towns. Grass grew between the cobblestones. Mangy, half-crazed prophets stalked the deserted streets, crying out judgment, and in truth nearly everyone believed God had sent the plague as a scourge for London's sins. At that time of crisis, Londoners flocked to Dean Donne for an explanation, or at least a word of comfort. And then the first spots of illness appeared on Donne's own body.

It was the plague, doctors told him. He had little time left. For six weeks he lay at the threshold of death. The prescribed treatments were as vile as the illness: bleedings, toxic poultices, the application of vipers and pigeons to remove "evil vapours." During this dark time Donne, forbidden to read or study but permitted to write, composed the book *Devotions*. While lying in bed, convinced he was dying, he carried on a no-holds-barred wrestling match with God Almighty and recorded it for posterity.

That ancient book has served me as an indispensable guide in thinking about pain. Not only when a friend dies, but whenever I feel overwhelmed by suffering, I turn to it for insight. John Donne is trenchant without being blasphemous, profound without being abstract or impersonal. He has changed forever the way I think about pain and death and how my faith speaks to these inevitable crises.

How shall they come to thee whom thou hast nailed to their bed?

No matter where I start, I usually end up writing about pain. My friends have suggested various reasons for this propensity: a deep scar from childhood, or perhaps a biochemical overdose of melancholy. I do not know. All I know is that I set out to write about something lovely, like the diaphanous wing of a mayfly, and before long I find myself back in the shadows, writing about the brief, tragic life of a mayfly.

"How can I write about anything else?" is the best explanation I can come up with. Is there a more fundamental fact of human existence? I was born in pain, squeezed out through torn and bloody tissues, and I offered up, as my first evidence of life, a wail. I will likely die in pain as well. Between those brackets of pain I live out my days, limping from the one toward the other. As Donne's contemporary George Herbert put it, "I cried when I was born and every day shows why."

John Donne's illness was only the latest encounter in a life marked by suffering. His father had died in John's fourth year. The Catholic faith of his family proved a crippling disability in those days of Protestant persecution: Catholics could not hold office, were fined for attending mass, and many were tortured for their beliefs. (The word "oppressed" derives from a popular torture technique: unrepentant Catholics were placed under a board on which heavy boulders were heaped to literally *press* the life out of the martyrs.) After distinguishing himself at Oxford and Cambridge, Donne was denied a degree because of his religious affiliation. His brother died in prison, serving time for having sheltered a priest.

At first Donne responded to these difficulties by rebelling against all faith. A notorious Don Juan, he celebrated his sexual exploits in some of the most frankly erotic poems in all of English literature. Finally, riven by guilt, he renounced his promiscuous ways in favor of marriage. He had fallen under the spell of a seventeen-year-old beauty so quick and bright that she reminded him of sunlight.

In a bitter irony, just as Donne decided to settle down, his life took a calamitous turn. Anne More's father determined to punish his new son-in-law, whom he thought unsuitable. He got Donne fired from his job as secretary to a nobleman and had him, along with the minister who performed the ceremony, thrown into prison. Disconsolate, Donne wrote his pithiest poem: "John Donne, Anne Donne, Undone."

Once released from jail, Donne, now blackballed, could not find further employment. He had lost any chance to fulfill his ambition to serve in the court of King James. For nearly a decade he and his wife lived in poverty, in a cramped house that filled with their offspring at the rate of one per year. Anne was subject to periodic depression, and more than once nearly died in childbirth. John, probably malnourished, suffered from acute headaches, intestinal cramps, and gout. His longest work during this period was an extended essay on the advantages of suicide.

Sometime during that gloomy decade, John Donne converted to the Church of England. His career blocked at every turn, he decided at the age of forty-two to seek ordination as an Anglican priest. Contemporaries gossiped about his "conversion of convenience" and scoffed that he had actually "wanted to be Ambassador to Venice, not Ambassador to God." But Donne considered it a true calling. He earned a Doctor of Divinity degree from Cambridge, promised to put aside his poetry for the sake of the priesthood, and devoted himself exclusively to parish work.

The year after Donne took his first church, Anne died. She had borne twelve children in all, five of whom died in infancy. John preached his wife's funeral sermon, choosing as his text words poignantly autobiographical from the Book of Lamentations: "Lo, I am the man that hath seen affliction." He made a solemn vow not to remarry, lest a stepmother bring his children further grief, which consequently meant he had to assume many household duties and use precious funds for outside help.

This, then, was the priest appointed to St. Paul's Cathedral in 1621: a lifelong melancholic, tormented by guilt over the sins of his youth, failed in all his ambitions (except poetry, which he had forsworn), sullied by accusations of insincerity. He hardly seemed a likely candidate to lift a nation's spirits in plague times. Nonetheless, Donne applied himself to his new task with vigor. He refused to join the many who were evacuating London and instead stayed with his beleaguered parishioners. He arose every morning at 4 A.M. and studied until 10. In the era of the King James Bible and William Shakespeare, educated Londoners honored eloquence and elocution, and in these John Donne had no equal. He delivered sermons of such power that soon, despite London's declining population, the vast cathedral was crowded with worshipers. Then came his disease, and the death sentence.

Some writers report that the knowledge of imminent death produces a state of heightened concentration, somewhat like an epileptic fit; perhaps Donne felt this as he worked on his journal of illness. The writing lacks his usual tight control. The sentences, dense, strung together in free association, overladen with concepts, mirror the feverish state of Donne's mind. He wrote as though he had to pour into the words every significant thought and emotion that had ever occurred to him.

"Variable, and therefore miserable condition of man! this minute I was well, and am ill, this minute," the book begins. Anyone confined to bed for more than a few days can identify with the circumstances, trivial yet overpowering, that Donne proceeds to describe: a sleepless night, boredom, doctors in whispered consultation, the false hope of remission followed by the dread reality of relapse.

The mood of the writing changes quickly and violently as the disease progresses. Fear, guilt, and the sadness of a broken heart take turns chasing away all inner peace. Donne worries over his past: Has God "nailed him to bed" as a mocking punishment for past sexual sins? In his prayers he tries to muster up praise, or at least gratitude, but often fails. For example, one meditation begins valiantly as Donne seizes upon the hopeful thought that, in sleep, God has given us a way to grow accustomed to the notion of death. We lose consciousness, yet rise again the next morning refreshed and mended: Is that not a picture of what will happen to us after death? Then he realizes with a start that the illness has taken away from him even this emblem of hope: "I sleep not day nor night . . . Why is none of the heaviness of my heart dispensed into mine eye-lids?" Insomnia has left him an unbroken span in which to worry over death, and no rest to renew him for that worrying.

Donne pictures himself as a sailor tossed about by the towering swells of an ocean in storm: he gets an occasional glimpse of faraway land, only to lose it with the next giant wave. Other writers have described the vicissitudes of illness with similar power; what sets

Donne's work apart is his intended audience: God himself. In the tradition of Job, Jeremiah, and the psalmists, Donne uses the arena of his personal trials as a staging ground for his great wrestling match with the Almighty. After spending a lifetime in confused wandering, he has finally reached a place where he can offer some service to God, and now, at that precise moment, he is struck by a deadly illness. Nothing appears on the horizon but fever, pain, and death. What to make of it?

In *Devotions*, John Donne calls God to task. "I have not the righteousness of Job, but I have the desire of Job: I would speak to the Almighty, and I would reason with God." Sometimes he taunts God, sometimes he grovels and pleads for forgiveness, sometimes he argues fiercely. Not once, though, does Donne leave God out of the process. The invisible stage manager looms like a shadow behind every thought, every sentence.

Give me, O Lord, a fear, of which I may not be afraid.

I have talked with many people whose lives are defined by suffering. In every case they describe to me a crisis of fear, a crisis of meaning, and a crisis of death. The central reason I keep returning to Donne's *Devotions*, as on the night of David's funeral, is that the book recounts each crisis in detail, and continues to yield new insights into these primal confrontations with the mystery of suffering.

Even as a visitor, I feel fear every time I open the doors and breathe in the familiar antiseptic scent of a hospital. My friend David told me what it was like to lie in a private room all day with nothing to fix on except misery. He reviewed all that he would miss when he died, and all that he had missed as he lived. Outside in the hallway he heard nurses and doctors discussing his case in lowered voices. They poked and prodded him every day, performing tests on his body that he barely understood.

John Donne likewise described the disconnected sensation that moves in when doctors hover over a patient. When he sensed fear in the physician, his own fears bubbled to the surface: "I overtake him, I overrun him, in his fear." As a patient, he felt like an object, like a map spread out across a table, pored over by cosmographers. He imagined himself separated from his own body and floating above it, from which vantage he could observe the disintegrating figure on the bed. As the illness advanced he saw himself as a statue of clay, its limbs and flesh melting off and crumbling into a handful of sand. Soon nothing would remain save a pile of bones.

Most of the time Donne had to battle such fears alone, for in those days doctors quarantined patients with contagious diseases, posting a warning notice on their doors. (Some in modern times were calling for the same treatment of AIDS patients like David.) As Donne lay inside he wondered if God, too, was participating in the quarantine. He cried out, but received no answer. Where was God's promised presence? His comfort? In each of the twenty-three meditations, Donne circles back to the main issue underlying his suffering. His real fear was not the tinny clamor of pain cells all over his body; he feared God.

Donne asked the question every sufferer asks: "Why me?" Calvinism was still new then, with its emphasis on God's absolute sovereignty, and Donne pondered the notion of plagues and wars as "God's angels." He soon recoiled: "Surely it is not thou, it is not thy hand. The devouring sword, the consuming fire, the winds from the wilderness, the diseases of the body, all that afflicted Job, were from the hands of Satan; it is not thou." Yet he never felt certain, and the not knowing caused much inner torment. Guilt from his spotted past lurked nearby, like a leering demon. Perhaps he was indeed suffering as a result of sin. And if so, was it better to be scarred by God or not visited at all? How could he worship, let alone love, such a God?

I quoted some of these passages at David's funeral, for at that time AIDS patients were hearing a steady stream of judgment from the church. Like Donne, I found comfort in the fact that not once did Jesus turn on a suffering person with a "You deserve it!" accusation. He offered instead forgiveness and healing.

Donne's book never resolves the "Why me?" questions, and after years of investigating the problem of pain I am convinced that none of us can resolve those questions. The Bible surely gives no clear answer. I have closely studied every passage on suffering, and even in God's summation speech to Job, at a moment that begged for such an answer, God refrained. Jesus contradicted the Pharisees' airtight theories that suffering comes to those who deserve it, yet avoided directly answering the question of cause. Resolution of the "Why?" questions lies beyond the reach of humanity—was that not God's main message to Job?

Although *Devotions* does not answer the philosophical questions, it does record Donne's emotional resolution, a gradual movement toward peace. At first—confined to bed, churning out prayers without answers, contemplating death, regurgitating guilt—he can find no relief from fear. Obsessed, he reviews every biblical occurrence of the word *fear*. As he does so, it dawns on him that life will always include circumstances that incite fear: if not illness, financial hardship, if not poverty, rejection, if not loneliness, failure. In such a world, Donne has a choice: to fear God, or to fear everything else.

In a passage reminiscent of Paul's litany in Romans 8 ("For I am convinced that neither death nor life . . . will be able to separate us from the love of God . . ."), Donne checks off his potential fears. Personal enemies pose no ultimate threat, for God can vanquish any enemy. Famine? No, for God can supply. Death? Even that, the worst human fear, offers no final barrier against God's love. Donne concludes his best course is to cultivate a proper fear of the Lord, which fear can supplant all others: "as thou hast given me a repentance, not to be repented of, so give me, O Lord, a fear, of which I may not be afraid." I learned from Donne, when faced with doubts, to review my alternatives. If for whatever reason I refuse to trust God, what, then, can I trust?

In his disputation with God, Donne has changed questions. He began with the question of *cause*—"Who caused this illness, this plague? And why?"—for which he found no answer. The meditations move ever so gradually toward the question of *response,* the defining issue that confronts every person who suffers. Will I trust God with my crisis, and the fear it provokes? Or will I turn away from God in bitterness and anger? Donne decided that in the most important sense it did not matter whether his sickness was a chastening or merely a natural occurrence. In either case he would trust God, for in the end *trust* represents the proper fear of the Lord.

Donne likened the process to his changing attitude toward physicians. Initially, as they probed his body for new symptoms and discussed their findings in hushed tones outside his room, he could not help feeling afraid. In time, however, sensing their compassionate concern, he became convinced that they deserved his trust. The same pattern applies to God. We often do not understand God's methods or the reasons behind them. The most important question, though, is whether God is a trustworthy "physician." Donne concluded yes.

Many people, such as those I addressed at David's funeral, do not envision a God worthy of trust. From the church, they hear mostly condemnation. That is why, following Donne, I turn for perspective to the central reason for trusting God: his son Jesus. How does God feel about those who die, even as a result of their own transgressions? Is God scowling, as the street prophets in John Donne's day warned, and some in our own day insist? Does God even care about the loss, anger, and fear that we feel? We need not wonder how God feels, because in Jesus, God gave us a face.

To learn how God views suffering on this planet, we need only look at the face of Jesus as he moves among paralytics, widows, and those with leprosy. In contrast to others in his day, Jesus showed an unusual tenderness toward those with a history of sexual sins—witness his approach to the Samaritan woman at the well, the woman of ill repute who washed his feet with her hair, the woman caught in the act of adultery. In Jesus, said Donne, we have a Great Physician "who knows our natural infirmities, for he had them, and knows the weight of our sins, for he paid a dear price for them."

How can we approach a God we fear? In answer, Donne holds up a phrase from Matthew's story of the women who discovered the empty tomb after Jesus' resurrection. They hurried away from the scene "with fear and yet great joy," and Donne saw in their "two legs of fear and joy" a pattern for himself. Those women had seen with their own eyes the vast distance between immortal God and mortal man, but suddenly it was a distance to inspire joy. God had used his great power to conquer the last enemy, death. For that reason the women felt both fear and great joy. And for that reason John Donne found at last a fear of which he need not be afraid.

Make this . . . very dejection and faintness of heart, a powerful cordial.

Viktor Frankl, survivor of a Nazi concentration camp, expressed well the second great crisis faced by people who suffer: the crisis of meaning. "Despair," he said, "is suffering without meaning." He had observed that fellow inmates could endure severe suffering if only they had some hope in its redemptive value. In a very different society such as ours, saturated with comfort, what possible meaning can we give to the great intruder, pain?

What is the meaning of a disease like AIDS? David and I had explored that very issue. At the time, a loud public debate was raging; his own church had turned away children with AIDS from their Sunday School. David freely admitted his illness traced back to behavioral choices he had made, and had repented of, but what about those children born with AIDS, or hemophiliacs who contracted the virus through a blood transfusion? What choice did they have?

In John Donne's day, it seemed that God's molten wrath was showering down on the entire planet. Two bright comets appeared in the sky each night—sure signs, said some, of God's hand behind the plague. Prophets roamed the streets, one echoing Jonah with his cry, "Yet forty days and London shall be destroyed!" We have our modern version of these prophets, quick to interpret plagues and disasters as specific signs of God's judgment. The past should teach us caution: theologians in Europe debated for *four centuries* God's message in the Great Plague, yet in the end a little rat poison silenced all their speculation.

What about the meaning of progeria, the tragic abnormality that speeds up the aging process and causes a six-year-old child to look and feel eighty? Or what is the meaning of cerebral palsy, or cystic fibrosis? What is the meaning of an earthquake in India, or a freak tidal wave that kills one hundred thousand people in Bangladesh? Does God withhold rains from Africa as a sign of his displeasure?

Most of us can see only a negative meaning to suffering, as an interruption of health, an unwelcome brake on our pursuit of life, liberty, and happiness. Any card shop conveys that message unmistakably. For suffering people, we can only wish that they "Get well!" As one woman with terminal cancer told me, "None of those cards apply to the people in my hospice. None of us will get well. We're all going to die soon. To the rest of the world, that makes us invalids. Think about that word. Not valid."

What is the meaning of terminal cancer?

John Donne, thinking himself terminally ill, asked such questions, and his book suggests the possibility of an answer. The first clues came to him through the open window of his bedroom as he heard church bells tolling out a doleful declaration of death. For an instant Donne wondered if his friends, knowing his condition to be more grave than they had disclosed, had ordered them rung for his own death. He soon realized that the bells were marking another person's death, one more victim of the plague.

A short time later, sounds from the funeral service drifted in among the street noises. Donne croaked out a feeble accompaniment to the congregational singing of psalms, and then he wrote Meditation XVII on the meaning of the church bells—the most famous portion of *Devotions,* and one of the most celebrated passages in English literature ("No man is an island . . ."). In stately, picturesque language, that meditation defines the loss we feel at any death: "If a clod be washed away by the sea, Europe is the less . . . any man's death diminishes me, because I am involved in mankind, and therefore never send to know for whom the bell tolls; it tolls for thee." We grieve at another's death because we ourselves are diminished. In the same event we sense a deep unity with others and also its rending.

Suffering has a singular ability to break through normal defenses and everyday routines, and to remind us of mortality. For some time I accompanied a friend to a life-threatening-illness support group, which met monthly in a hospital waiting room. I cannot say I "enjoyed" those meetings, yet every month, walking home, I had the sense that the evening was one of the most meaningful I had spent. We skipped trivialities and faced into the issues most urgent to everyone in that room—death and life, and how best to spend what time remained.

As Donne said, "I need thy thunder, O my God; thy music will not serve thee." The tolling of the bell was, for him, an advance echo of his own death. For the dead man, it was a period, the end of a life; for Donne, clinging to life, it was a penetrating question mark. Was he ready to meet God?

When people asked Jesus about a contemporary tragedy, here is how he responded:

> Do you think that these Galileans were worse sinners than all
> the other Galileans because they suffered this way? I tell you,
> no! But unless you repent, you too will all perish. Or those eigh-
> teen who died when the tower in Siloam fell on them—do you
> think they were more guilty than all the others living in Jeru-
> salem? I tell you, no! But unless you repent, you too will
> all perish.   (Luke 13:2–5)

Jesus followed up those comments with a parable about God's restraining mercy. He seems to imply that we bystanders of catastrophe have as much to learn from the event as do the victims. What should a plague or contemporary disaster teach me? Humility, for one thing. And gratitude for the life that I still enjoy. And compassion, the compassion that Jesus conveyed to all who mourned and suffered. Finally, catastrophe joins together victim and bystander in a common call to repentance, by abruptly reminding us of the brevity of life.

The tolling of that bell worked a curious twist in Donne's thinking. To that point, he had been wondering about the meaning of illness and what lessons to learn from it. Now he began contemplating the meaning of health. The bell called into question how he had spent his entire life. Had he hallowed the gift of health by serving others and God?

Had he viewed life as a preparation, a training ground, for a far longer and more important life to come—or as an end in itself?

As Donne began to reexamine his life, surprises came to light. "I am the man that hath seen affliction," Donne had told the congregation at his wife's funeral. It now seemed clear, though, that those times of affliction, the circumstances he most resented at the time, turned out to be the very occasions of spiritual growth. Trials had purged sin and developed character; poverty had taught him dependence on God and cleansed him of greed; failure and public disgrace had helped cure pride and ambition. Perhaps God's own hand had blocked his career— a devastating disappointment at the time—in order to prepare him for the ministry? A definite pattern emerged: pain could be transformed, even redeemed, and apparent evil sometimes results in actual good. Suffering not removed may serve as God's tool.

Donne's systematic review brought him up to his present circumstances. Could even *this* pain be redeemed? His illness limited him, of course, but the physical incapacity surely did not inhibit all spiritual growth. He had much time for prayer: the bell had reminded him of his less fortunate neighbor, and the many others afflicted in London. He could learn humility, and trust, and gratitude, and faith. Donne made a kind of game of it: he envisioned his soul growing strong, rising from the bed, and walking about the room even as his body lay flat.

In a word, Donne realized he was not "in-valid." He directed his energy toward spiritual disciplines: prayer, confession of sins, keeping a journal (which became *Devotions*). He got his mind off himself and onto others. The *Devotions* thus record a crucial shift in Donne's attitude toward pain. He began with prayers that the pain be removed; he ends with prayers that the pain be redeemed, that he be "catechized by affliction." Such redemption might take the form of miraculous cure—he still hoped so—but even if it did not, God could take a crude lump and through the refiner's fire of suffering make of it pure gold.

> *Though so disobedient a servant as I may be afraid to die,*
> *yet to so merciful a master as thou I cannot be afraid to come.*

Two great crises spawned by Donne's illness, the crisis of fear and the crisis of meaning, converged in a third and final crisis: death. The poet truly believed that he would die from his illness, and that dark cloud hangs over every page of *Devotions*. "I tune my instrument here at the door," he wrote—the door of death.

We moderns have perfected techniques for coping with this crisis, techniques that doubtless would cause John Donne much puzzlement. Most of us construct elaborate means of avoiding death altogether. Health clubs are a booming industry, as are nutrition and health food stores. We treat physical health like a religion, while simultaneously walling off death's blunt reminders—mortuaries, intensive care units, cemeteries. Living in plague times, Donne did not have the luxury of denial. Each night horse drawn carts rumbled through the streets to collect the bodies of that day's victims; their names—over a thousand each day at the plague's height—appeared in long columns in the next day's newspaper. No one could live as though death did not exist. Like others from his time, Donne kept a skull on his desk as a reminder, *memento mori*.

On the other hand, some modern health workers have taken the opposite tack, recommending acceptance, not denial, as the ideal attitude toward death. After Elisabeth Kübler-Ross labeled acceptance the final stage in the grief process, scores of self-help groups sprang up to help terminally ill patients attain that stage. One need not read long in John Donne's work to realize how foreign such an idea might seem to him. Some have accused Donne of an obsession with death (thirty-two of his fifty-four songs and sonnets center on the theme), but for Donne death loomed as the great enemy to be resisted, not a friend to be welcomed as a natural part of life's cycle. From the times that I have watched, week by week, a friend or loved one deteriorate, I know death as an enemy too.

The *Devotions* record Donne's active struggle against accepting death. Despite his best efforts, he could not really imagine an afterlife. The pleasures that he knew so well, that filled his writings, all depended on a physical body and its ability to smell and see and hear and touch and taste.

Donne took some comfort in the example of Jesus, "my master in the science of death," for the account of the Garden of Gethsemane hardly presents a scene of calm acceptance either. There, Jesus sweat drops of blood and begged the Father for some other way. He too felt the loneliness and fear that now haunted Donne's deathbed. And why had he chosen that death? The purpose of Christ's death brought Donne some solace at last: he had died in order to effect a cure.

A turning point came for Donne as he began to view death not as the disease that permanently spoils life, rather as the only cure to the disease of life, the final stage in the journey that brings us to God. Evil infects all of life on this fallen planet, and only through death— Christ's death and our own—can we realize a cured state. Donne explored that thought in "A Hymn to God the Father," the only other writing known to survive from his time of illness:

> Wilt thou forgive that sin where I begun,
>   Which was my sin, though it were done before?
> Wilt thou forgive that sin, through which I run,
>   And do run still: though still I do deplore?
>   When thou hast done, thou hast not done,
>   For, I have more.

> Wilt thou forgive that sin which I have won
>   Others to sin? and, made my sin their door?
> Wilt thou forgive that sin which I did shun
>   A year, or two: but wallowed in, a score?
>   When thou hast done, thou hast not done,
>   For I have more.

> I have a sin of fear, that when I have spun
>   My last thread, I shall perish on the shore;
> But swear by thy self, that at my death thy son
>   Shall shine as he shines now, and heretofore;
>   And, having done that, thou hast done,
>   I fear no more.

The word-play on the poet's name ("thou hast *done*") reveals a kind of acceptance at last: not an acceptance of death as a natural end, but a willingness to trust God with the future, no matter what. "That voice, that I must die now, is not the voice of a judge that speaks by way of condemnation, but of a physician that presents health."

As it happened, to everyone's astonishment John Donne did not die from the illness of 1623. His illness, misdiagnosed, proved to be a spotted fever like typhus, not bubonic plague. He survived the physicians' bizarre treatments, recovered, and put in eight more years as dean of St. Paul's.

Donne's later sermons and writings often returned to the themes touched upon in *Devotions,* especially the theme of death, yet never again did they express the same sort of inner turmoil. In his crisis, Donne managed to achieve a "holy indifference" to death: not by a discounting of death's horror—his later sermons contain vivid depictions of those horrors—but rather by a renewed confidence in resurrection. Death, which appears to sever life, actually opens a door to new life. "O death, where is thy sting? O grave, where is thy victory?"

If Donne could somehow time-travel into modern times, he would no doubt be aghast at how little attention we give to the afterlife. Today, people are almost embarrassed to talk about such a belief. We fear heaven as our ancestors feared hell. The notion seems quaint, cowardly, an escape from this world's problems. What inversion of values, I wonder, has led us to commend a belief in annihilation as brave and dismiss a hope for blissful eternity as cowardly? Heaven holds out a promise of a time, far longer and more substantial than this time on earth, of wholeness and justice and pleasure and peace. If we do not believe that, then, as the apostle Paul argued in 1 Corinthians 15, there's little reason for being a Christian in the first place. If we do believe, it should change our lives, as it changed John Donne's.

God knows all this world's weight and burden and heaviness, said Donne in a sermon; "And if there were not a weight of future glory to counterpoise it, we should all sink into nothing."

Death be not proud, though some have called thee
Mighty and dreadful, for, thou art not so . . .

. . . One short sleep past, we wake eternally,
And death shall be no more, Death thou shalt die.

Seven years after the illness that inspired *Devotions*, Donne suffered another illness, which would severely test all that he had learned about pain. He spent most of the winter of 1630 out of the pulpit, confined to a house in Essex. But when the time of the Passion approached on the church calendar, Donne insisted on traveling to London to deliver a sermon on the first Friday of Lent. The friends who greeted him there saw an emaciated man, looking much older than his fifty-eight years. A lifetime of suffering had taken its toll. Although the friends urged Donne to cancel the scheduled sermon, he refused.

Donne's first biographer, his contemporary Izaac Walton, sets the scene at Whitehall Palace on the day of Donne's last sermon:

> Doubtless many did secretly ask that question in Ezekiel, "Do these bones live?" Or can that soul organise that tongue? . . . Doubtless it cannot. And yet, after some faint pauses in his zealous prayer, his strong desires enabled his weak body to discharge his memory of his preconceived meditations, which were of dying; the text being, "To God the Lord belong the issues from death." Many that then saw his tears, and heard his faint and hollow voice, professing they thought the text prophetically chosen, and that Dr. Donne had preached his own Funeral Sermon.
> (From *The Life of Dr. John Donne*)

Donne had often expressed the desire to die in the pulpit, and so he nearly did. The impact of that sermon, "Death's Duel," one of Donne's finest, did not soon fade from those who heard it. To John Donne, death was an enemy he would fight as long as strength remained in his bones. He fought with the confident faith that the enemy would ultimately be defeated.

Carried to his house, Donne spent the next five weeks preparing for his death. He dictated letters to friends, wrote a few poems, and composed his own epitaph. Acquaintances dropped by, and he reminisced. "I cannot plead innocency of life, especially of my youth," he told one friend, "but I am to be judged by a merciful God, who is not willing to see what I have done amiss. And though of myself I have nothing to present to Him but sins and misery, yet I know He looks upon me not as I am of myself, but as I am in my Savior . . . I am therefore full of inexpressible joy, and shall die in peace."

Izaac Walton contrasted the image of John Donne in those final days—his body gaunt and wasted but his spirit at rest—with a portrait he had seen of Donne at age eighteen, as a dashing young cavalier, bedecked in finery, brandishing a sword. Its inscription, notes Walton, had proved ironically prophetic of Donne's difficult life: "How much shall I be changed before I am changed!"

A carver came by during those last few weeks, under orders from the church to design a monument. Donne posed for him in the posture of death, a winding sheet wrapped around him, his hands folded over his stomach, his eyes closed. The effigy was carved out of a single piece of white marble, and after Donne's death workmen mounted it over his funeral urn in St. Paul's Cathedral.

It is still there, John Donne's monument. I have seen it. It was, in fact, the only object in St. Paul's to survive the Great Fire of 1666, and it can be viewed in the ambulatory of the cathedral rebuilt by Christopher Wren, behind the choir stalls, an ivory-colored monument set in a niche in the old gray stone. Tour guides point out a brown scorch mark on the urn dating from the fire. Donne's face wears an expression of serenity, as though he attained at last in death the peace that eluded him for so much of life.

> Our last day is our first day; our Saturday is our Sunday; our eve
> is our holy day; our sunsetting is our morning; the day of our
> death is the first day of our eternal life. The next day after
> that . . . comes that day that shall show me to myself. Here I
> never saw myself but in disguises; there, then, I shall see myself,
> but I shall see God too. . . . Here I have one faculty enlightened,
> and another left in darkness; mine understanding sometimes

cleared, my will at the same time perverted. There I shall be all
light, no shadow upon me; my soul invested in the light of joy,
and my body in the light of glory.   (From Donne's *Sermons*)

Another monument lives on in Donne's writings. I have read many
words on the problem of pain, and written some myself. Nowhere,
however, have I found such a concentrated, wise meditation on the
human condition as in the journal John Donne kept during the weeks
of his illness, as he lay preparing to die. Having braced himself to
wrestle with God, he instead found himself in the arms of a merciful
Physician, who tenderly guided him through the crisis so that he could
emerge to give comfort and hope to others.

At David's funeral, a Chicago stockbroker came up to me and
asked if he could see the book I had been quoting from. He thumbed
through my well-worn copy. "I had no idea there were Christians like
this," he said.

GETTING STARTED WITH JOHN DONNE:

Devotions Upon Emergent Occasions has remained in print for almost
four centuries, a token of its status as a classic. And Internet users can
find the complete text at *http://www.ccel.org/d/donne/devotions/*.
Donne's poems and prose writings can be found in numerous collections in the Literature section of good bookstores. Unfortunately, collections of his sermons, as well as most reliable biographies of Donne,
have gone out of print and can be found only in libraries or in used
bookstores. If you get the chance, by all means see the Pulitzer-Prize-
winning play *Wit*, by Margaret Edson, which depicts the final days of
a John Donne scholar dying of ovarian cancer. HBO television also
produced a version starring Emma Thompson.

I cannot resist telling a story of my very first venture at writing
books. In 1973, while I was editor of *Campus Life* magazine, I attempted a paraphrase of *Devotions*. I had given the book to friends, but

many found the King James language difficult. Just as others were paraphrasing the version of the Bible composed in that era, I decided to do an updated version of this classic work on suffering: John Donne Redone, if you will. I paraphrased six of its twenty-three sections and mailed them off to a publisher with a proposal. A few weeks later I got a three-paragraph letter in response. The first paragraph, probably boiler-plate, informed me that although the editors loved my work, regretfully the marketing department had determined that projected sales would not justify their publishing it. The second paragraph read, "Please make this sound anguished and personal, as this is an important magazine source." The third paragraph asked me to keep them in mind for any future projects. I read that second paragraph over several times, trying to make sense of it, before it dawned on me what had happened. In dictating the letter, the publisher had intended that sentence for the ears of the stenographer, who was supposed to work at making my rejection sound anguished and personal. Instead, she typed his comments verbatim! Ten years later, I showed the letter to the publisher who had dictated it. I imagine he lost several nights' sleep wondering what else he had remarked in asides that inadvertently ended up in letters to writers.

My image of Annie Dillard forever changed when we met for the first time in 1977. Acquainted with her only through her writing, I expected to find a fey, neurotic poet like Emily Dickinson or a gaunt mystic like Simone Weil. We had arranged to meet in her office, which I envisioned as a one-room cabin tucked in a grove of Douglas firs.

The office turned out to be a garish institutional cell in a low-rise classroom building, with not a single decoration adorning the walls, one of which was painted orange and one blue. Dillard herself, barely thirty years old, wore blue jeans and an embroidered shirt. She was funny, and used conversational slang. She chain-smoked. She loved Ping-Pong and white-water rafting and dancing. She reveled in a good joke. Neither Dickinsonian nor professorial, she was rather the kind of person to include on your guest list to liven up a dinner party.

Dillard, too, had expectations. "I'm so glad it's you," she said when I entered her office. "I didn't know what to expect from a magazine called *Christianity Today*. When I saw a sixty-year-old bald man walking across campus I thought, 'Uh oh, what have I agreed to?'" At the time I was half the bald man's age and my abundant hair stuck out like a Brillo pad; what she had agreed to was a lengthy interview for that magazine.

I had just studied John Donne, published *Where Is God When It Hurts?*, and begun writing with Dr. Brand. I had a notebook full of

Chapter 10

ANNIE

DILLARD

THE

SPLENDOR

OF THE

ORDINARY

questions to ask her: about the problem of pain, nature, the theological argument from design, the writing life. We talked long past the time we had agreed on, and at the end she let out a deep sigh and said, "How delightful to talk about ideas, especially with someone laboring in the same vineyard. Most reporters want to know about my bank account and my sex life." That, of course, opened up a whole new line of questioning.

Working as a magazine journalist at the time, I viewed writing as both career and hobby, something you do as well as you can under tight deadlines. Dillard approached it as a holy calling, as seen in this passage from her book *Holy the Firm*:

> How many of you, I asked the people in my class, which of you want to give your lives and be writers? I was trembling from coffee, or cigarettes, or the closeness of faces all around me. . . . All hands rose to the question. And then I tried to tell them what the choice must mean: you can't be anything else. You must go at your life with a broadax. . . . They had no idea what I was saying. (. . . I'll do it in the evenings, after skiing, or on the way home from the bank, or after the children are asleep. . . .) They thought I was raving again. It's just as well.

Although Annie Dillard and I have met only one time since, we have kept up an occasional correspondence and I have followed her work closely. No, make that fanatically. She is a guiding light for writers who still care about words, sentences, paragraphs, and ideas, and a singular beacon for writers of faith. After that conversation, I never again looked on writing as a hobby. She taught me to see the craft, and indeed the world, with new eyes.

Dillard's memoir *An American Childhood* sketches some of the details of her life. She grew up in an upper-middle-class home in Pittsburgh, Pennsylvania, where loving parents indulged her in a comfortable life of private girls' schools and the country club. They talked ideas at the dinner table, took Annie to an upper-crust Presbyterian church, and gave her intellectual curiosity free rein. Annie squirmed through adolescence in the early 1960s: she got kicked out of school for smoking, and landed in a hospital after a drag racing incident. She showed a fondness for nature, yes, but also for baseball and the French and Indian Wars. "Works only on what interests her," scolded one of her high school teachers. When her parents sent her away to Hollins College in Virginia, she married her creative-writing teacher during her sophomore year.

To this day Dillard can recite the first poem she attempted, a product of that sultry adolescence when she had fallen under the spell of the French Symbolist poet Arthur Rimbaud:

Once, if I remember well,
My flesh did lay confined in Hell.
A cell of darkness prison damp,
A cell in need of fire and lamp.
My hand did drop, my body fell
And in my filth did I lie still.

Nothing in that poem or in Dillard's early life gave a clue that she would win a Pulitzer Prize before turning thirty and emerge as one of the premier nature writers of modern times. But she does credit her adolescence for awakening her spirituality and whetting her appetite for the abstract themes that would infuse her later works. Her memoir begins with this inscription from Psalm 26: "I have loved, O Lord, the beauty of thy house and the place where dwelleth thy glory."

Church mainly provided a social setting for tidily dressed families to "accumulate dignity by being seen" every Sunday. Summers, however, Annie trotted off with her sister to a religious camp in the pines. "If our parents had known how pious and low-church this camp was, they would have yanked us," she recalls. "We memorized Bible chapters, sang rollicking hymns around the clock, held nightly devotions including extemporaneous prayer, and filed out of the woods to chapel twice on Sundays dressed in white shorts. The faith-filled theology

there was only half a step out of a tent; you could still smell the sawdust."

As we compared backgrounds, I realized how different it is to step
into a subculture for a summer as compared to feeling trapped inside
that tent, the air always reeking of sawdust. My summers at a low-
church camp served to harden me against further indoctrination. In
contrast, Dillard felt drawn to religious ideas, which to her "made other
ideas seem mean." Memorizing long passages from the King James Version, she wrote poems in deliberate imitation of its rhythms. Back
home in the staid Pittsburgh church, she occasionally felt "despite myself, some faint, thin stream of spirit braiding forward from the pews."

Annie did have one short fling of rebellion against God, she told
me. After four consecutive summers at the church camp, she got fed
up with the hypocrisy of people coming to church to show off their
clothes and, wanting to make a major statement, she decided to confront the ministers head-on. The senior minister ("He looked exactly
like James Mason in *A Star Is Born* and his idea of a sermon was a
book review") terrified her, so she marched into the assistant minister's
office and delivered her spiel about hypocrisy.

A wise man, in one fell swoop he accomplished for her what took
me many years: he separated the church from God, and did so in a way
that dignified, rather than demeaned, his teenage critic. "He was an
experienced, calm man in a three-piece suit; he had a mustache and
wore glasses. I was this little high school kid who thought I was the
only person in the world with complaints against the church. He heard
me out and then said, 'You're right, honey, there is a lot of hypocrisy.'"
Annie felt her arguments dissolve. Then the minister proceeded to
load her down with books by C. S. Lewis, which, he suggested, she
might find useful for a senior class paper. "This is rather early of you,
to be quitting the church," he remarked as they shook hands in parting. "I suppose you'll be back soon."

To Annie's consternation, he was right. After plowing through four
straight volumes by C. S. Lewis she fell right back in the arms of
Christianity. Her rebellion had lasted one month.

Twelve books now bear Annie Dillard's name, and they include poems, essays, a memoir, a journalistic account of a visit to China,
historical fiction, and literary criticism. Some forms succeed better
than others, but all bear her mark: a piercing gaze, terrific sentences,
mystical intensity, the sense of writing as a calling.

No matter what else she achieves, Dillard will doubtless have to
live with the tag "nature writer." *Pilgrim at Tinker Creek* hit the reading public in 1974 with the impact of an asteroid: a new genre, fused
somewhere in outer space, scattering fragments of itself throughout
the atmosphere. In quick succession it got featured by the Book-of-
the-Month Club, won the Pulitzer Prize, was named Best Foreign
Book in France, and went on to become a surprise best-seller (nearly
half a million copies). Dillard was the new darling of the literary establishment. Reviewers compared her work to that of Virginia Woolf,
Gerard Manley Hopkins, William Blake, and Henry David Thoreau. A
slim young woman with wispy blond hair, blue eyes, and a penchant
for felt hats, she fit the role photogenically.

Pilgrim begins with the faculty of sight. In another work, Dillard
recalls the story of Noah Very, a septuagenarian hermit who lives in a
cottage in Appalachia. "One time when my children were young,"
Noah told her,

> . . . and we were all living where I live now, I looked out of the
> window and saw the children playing by the river. There is a lit-
> tle patch of sand on the bank there. The children were all very
> young, very small, and they were playing with buckets, and pour-
> ing water, and piling sand on each other's feet. . . . I said to my-
> self, "Noah, now you remember this sight, the children being so
> young together and playing by the river this particular morning.
> You remember it." And I remember it as if it happened this
> morning. It must have been summer. There are another twenty
> years in there I don't remember at all.
>
> (From *Teaching a Stone to Talk*)

The act of remembering, Dillard the writer adopts as a kind of sacred
mission. *Annie, you remember this sight,* one can imagine her saying to

herself over and over again. *You remember it, and write it down for others, as if it happened this morning.* She remembers with such vivid detail, in fact, that she teaches the rest of us to see. Readers keep returning to her work because she describes what no one else has noticed with quite the same acuity: a mockingbird's free-fall descent from a four-story building, a shearwater's "bank shot" plunge into a nest on a cliff, the texture of onrushing shadow in a solar eclipse, a luminous "tree with the lights in it." Dillard helps us slow down, look closer, and breathe deeper as we stride through the natural world. Such experiences, she says, can be "less like seeing than like being for the first time seen, knocked breathless by a powerful glance."

Emily Dickinson once wrote a friend that "Consider the lilies of the field" is the only commandment she never broke. It took Annie Dillard to teach me how to keep that commandment. I first read *Pilgrim at Tinker Creek* while living in an aluminum trailer in the wastelands of Chicago's suburbs. Recently married and paying off school debts, I was just getting my career as a journalist underway. I missed the lushness of the South: long-needle pines, honeysuckle vines, dogwood and redbud strewn in the forests. In Illinois I rarely bothered going outside, for what was there to see—cornfields? Tire tracks in dirty snow? As I read her accounts of nature, more exciting than an adventure novel, it struck me that everything she was describing took place beside a muddy creek in a nondescript field in Virginia. "It's all a matter of keeping my eyes open," she says. "Beauty and grace are performed whether or not we will sense them. The least we can do is try to be there . . . so that creation need not play to an empty house."

After reading the book, I made a vow to take a half-hour walk every day on the Illinois Prairie Path, a crushed gravel trail that followed an old railroad bed through the prairie and marshes near my home. Some days, I saw nothing special. Other days, the bare landscape I had always hurried past came alive. In winter, horsetail grasses collected a skin of ice that caught the sun like diamonds, and snow transformed common trees into works of abstract art. In spring, thousands of tiny spiders scurried under the mat of vegetation pressed down by the winter. In summer the marshes came alive with the sound of birds and insects, and I began to learn the range of territory patrolled by each red-winged blackbird. In fall, a solitary maple tree beside a fetid pool became a blaze of fire, a "tree with the lights in it." I took up photography to keep a record of all that I newly saw.

Annie Dillard comes to nature not merely to observe but also to learn, to wrest meaning out of a text that mulishly resists all such attempts. A careful guide, she took me by the hand down a familiar path that I had walked with others, such as Paul Brand and G. K. Chesterton, and even John Donne (who called nature a "subordinate John the Baptist to Christ"). Dillard likewise acknowledges the world as the Creator's work and then considers the consequences. What joke is this Creator playing on us? she asks. The mother octopus laying a million eggs to produce one survivor, killer whales slashing through a pod of sea lions, the female praying mantis consuming the male as he, now headless, continues to mount her—what lesson can we draw from such a work?

The problem, as always, is that nature gives off mixed signals. Like an unruly child, the natural world both reveals and obscures God; creation *groans*, to use the apostle Paul's term. Dillard lacks the optimism of a Chesterton, who sees God's smile even among the shadows, or of a Donne, who longs for a new home in an afterlife. She says, "I alternate between thinking of the planet as home—dear and familiar stone hearth and garden—and as a hard land of exile in which we are all sojourners." God must prefer working with one hand tied behind his back, she concludes.

As she was writing *Pilgrim,* Dillard lost a brother-in-law to leukemia. The tests had come back positive the day before his wedding, then took three years for him to die. Against that background, Dillard says, "I could not write this little cheerful nature book, nor could I write a new version of the argument from design. I had to write for people who are dying or grieving—that's everybody. The images of my sister and her husband were right there in the room as I wrote the book. How can I talk to my sister who didn't believe in God about God?"

Hence, the joyful scenes in *Pilgrim* are interspersed with, and sometimes overwhelmed by, scenes of violence. She gazes at a small green frog floating on the surface of the water until suddenly it transmogrifies before her, its skull collapsing inward "like a kicked tent," its body "shrinking before my eyes like a deflating football." The villain, she sees, is a giant water beetle, which has punctured, poisoned, and sucked the insides out of the frog. As she walks the well-worn route along Tinker Creek, thoughts of her brother-in-law wasting away from leukemia are never far away.

After *Pilgrim at Tinker Creek* came *Holy the Firm*. Dillard began the project while living on an island in Puget Sound near Seattle, working in a room furnished with "one enormous window, one cat, one spider and one person." The pressures that followed in the wake of *Pilgrim*'s huge success all bore in on that solitary room. "I was hideously self-conscious," she recalls. "I worked sixteen months full time, eight hours a day. Whenever I had the sheer nerve to even approach the stack of papers, I'd read what I'd written on the last couple of pages, and even I didn't understand it. I'd read it about 800 times until I understood enough to squeeze out a few more words. At the end of that time, I had forty-three pages. I was getting like Beckett: fewer and fewer words, more and more silence."

Holy the Firm records Dillard's daily routine—teaching, musing, walking to the store to buy Communion wine—interlacing the narrative with her metaphysical speculation. She had decided to write about whatever happened in her life during the next three days. What is the particular brand of holiness that each day brings? What is the relationship between time and eternity, between God and daily events? On the second day, though, a plane went down, and Annie Dillard found herself having to cover the same ground she had trod in *Pilgrim*. "When the plane went down, I thought, *Oh no, God is making me write about this damn problem of pain again.* I felt I was too young, I didn't know the answer, and I didn't want to do it. But, again, I had to."

In a borrowed cabin with no electricity, heated by the alder wood she had chopped that morning, she wrote about pain, the incarnation of Christ, the sacramental nature of existence, the ultimate mysteries of the universe. How can we, how dare we, love the God who allows a child to burn grotesquely in a plane wreck? Dillard had written in *Pilgrim:* "In the Koran, Allah asks, 'The heaven and the earth and all in between, thinkest thou I made them *in jest?*' It's a good question."

When I talked about these matters with Dillard in person, we discussed C. S. Lewis's notion that we must not go to nature to construct theology; she will fail us every time. Rather, we go to nature once we have our theology and let her fill the words—awe, glory, beauty, terror—with meaning. "I like that," she said. "But you see, I'm trained as a literary critic, and I approach the whole chaos of nature as if it were God's book. For many of my readers, that's the only book of God they will read. I must start there."

I first felt attracted to Dillard's writings because in modern times nature and supernature have split apart, and she seeks somehow to stitch them back together. By and large, the church has abandoned nature to physicists and geologists and biologists. Writers of faith tend to tiptoe around God's creation, dismissing it as mere matter, unworthy of the attention granted the mind and spirit. Doing so, we forfeit one of God's main texts. "Plunge into matter," said Teilhard de Chardin. "By means of all created things, without exception, the divine assails us, penetrates us, and molds us. We imagine it as distant and inaccessible, whereas in fact we live steeped in its burning layers."

Dillard reopens the text, as a script of the spirit. She writes about nature as a work of God, while admitting that nature gives muddled hints. "I paddle my canoe out to the edge of mystery where words fail and reason fails," she says. Her approach brings to mind once again God's own approach in the Book of Job. To a suffering man burdened with urgent existential questions, God replied with a stunning lecture on the natural world. Consider the ostrich, he told Job, and the mountain goats giving birth, and the wild oxen and feral horses and soaring eagles; observe the behemoth and leviathan. Look at the text; what does it tell you? As for the subtext, that requires faith; you must have eyes to see, ears to hear. Not even God reduced the message of creation. He simply pointed to it, as an item in his résumé.

Annie Dillard starts with the bad news about the world because that way, she says, when you eventually give the good news it proves far more convincing. The reader needs to trust that the writer knows how grim it can get—and yet still believe. Her most recent book, *For the Time Being*, stirs the pot yet again. She records how many suicides take place each day and what percentage of the population is mentally retarded. She describes birth defects in clinical detail, and details slaughter techniques practiced by tyrants throughout history. She notes that there are nine galaxies for each person alive on earth. She gives roughly equal attention to the secrets of dust and ocean waves and the life of the Catholic paleontologist/theologian Teilhard de Chardin.

Traveling an uncharted zone between skepticism and belief, Dillard turns repeatedly to the common language of nature. She points back to the Hasidic practice of an observer "hallowing" creation by recognizing the "holy sparks" hidden within it. As an artist, she reimagines a world that contains far more than we can see, a sacramental world. While theologians debate miracles and the supernatural, she renders the splendor of the ordinary.

"I have no problem with miracles," Dillard says; "I'm a long way from agnosticism, and no longer even remember how a lot of things that used to be problems for me were. But that isn't the question I struggle with. To me, the real question is, How in the world can we *remember* God. I like that part of the Bible that lists kings as good and bad. Suddenly there comes this one, King Josiah, who orders the temple to be cleaned up and inadvertently discovers the law. This happens after generations of rulers and after the Israelites followed God through the Exodus. Somehow they had forgotten the whole thing, every piece of it. A whole nation simply forgot God. That famous prayer 'I will in the course of this day forget thee; forget thou not me' is sometimes thought of as a warm Christian joke. I don't think it is so warm. I think that is a lot to ask." As a member of post-modern academia, she realizes that, with a worldview light-years away from that of the Hasidim, a whole civilization is in danger of forgetting God.

Part of Dillard's appeal lies in her ability to enrich the faith of serious Christians while still seeming credible to the cultured despisers of religion. In the United States, Christians tend to create subcultures, reading their own books, listening to their own music, educating their children in their own schools. Little cross-fertilization takes place between that subculture and the wider, secular culture. By combining stubborn doubt with an equally stubborn insistence on faith, Dillard serves as a bridge between two worlds, the literary establishment and conservative Christians.

Reading religious books sometimes reminds me of traveling through a mile-long mountain tunnel. Inside the tunnel, headlights provide crucial illumination; without them I might crash into the tunnel walls. But as I near the tunnel exit, a bright spot of light appears that soon engulfs my headlights and renders them so useless that, when I emerge, a Check Headlights sign reminds me to switch them off. In comparison to the light of day, they are so faint that I lose awareness of them. Christian books are usually written from a perspective outside the tunnel. Flooded with light, the author forgets the blank darkness inside the tunnel where many readers journey. Annie Dillard remembers, and aims her headlights precisely.

She writes with the agnostic intellectual in mind, hoping to get him or her to consider "that it's not only stupid people who are Christians." She sees one of her tasks as "trying to mediate a bit between Christians and humanists—especially between evangelical Christians and my colleagues in academia and the arts who think a Christian is a madman with a white sheet and a gun. . . ." Almost uniquely, she treats evangelicals and even fundamentalists with respect and kindness. While teaching at Hollins College in Virginia early in her career, she spent time reading to the blind at Shenandoah Bible College, where she learned the more compassionate side of fundamentalism. Now she volunteers in a soup kitchen.

"I know only enough of God to want to worship him, by any means ready at hand," Dillard wrote in *Holy the Firm*. She never fails to identify herself openly as a Christian, although she confesses that epiphanous religious experiences occur less frequently now. A few years ago she took the very public step of converting to Roman Catholicism. As she explained to the *New York Times*, "What I like about the Catholics is that they have this sort of mussed-up human way. You go to the Episcopal church, and people are pretty much all alike. You go to a Catholic church, and there are people of all different colors and ages, and babies squalling. You're taking a stand with these people. You're saying: 'Here I am. One of the people who love God.' "

Just as nature both reveals and obscures God, so does the church, and more and more Dillard writes directly about her community of faith. She told a gathering of Christian artists, "I feel I was set here on earth to describe church services, and there's something intrinsically hilarious about them. Often I have almost died in church in the effort to keep from laughing out loud. I wrote about this in 'An Expedition to the Pole.' What's so funny? The gap between what we're doing and what we're trying to do. The relationship between the incongruity of who we are and who we're trying to move with our prayers. It's a sort of dancing bear act."

The essay she refers to contains this lament:

> I have been attending Catholic Mass for only a year. Before that, the handiest church was Congregational. . . . Week after week I was moved by the pitiableness of the bare linoleum-floored sacristy which no flowers could cheer or soften, by the terrible singing I so loved, by the fatigued Bible readings, the lagging emptiness and dilution of the liturgy, the horrifying vacuity of the sermon, and by the fog of dreary senselessness pervading the whole, which existed alongside, and probably caused, the wonder of the fact that we came; we returned; we showed up; week after week, we went through with it.
>
> (From *Teaching a Stone to Talk*)

On Puget Sound, she attended a tiny church in which she was often the only person under sixty, and felt as if she were on an archaeological tour of Soviet Russia. The Catholic church proved more innovative. On one occasion parishioners partook of sacred mass to the piano accompaniment of tunes from *The Sound of Music*. Dillard sighs, "I would rather, I think, undergo the famous dark night of the soul than encounter in church the hootenanny." She adds, "In two thousand years, we have not worked out the kinks. We positively glorify them. Week after week we witness the same miracle: that God is so mighty he can stifle his own laughter."

She lodges against the church not the dreary complaint of so many modern writers—its irrelevance to our age—but rather the opposite: If Christianity is true, why on earth don't we act like it? "Does anyone have the foggiest idea what sort of power we so blithely invoke?" For Dillard, the monks at a Benedictine monastery come closest. On visits there she does the liturgy and sings the Divine Office seven times a day, and finds that in between the monks spend an inordinate amount of time laughing. They laugh at anything. They don't talk much, but they do laugh.

Some Christians do not know quite what to make of Annie Dillard. Writing works of art, not theology, she uses obliqueness and indirection. "If I wanted to make a theological statement or a statement of what I think, I would have hired a skywriter," she says. "Instead I knock myself out trying to do art—not that it is so good—but by its very nature it is not reducible to a sealed system. It's not so airtight. People will say, 'What do you think about this?' and I'll say, 'I don't know, here are 271 pages, you'll have to take them all.' "

Søren Kierkegaard described himself as a spy, an unholy man who kept his eye on suspicious characters, including himself. The police, he said, make good use of cunning people who can nose anything out, follow a clue, and bring things to light. In one sense, every writer works at espionage, taking notes, observing particulars that everyone else overlooks, scouring the world for clues of meaning. For a writer of faith, to labor in a secular culture vastly complicates the task. Writing books that appear only in Christian bookstores to be read only by church people requires little cunning; writing books of faith for a readership that has only vestigial organs of perception—that requires a particular kind of shrewdness.

Annie Dillard never denies her identity, but neither does she tell the whole story. She knows her audience, and herself. I thought of Kierkegaard's spy analogy not long ago when I picked up an article Dillard wrote for *The Yale Review* back in 1985. "Singing with the Fundamentalists" recalls the time she taught at the university in Bellingham, Washington. Early one morning she heard singing, and looked out her window to see a group of students gathered around a fountain.

> I know who these singing students are: they are the Fundamentalists. This campus has a lot of them. Mornings they sing on the Square; it is their only perceptible activity. What are they singing? Whatever it is, I want to join them, for I like to sing; whatever it is, I want to take my stand with them, for I am drawn to their very absurdity, their innocent indifference to what people think. My colleagues and students here, and my friends everywhere, dislike and fear Christian fundamentalists. You may never have met such people, but you've heard what they do: they pile up money, vote in blocs, and elect right-wing crazies; they censor books; they carry handguns; they fight fluoride in the drinking water and evolution in the schools; probably they would lynch people if they could get away with it. I'm not sure my friends are correct. I close my pen and join the singers on the Square.

In the remainder of the article, Dillard relates what she learned singing with the Fundamentalists at quarter to nine every morning throughout the spring. She studies the magazines these students read—*Christianity Today, Campus Life, Eternity*—and describes the students she gets to know. They are bright kids, not ignoramuses; they read the Bible, but also books of literary theory. Some support moderate Democrats; some support moderate Republicans.

In the course of the article Dillard also reproduces the lyrics to the songs that are sung, including these:

> *Give praise to the king.*
> *Singing alleluia—*
> *He is the king of kings . . .*

And

> *He is my peace*
> *Who has broken down every wall . . .*
> *Cast all your cares on him,*
> *For he careth for you-oo-oo . . .*

And

> *In my life, Lord,*
> *Be glorified, be glorified, today.*

And

> *I will eat from abundance of your household.*
> *I will dream beside your streams of righteousness.*
> *You are my king.*
> *Enter his gates*
> *with thanksgiving in your heart;*
> *come before his courts with praise.*
>
> *He is the king of kings.*
>
> *Thou art the Lord.*

Dillard tells us why she chooses to sing with the Fundamentalists all spring: ". . . they come pretty much for the same reasons I do: each has a private relationship with 'the Lord' and will put up with a lot of junk for it."

Even for a spy, it is quite a feat to work the text of eight different praise songs into an intellectual journal published by Yale University. "I just about fainted when they took it," Dillard told me later. "Actually," she went on to say, "I'm coming out of the closet more every year."

From the letters I receive, and from stray comments I pick up at parties and book signings, I gather that people have a glamorized image of a writer's life. These people have never sat and watched a writer staring at a thesaurus for fifteen minutes in search of one word. By necessity, writers lead a solitary life. We work alone, rebuffing all distractions, and create our own private reality, exploring and domesticating it until the time comes for a publisher to entice other people to join us—by which time, of course, we're merrily constructing another false reality. Most of the time the world we create is far more interesting than dull reality we live in.

I sometimes have the sense that my writer's life has taken over my real life. I wonder, *If I did not write, would I even exist?* How do I know what I think or feel unless I open my notebook and begin to write about it? I remember working on a short story early one morning. For three hours I strained to develop three-dimensional characters and to purge all clichés from their dialogue. A raw beginner at fiction, I was getting a terrific headache from the effort. Naturally I used the excuse to stop writing and walk across the street to a coffee shop. Imagine my surprise when I discovered that all the people in the coffee shop were two-dimensional characters who talked in clichés! None of them seemed nearly as interesting to me as the people who populated my story. I fled back to the security of the false reality awaiting me (and only me) in my basement office.

Annie Dillard knows this syndrome well. She prefers working in cinder-block offices without windows—so dull, she says, that sometimes she changes the color of her pen for excitement:

> It should surprise no one that the life of the writer—such as it
> is—is colorless to the point of sensory deprivation. Many writers
> do little else but sit in small rooms recalling the real world. This

explains why so many books describe the author's childhood. A writer's childhood may well have been the occasion of his only firsthand experience. Writers read literary biography, and surround themselves with other writers, deliberately to enforce in themselves the ludicrous notion that a reasonable option for occupying yourself on the planet until your life span plays itself out is sitting in a small room for the duration, in the company of pieces of paper. (From *The Writing Life*)

Dillard understands that those of us who write about life have very little energy left over actually to live. Most of us, in fact, aren't very well equipped to live, and genuinely prefer sitting in small rooms in the company of pieces of paper. At an early age, however, she suddenly emerged from her room to find tape recorders clicking on every time she opened her mouth, and readers from all over the world writing to ask her advice. For Dillard, winning the Pulitzer Prize changed everything overnight. "I was in my twenties and I'd won a Pulitzer—I didn't mean to, it was an accident, these things just fall down on your head. I was horribly embarrassed and hid myself as far as I could." While she sought to be a pilgrim, the world kept trying to turn her into a saint.

All the attention was terribly confusing at first. Offers came in for her to endorse books and products, to write Hollywood scripts, to write ballets and songs. Invitations for her to speak and to teach filled her mailbox. For a time she fled, moving across the continent from Virginia to live in the one-room house on Puget Sound. She made a vow she still honors, to give only two public readings a year. "Would Christ have gone on television?" Dillard once asked. She turned down an appearance on the "Today" show, but decided to grant selective interviews to print journalists.

Interviews distress her, especially those that bore in on her personal life. When a *New York Times* reporter spent a weekend with Dillard in Connecticut, Annie stayed up half the night crying uncontrollably, troubled by questions the interviewer had asked about her faith. Still she cooperates, a pilgrim submitting to emotional martyrdom.

Surely the years in the spotlight have taken a personal toll. She has had three marriages. Her voice betrays the decades of smoking. In person, she strikes me as strangely fragile, and her thin eyebrows, thin hair, and pale skin all contribute to that sense of fragility. Throughout her career, Dillard has made her personal struggles—with fame, with the harsh demands of the writing life, with doubt and faith—transparent. In the face of America's relentless celebrity machine, a serious writer has few options: he or she can give in, like Truman Capote, Norman Mailer, and Gore Vidal—or simply disappear, like J. D. Salinger and Thomas Pynchon. Dillard has chosen something of a middle road. The word *Pilgrim* in the title of Dillard's first major book gives a clue to how she sees herself.

I last met Annie Dillard at a conference in Kansas where she received the ten-thousand-dollar Milton Center Prize for distinction in Christian literature. She told jokes, engaged in witty repartee with the audience, and worked the crowd like a stand-up comic. Her fans, mostly aspiring writers, lapped it up. Now in her mid-fifties, with a maturing body of work to her credit, Dillard has become part of the literary establishment that once welcomed her as a dazzling newcomer. In some ways she has lived up to her promise; in other ways, the critics assess, she has not. When your first book wins worldwide acclaim, what do you do for an encore?

Readers by the thousands write Dillard. *Pilgrim at Tinker Creek,* after all, came out at a time when spirituality had no place on the literary landscape, and in that desert *Pilgrim* shimmered like an oasis for the soul. It did for some readers what fantasy literature does for others: it pointed convincingly to a world beyond. Most involuntarily, Annie Dillard became a modern saint, an icon.

A college student wrote to ask, What is transcendence, and how can I get more of it in my writing? A priest sent her an envelope in which she could see, holding it up to the light, a cross in silhouette. When she opened the envelope, "instead of a cross, a little agonized Christ fell out in my palm. I jumped. He must have fallen off his cross in the mail." Nuns sent religious medals and shreds of fabric from Veronica's veil. A woman wrote from her dying grandson's bedside asking for Dillard to settle one question: Was the United States right or wrong to drop the atomic bomb on Hiroshima? A well-known artist inquired, "I don't mean to bother you, but would you tell me if God is here watching his creation and deciding who lives and who dies, or is he gone?" The artist's son had drowned sailing a small, one-person sailboat.

Is it any wonder she moved three thousand miles away? She moved to Washington knowing no one in the state, and she hardly fit in: "The women out there had a kind of culture I couldn't share. They used chain saws and canned things and they breast-fed. I thought I was a hippie until I went out there. Out there I was suddenly a bluestocking."

She felt more than a twinge of guilt about the kind of writing she did, which, she admits, is "appallingly isolated from political, social, and economic affairs." When a person writes about religious faith, especially, complications arise, for writing requires a self-consciousness that destroys the sublime self-surrender every pilgrim seeks. Every writer who touches on spirituality can identify with Thomas Merton's concern that his books expressed the spiritual life so confidently and surely when actually he was plagued by insecurities, doubts, and even terrors. Is there room for a pilgrim—just that, a pilgrim and not an expert or a saint?

In *Holy the Firm,* Dillard even inserts a disclaimer: "I do not live well, I merely point to the vision." She once explained to me, "Holy people ask me to speak at their monasteries and I write back and say no, keep your vision. In *The Wizard of Oz* there's a giant machine and behind the curtain a little man is cranking it and pushing buttons. When the dog pulls back the curtain to expose the little man, the machine says, 'Pay no attention to that man behind the curtain! Look at the light show.' So I ask the monks to keep their vision of power, holiness, and purity. We all have glimpses of the vision, but the truth is that no one has ever lived the vision."

Some twenty years ago I told her that I would pray for her one day a week because I imagined the kind of pressures she would face. "No one had ever once said he was praying for me," she told me recently. "Consequently I felt obligated to be worthy of your prayers, to remain a Christian writer, to do it as well as I could."

When a struggling writer found unexpected success and wrote Dillard for advice, she got this reply: "I have an urgent message for you. *Everyone* feels like a fraud. . . . Separate yourself from your work. A book you made isn't you any more than is a chair you made, or a soup. It's just something you made once. If you ever want to make another one, it, too, will be just another hat in the ring, another widow's mite, another broken offering which God has long understood is the best we humans can do—we're forgiven in advance."

Dillard's own work bears out her advice. In the alchemy of the written word, a faithful pilgrim's struggles have become to others a source of comfort and her doubts have strengthened others' faith. As a writer all too conscious of my own failings in life, that mysterious alchemy offers hope. "What is a poet?" asked Kierkegaard. "A poet is an unhappy being whose heart is torn by secret sufferings, but whose lips are so strangely formed that when the sighs and the cries escape them, they sound like beautiful music . . ."

GETTING STARTED WITH ANNIE DILLARD:

Pilgrim at Tinker Creek, one of Dillard's earliest books, still offers the best introduction to her style and thought. As a writer, she is willing to try just about anything. *The Writing Life* and *Living by Fiction* offer rich material for those interested in the craft of writing and *An American Childhood* satisfies readers interested in Annie Dillard herself. She has also published a full-length novel, *The Living,* which received mixed reviews, and several volumes of poetry. *The Annie Dillard Reader* gathers together excerpts from various works—a sampling chosen by the author herself—which devoted readers can then pursue in their original sources.

I remember the day I picked up my first book by Frederick Buechner. It came in a clump of books as a gift from a friend, and I selected it mainly because of its brevity (just under a hundred pages). It was a book of sermons, of all things, adapted from actual sermons Buechner had delivered as the Beecher Lectures on preaching at Yale. These, however, bore about as much resemblance to the average sermon as Shakespeare's plays do to the average church Christmas pageant.

> In the front pews the old ladies turn up
> their hearing aids, and a young lady slips
> her six year old a Lifesaver and a Magic
> Marker. A college sophomore home for
> vacation, who is there because he was
> dragged there, slumps forward with his
> chin in his hand. The vice-president of a
> bank who twice that week has seriously
> contemplated suicide places his hymnal in
> the rack. A pregnant girl feels the life stir
> inside her. A high-school math teacher,
> who for twenty years has managed to keep
> his homosexuality a secret for the most
> part even from himself, creases his order
> of service down the center with his
> thumbnail and tucks it under his knee. . . .
> The preacher pulls the little cord that
> turns on the lectern light and deals out his
> note cards like a riverboat gambler. The
> stakes have never been higher.

The book reads more like a novel than a sermon, which makes sense because, as I would

Chapter 11

FREDERICK

BUECHNER

WHISPERS

FROM THE

WINGS

learn, Buechner was a novelist long before becoming a preacher. No matter what he writes, he relies on the techniques of fiction: sensory detail, an intriguing story line, the taut tug of suspense. In my first encounter, though, I took little notice of prose technique, being instead swept along in the sheer drama of the old, old story told in a very new way. That slim book, *Telling the Truth,* carries the subtitle *The Gospel as Tragedy, Comedy, and Fairy Tale,* a three-part division through which Buechner recapitulates the entire Christian story. He quotes *King Lear* and *The Wizard of Oz* as often as he quotes Isaiah or Matthew, and for some reason I found that made the gospel all the more believable.

Walker Percy used to say that good fiction tells us what we know but don't quite know that we know. So does good theology. Frederick Buechner reminded me that the gospel is not a systematic overlay imposed on life, but rather a summary of all that is most true about it. Life is as tragic as the last sad days of King Lear and of Jesus; as comic as an armadillo, or the old-lady pregnancy of a Jewish matriarch named Sarah. If the story of Jesus holds any promise at all, life is also a fairy tale, a story with an ending too good not to be true, a whiff of "joy beyond the walls of the world more poignant than grief."

Buechner became for me a mentor in rediscovering a gospel that had grown all too familiar. Unlike me, he did not have to unlearn what he had learned in church, since he had never learned much in church. His pilgrimage he undertook voluntarily as an adult, a journey fraught with risk and danger, not a group tour with a prearranged itinerary. As a result, he makes the basic facts of the gospel glow as though he has just discovered them in a pottery jar in the Middle East. The Christian faith strikes him as good news because it presents the truth of the world as he has experienced it, giving words to the deepest things he has felt by living on this planet.

A minister, says Buechner, has two stories to tell: Jesus' story and the minister's own. In Buechner's case, the minister's own story illumines how he tells the other, for a few defining events in his life provide background lighting to virtually everything Buechner has written.

At the age of ten, Fred and his younger brother Jamie watched from their upstairs bedroom window as their mother and grandmother, barefoot and in their nightgowns, tried to revive a motionless body, dressed in gray slacks and a maroon sweater, lying face up in the driveway. It was the boys' father, dead of carbon monoxide poisoning from a car engine running in a closed garage. A few years later the father's younger brother, Fred's uncle, also took his own life.

Fred was, in his own words, "a bookish, rain-loving, inward-looking child," and the deaths of his father and uncle stirred in him a sense of his own mortality that has never gone away. For a time he wondered whether the family was afflicted with some fatal suicide gene. As he grew up, the family tragedies also helped convince him that most of us are shaped less by the global forces described each night on the television news than by the intimate forces of family, friends, and shared secrets. He learned, like every good novelist, that human behavior can neither be explained nor predicted, only rendered.

A very different kind of disruption occurred when he reached the age of twenty-seven. With two novels under his belt, one (*A Long Day's Dying*) extravagantly praised by the critics, Buechner moved to New York City to try his hand at full-time writing. He hit a creative block, found himself unable to write anything, grew depressed, and contemplated other careers—in advertising, perhaps, or working for the CIA. Uncharacteristically, simply because the impressive building stood a block from his apartment, he began attending the Madison Avenue Presbyterian Church, home of the celebrated preacher George Buttrick. In 1953, around the time of the coronation of Queen Elizabeth II, Buechner heard a sermon that changed his life. Buttrick was contrasting Elizabeth's coronation with the coronation of Jesus in the believer's heart, which, he said, should take place among confession and tears. So far so good.

And then with his head bobbing up and down so that his glasses glittered, he said in his odd, sandy voice, the voice of an old nurse, that the coronation of Jesus took place among confession and tears and then, as God was and is my witness, *great laughter,* he said. Jesus is crowned among confession and tears and great laughter, and at the phrase *great laughter*, for reasons that I have never satisfactorily understood, the great wall of China crumbled and Atlantis rose up out of the sea, and on Madison Avenue, at 73rd Street, tears leapt from my eyes as though I had been struck across the face.　　　　(From *The Alphabet of Grace*)

A week later the young novelist was asking Buttrick what seminary he should attend. Buttrick drove him to Union Theological Seminary, where the following fall Buechner enrolled as a student to learn from the likes of Reinhold Niebuhr, James Muilenburg, and Paul Tillich, and ultimately to seek ordination as a Presbyterian minister. His family and acquaintances thought him foolish for apparently trading in a promising career as a writer. "Freddy, did you make this decision on your own, or were you poorly advised?" asked one condescending matron at a cocktail party.

At times Buechner has been tempted to interpret his conversion experience in Freudian terms as a search for a missing father, or in existentialist terms as a leap-of-faith response to anxiety over career failure. He resists the temptation, viewing it instead as an exemplar of the "crazy, holy grace" that wells up from time to time "through flaws and fissures in the bedrock harshness of things."

Many modern writers have plumbed the despair in a world where God seems largely absent, but very few have tried to tackle the reality of what God's *presence* might mean. Buechner has never forgotten that Christ was crowned in a spirit of laughter. He writes of a magic kingdom, of an end to our weary journey, of a home that will heal at last the homesickness that marks our days. As a preacher and a writer, he tries to reawaken the child in people: the one who naïvely trusts, who will at least go and look for the magic place, who is not ashamed of not knowing the answers because he is not expected to know the answers. Given my own melancholy, my obsession with the problem of pain, and my emotionally truncated childhood, it was a message that breathed life into me.

"I have been spared the deep, visceral look into the abyss," Buechner says. "Perhaps God indeed saves his deepest silence for his saints, and if so I do not merit that silence. I have intellectual doubts, of course. But as John Updike puts it, if there is no God then the universe is a freak show, and I do not experience it as a freak show. Though I have had neither the maleficent or the beatific vision, I have heard whispers from the wings of the stage."

I first met Buechner during the early 1980s, about the time he decided to donate his correspondence and original manuscripts to Wheaton College to repose in the college's Wade Collection alongside papers from C. S. Lewis, G. K. Chesterton, Charles Williams, J. R. R. Tolkien, and Dorothy L. Sayers. Buechner knew almost nothing about the school—in our phone conversations he kept calling it "Wheatland College"—but his alma mater, Princeton, had shown little interest while the folks at the Wade Collection had been warm and solicitous. After he traveled to Wheaton and toured the campus, I asked him what he thought of his decision. "Well, it seems a good place for my literary remains to molder," he said. "A safe place, where at least they will rest in very distinguished company."

He returned to the campus several years later as a visiting professor. For the first time, he was getting regular exposure to evangelical Christians, a breed he had never before met. Some, he told me, reminded him of American tourists in Europe who, not knowing the language of their listeners, simply raise their voices. Such Christians spoke confidently about matters Buechner thought veiled in mystery, and their certitude both fascinated and alarmed him. "I was astonished to hear students shift casually from small talk about the weather and movies to a discussion of what God was doing in their lives. They spoke of 'prayer diaries' and used phrases like 'God told me . . .' If anybody said anything like that in my part of the world, the ceiling would fall in, the house would catch fire, and people's eyes would roll up in their heads."

Buechner contrasts that environment with what he has found as a guest lecturer at places like Harvard Divinity School. "There you meet students who are militant homosexuals or proud atheists, and some who are witches hold covens outside of chapel. I once opened a class on preaching with a simple prayer, and the students fell over in shock. Evidently, nobody prays at Harvard Divinity School."

Although he has learned to appreciate the fervor of evangelicals, Buechner speaks of his own faith in more muted tones. He deeply believes that God is alive and present in the world, yet it surprises him not at all that God gives us only "momentary glimpses into a mystery of such depth, power and beauty that if we were to see it head on, in any way other than in glimpses, I suspect we would be annihilated."

There are two ways to picture how God interacts with history. The traditional model shows a God up in heaven who periodically dispatches a lightning bolt of intervention: the calling of Moses from a burning bush, the Ten Plagues, the prophets, the birth of Jesus. The Bible indeed portrays such divine interventions, although they usually follow years of waiting and doubt. Another model shows God beneath history, continuously sustaining it and occasionally breaking the surface with a visible act that emerges into plain sight, like the tip of an iceberg. Anyone can notice the dramatic upthrusts—Egypt's Pharaoh certainly had no trouble noticing the Ten Plagues—but the life of faith involves a search below the surface as well, an ear fine-tuned to rumors of transcendence.

Buechner has spoken of his quest for that subterranean presence of grace in the world. He writes of an anxious moment in an airport (he battles a fear of flying) when suddenly he notices on the counter a tiepin engraved, against all odds, with his own initials, "C. F. B."; and of a good friend who dies in his sleep and then visits Buechner in a dream, leaving behind a strand of blue wool from his jersey, which Buechner finds on the carpet the next morning; and of sitting parked by the side of the road in a moment of personal crisis when a car barrels down the road with a license plate bearing the simple message "T-R-U-S-T."

Each of these occurrences, Buechner grants, allows for a more reductionist interpretation. Perhaps nothing happened beyond a cat dragging in a wool thread, or a passenger leaving a tiepin on a counter, or a trust officer of a bank driving down the highway. Buechner, however, prefers to see in such occurrences hints—upthrusts—of an underlying Providence. For example, when the car drove by, "Of all the entries in the entire lexicon it was the word *trust* that I needed most to hear. It was a chance thing, but also a moment of epiphany—revelation—telling me, 'trust your children, trust yourself, trust God, trust life; just *trust*.' "

In ways like these, ambiguous, elusive, and subject to different interpretations, God edges into our lives. For Buechner, such random events present a kind of Pascalian gamble: he can either bet yes on a God who gives life mystery and meaning, or no, concluding that whatever happens happens, with no meaning beyond. Either way, the evidence remains fragmentary and inconclusive, and demands faith. Were there no room for doubt, there would be no room for faith either.

> Faith is homesickness. Faith is a lump in the throat. Faith is less a position *on* than a movement *toward*, less a sure thing than a hunch. Faith is waiting. Faith is journeying through space and time.
>
> So if someone (and this frequently happens) were to come up and ask me to talk about my faith, it's exactly that journey through space and time I'd have to talk about. The ups and downs of the years, the dreams, the odd moment, the intuitions. I'd have to talk about the occasional sense I have that life isn't just a series of events causing other events as haphazardly as a break shot in pool causes billiard balls to go off in many directions, but that life has a plot the way a novel has a plot—that events are somehow leading somewhere. (From *Going on Faith*)

I find companionship in Buechner's writings because for me, too, faith is a Pascalian gamble. Though I spend my life in pursuit of God, I often sense that God lies just around the next bend in the trail, just behind the next tree in the forest. I keep walking because I like where the journey has led me thus far, because other paths seem more problematic than my own, and because I yearn for the resolution of the plot. I know a little of life's tragedy. I have tasted of its comedy. I keep walking because I believe in the fairy tale, that a God strong and wise enough to create a world stamped with such beauty and goodness will be faithful in restoring it to the original design. With Buechner, I place a bet on God's firm promise that in the end, all will be well.

On one of Buechner's visits to Wheaton, I talked him into speaking at my church in downtown Chicago. I grew more and more uneasy as the day approached. Our worship services were decidedly low-church affairs, planned by a lay committee, and music styles ranged from a black gospel group to classical violin to a blasting rock band—or perhaps all three in the same service. Liturgical readings, the committee usually edited into contemporary language, with petitions for the homeless and the Chicago public schools shoehorned into lofty prose from the Book of Common Prayer. Street people often wandered into the service and, appreciating the warmth they found indoors, stretched out on the pews to take a nap. I doubted that Buechner's community in rural Vermont offered anything quite like our urban church scene.

Sure enough, the worship committee outdid themselves in Buechner's honor. New banners hung from the ceiling. A sloppily dressed, overweight woman led us in jazzed-up readings, prayers, and songs. During the offertory music, a slender young lass in clinging chiffon danced a sacred dance. After watching all this from his pulpit chair, as a visitor to India might watch an elaborate temple ritual, Buechner stood and delivered an eloquent sermon. Afterward, he had two comments. About the woman who led worship he said, "How can anyone let herself get that fat!" About the dance he said, "I know it is supposed to enhance my worship. Instead, I spent the whole time wondering whether she had on any underwear." From then on I knew I liked this guy, who alone felt free to say what everyone else was thinking.

I soon learned that Buechner has definite opinions on nearly everything—on politics, movies, other writers, his own profession as a minister/writer—and freely offers them. "I'm sick of religious language," he once told an interviewer. "I'm sick of sermons right now." Because he kept agreeing to preach despite the illness, he sought out new carriers for his beliefs. He looked to Dostoevsky and Henry James to make his points, as well as to Jacob and to Paul. Most importantly, in his nonfiction prose he stuck to a lesson he had learned in writing fiction: nothing alienates an audience faster than a slight note of falsity or unrealism. To write or speak about the Christian faith, he must do so with undiluted honesty.

Raised in a nonreligious home, Buechner got baptized "less from any religious motive, I think, than from simply a sense that like getting your inoculations and going to school, it was something you did." The baptism had a paradoxical effect, inoculating him against a Christianity of symbol and no substance, against the cozy imagery of stained glass and statues, against the trappings of church for church's sake, against the repetition of stale words long since desiccated of meaning. When he finally gained a personal faith, he had to locate a new vocabulary in which to express it.

That fresh style seasons Buechner's writing. When he writes of biblical characters or of abstract theology, he struggles to cut through the mustiness and excess piety. It takes a vivid image, a twist of words, or a phrase that hangs in the air, to get a reader to stop and take notice. A few examples:

- A Christian is one who is on the way, though not necessarily very far along it, and who has at least some dim and half-baked idea of whom to thank.

- Lust is the craving for salt of a man who is dying of thirst.

- God doesn't explain. He explodes. He asks Job who he thinks he is anyway. He says that to try to explain the kind of things Job wants explained would be like trying to explain Einstein to a little-neck clam.

- And as for the king of the kingdom himself, whoever would recog-

nize him? He has no form or comeliness. His clothes are what
he picked up at a rummage sale. He hasn't shaved for weeks. He
smells of mortality. We have romanticized his raggedness so long
that we can catch echoes only of the way it must have scandalized
his time in the horrified question of the Baptist's disciples, "Are
you he who is to come?"—in Pilate's "Are you the king of the
Jews?" you with pants that don't fit and a split lip; in the black
comedy of the sign they nailed over his head where the joke was
written out in three languages so nobody would miss the laugh.

Buechner the novelist has, in many ways, carved out a new genre with
his nonfiction. With some notable exceptions, nonfiction writing by
Christians tends to fall into a few well-defined categories. Persuasive
literature, whether sermons, jeremiads, essays, or rational apologetics,
is a genre well practiced by Buechner's esteemed companions in the
Wade Collection at Wheaton. Others write memoirs or personal testi-
mony, often compelling but with the drawback of having a predictable
plot: sinner gets saved. Buechner's own style combines the skills he
learned as a novelist with the Christian discipline of inward reflection.

A novel and a life of faith—the two, Buechner concluded, have
much in common. Faith and fiction both rely on the concrete and particular more than the abstract and cerebral, both deal with seeming
contradictions, and both involve a sustained process of reordering
those particulars and contradictions into some pattern of meaning.
Finding the appropriate voice took a while. Even after ordination Buechner found it difficult to write about his personal faith. Raised in a nonreligious home, living in a nonreligious part of the country, he felt
reticent and embarrassed, as if faith should stay in a closet, one of
those family secrets no one mentions in public. The change came
about, appropriately, through an odd coincidence.

Buechner was going through a dark time, something approaching
a nervous breakdown. He had just moved his family to an isolated
farm in Vermont, leaving a comfortable position with a private school
in order to write full time. Before long he had written himself into a
corner, facing blank walls each day. The muses would not show up on

schedule. Everything he wrote made him so depressed he could not continue. Then a letter from Harvard arrived inviting him to deliver the school's Noble Lectures on theology. Perhaps, suggested the chaplain, Buechner could do something on "religion and letters."

The chaplain no doubt meant the phrase in the sense of letters as literature or learning. As he stared at the invitation, though, Buechner saw the word in its most basic, literal essence: the letters of the alphabet, building blocks of all language. The more he thought about it, the more he saw that faith consists of God using the humdrum events of our lives as a kind of alphabet, the scraps of a language that, if listened to properly, can convey God's self to us. His eye turned inward. Out of those musings came *The Alphabet of Grace,* an adaptation of the Noble Lectures in which Buechner picks one by one through the fragments of a single day: shaving, getting dressed, staring in a mirror, starting the coffee, dressing the kids, stalling to avoid writing, meeting a friend for lunch, watching the news, growing sleepy, turning out the lights on the day.

At last Buechner had found a voice for his nonfiction. He need not be a theologian like his teachers at Union. He need not be a preacher of sermons. He could simply fashion stories and meaning out of the material of his own life, just as he already did in his fiction. He began producing his own quieter, more subtle "letters" of faith (*The Alphabet of Grace, Telling the Truth, A Room Called Remember*), as well as a series of memoirs. Sometimes he would experiment with other forms, such as collected sermons or the "theological ABC" books (*Peculiar Treasures, Wishful Thinking, Whistling in the Dark*). All of them convey Buechner's personal voice, his deliberate mining of subterranean strata for the hidden message of God. Like a beachcomber, he goes over and over the same patch of sand, seeking buried treasure.

"Literature deals with the ordinary," said James Joyce; "the unusual and extraordinary belong to journalism." By that definition, Buechner's work fits the category of literature. Annie Dillard chose the world of nature as her text; Buechner chose his own life. For him writing is a form of self-discovery, a "conscious remembering" as he once called it. He writes not about Iraq, China, or the crisis of postmodernism, rather about a faint memory of his grandmother Naya, or about the old mill down the road, or about two apple tree limbs clacking together in the backyard.

His approach harks back to the Middle Ages, to mystics who sat in cells all day, gazing inward and exploring the soul's inner depths. Buechner at least walks outdoors, strikes up conversations, has a family to fuss over, and takes an occasional trip. From this raw material he forges memoirs-in-process. The reader has no idea where the words are going, and sometimes gets the sense that neither does Buechner. He assumes the role of an unobtrusive observer who peers out on the world—sometimes bemused, sometimes bewildered, always surprised—rather than a stage manager who manipulates props to fit his personal point of view.

The same silent-observer style, Buechner claims, also drives his fiction. " 'Be still and know that I am God,' is the advice of the Psalmist, and I've always taken it to be good literary advice too. Be still the way Tolstoy is still, or Anthony Trollope is still, so your characters can speak for themselves and come alive in their own immortal way. If you're a writer like me, you try less to impose a shape on the hodgepodge than to see what shape emerges from it, is hidden in it. If minor characters show signs of becoming major characters, you at least give them a shot at it because in the world of fiction it may take many pages before you find out who the major characters really are just as in the real world it may take you many years to find out that the stranger you talked to for half an hour once in a railway station may have done more to point you to where your true homeland lies than your closest friend or your psychiatrist."

In his recent volume *The Longing for Home,* Buechner draws a contrast between the news of the day reported on television each night—wars, elections, natural disasters—and the news of the day that transpires in our private worlds. Some of the things that happen there are so small that we hardly notice them, yet they help compose the day-by-day story of who we are. "Their news is the news of what we are becoming or failing to become," he says, which may be the most important news of all.

In the same vein, Buechner believes that if God speaks at all in this world, it is into our everyday personal lives. In searching for God, many people tend to look for the miraculous and supernatural. Instead we should be attending to the ordinary: waking and sleeping and above all dreaming, what we remember and what we forget, what makes us smile and what makes us cry, what delights and what depresses us. In the most commonplace events of a day, God speaks, and Buechner demonstrates through his writing how to listen.

Buechner recommends reviewing this more intimate news during the nightly interval when you first turn out the light and lie in the dark waiting for sleep to come. That is when the events of the day—an unanswered letter, a phone conversation, a tone of voice, a chance meeting at the post office, an unexpected lump in the throat—hint at other, sub-surface meanings.

> If I were called upon to state in a few words the essence of everything I was trying to say both as a novelist and as a preacher, it would be something like this: Listen to your life. See it for the fathomless mystery it is. In the boredom and pain of it no less than in the excitement and gladness: touch, taste, smell your way to the holy and hidden heart of it because in the last analysis all moments are key moments, and life itself is grace.
>
> (From *Now and Then*)

That very notion of Buechner's prompted me to move halfway across the country. I had lived happily for thirteen years in downtown Chicago, a lively and underrated city. I went to concerts, movies, and plays, and could choose from two dozen ethnic restaurants within walking distance. I wrote in coffee shops and on benches in Lincoln Park. I got to know the neighbors and shopkeepers, and even the panhandlers. Life was rich—so rich in fact, that it ultimately drowned out any inner voice. In the cacophony of car alarms, bus horns, and drunken Cubs baseball fans, I could no longer listen to my life in the sense Buechner advocates. Chicago gave me plenty to write about—I need only take a walk to meet the beggar who called himself Tut Uncommon and the shop owner down the street who, I found out, was the notorious Tokyo Rose of World War II infamy—but always other people's stories, not my own.

I moved to Colorado to explore, as Buechner suggests, the ordinary life that lies hidden inside each one of us. Amid the tedium and pain there lies mystery, and grace to be mined. I wanted to find my own voice, to peer inside rather than out, and to do so I needed a more nurturing environment, a place of quietness and solitude.

On the average day now, I see more wild animals than people. When the writing stalls, I take a walk, only instead of plunging into the sensory overload of Clark Street I now walk on a soft carpet of pine needles or in untracked snow. I understand the change Buechner describes after his move from New York to Vermont. After eight years, I am just now learning to listen.

I t is one thing to spill your own secrets, and quite another to spill someone else's. Several times Buechner and I have discussed the occupational hazards of writing, especially the unavoidable wounds we inflict on people close to us.

For this reason, only late in his career did Buechner dredge up certain family secrets. He began to write of other family members' depression, and his own; and of a daughter's life-threatening battle with anorexia. Out of consideration for his mother, who jealously guarded family secrets, Buechner did not write directly of his father's suicide for decades, though scenes of suicide haunt his novels. His mother reacted with fury to one such scene, and could barely speak to him for days. Finally Buechner decided that he had as much right to tell his father's story as his mother had not to tell her husband's story, and his memoirs began to probe the family tragedy. To Fred's amazement, his mother simply refused to read the accounts he had feared to write for so long.

Janet Malcolm, writing in the *New Yorker,* suggests that an author initially functions like a nourishing, supportive mother. We coax out a person's deepest secrets, nodding sympathetically, gently pressing for more details. "You can trust me," we imply. "Tell me everything." But when we move into the writing phase, we switch roles and become the authoritarian, objective father. We make judgments, and cull our material until we have a thematic whole to present. That process inevitably distorts, and often wounds.

I felt something of this shift, in fact, when I decided to write about Frederick Buechner. For more than two decades we had been friends, corresponding, occasionally talking on the telephone, visiting in person when our travel paths crossed. Suddenly I stepped out of the friendship and began evaluating him as a writer, sorting through his life for themes and patterns. I "objectified" him, and quite naturally he disagreed with some of my judgments. Our friendship survived intact, but the experience reminded me of the unfair power that writers wield.

Why do we do it, we writers? "Of making many books there is no end," sighed the Teacher of Ecclesiastes some three millennia ago, and fifty thousand new ones will appear this year alone. Yet we keep at it, cranking out more and more words, with the potential to bring harm as well as comfort. I think we do it because each of us has nothing else to offer than a living point of view that differentiates us from every other person on this planet. We must tell our stories to someone.

Dying people—a passenger on a Japanese airliner falling from the skies in 1985, a crew member on a Russian submarine that sank in 2000, Jewish prisoners in the extermination camps, zeks in the Soviet Gulag—write as if by instinct to record something of their lives for posterity. Those of us who make a living at it cultivate that instinct every day. We are called to be stewards of our singular point of view, and stewards of the strange power of words through which we express it.

Every writer must overcome a kind of shyness, putting out of mind the fear that we are being arrogant by thrusting ourselves upon you the reader, and egotistical by assuming our words are worth your time. Why should you care about what I have to say? What right have I to impose myself on you? In another context, Simone Weil presents a kind of answer: "I cannot conceive the necessity for God to love me, when I feel so clearly that even with human beings affection for me can only be a mistake. But I can easily imagine that he loves that perspective of creation which can only be seen from the point where I am." That is all any writer can offer, especially a writer of faith: a unique perspective of creation, a point of view visible only from the point where I am.

Everything I write is colored by my family dysfunctions, my upbringing in Southern fundamentalism, my halting pilgrimage—indeed, every writer represented in this book sees the world through a unique set of eyes. We can only write with passion about our own experiences, no one else's. I find that readers respond not to the specifics of my experience, but rather to what they summon up. In the reader, words work a different effect than they worked in me as I composed them. I write about fundamentalism: readers respond with stories about a strict Roman Catholic or Plymouth Brethren upbringing. Somehow my rendering of church, family, and my tentative steps toward faith strikes a sympathetic chord; it *provokes* something.

As I compare my background with Frederick Buechner's, on the surface I find little in common. He came from upper-class roots, lost a father to suicide, wintered in Bermuda, attended a private school, found instant success as a novelist, moved to a sylvan estate in rural New England. Yet such is the power of his evocation that when he describes his life he may as well be describing my own.

A time came, nonetheless, when Buechner felt the need to change his writing. Enough of introspection, he thought. Enough of flawed, sin-prone moderns like himself. With no conscious thought of what to write next, he picked up the *Penguin Dictionary of Saints,* hoping to come across some historical saint of the past, perhaps a truly holy person. The book opened to Godric, an eleventh-century English saint and a figure unknown to him. As he read, it struck him that Godric was Leo Bebb, one of Buechner's oddball, earthy fictional characters, in an earlier incarnation: yes, a holy man, a missionary, a body-torturing ascetic who kept two pet snakes, a rough man who became per-

haps England's first great lyric poet; but also a man who took his own
sister to bed and who waged a lifelong war against lust, the "ape gib-
bering in his loins," as Buechner would later put it.

Buechner emerged from this book with a new definition of saint: a
"life-giver" who makes others come alive in a new way, a garden-vari-
ety human being through whose life the power and the glory of God
are made manifest even though the saint himself may be standing
knee-deep in muck. That definition, of course, applies potentially to
all of us—which is precisely why Buechner urges us to look to the ordinary, to listen to our lives and seek God in the most unexpected
places, for there will God most likely be found.

Buechner came across a similar character in the sixth-century Irish
saint known as Brendan the Navigator, and wrote a book about him
too. "He was a haggard sort of man as I pictured him, in many of the
ways that I also am haggard, a loose-footed sort of a red-headed, in-
hibited, nimble-tongued, miracle-working man." And when he later
chose to write about a biblical character *(Son of Laughter)*, he settled
on Jacob, the inveterate conniver who challenged God to a wrestling
match and got a new name the next morning. Is it any accident that
God identified his chosen people as the children of Israel, "the
wrestler's children," the offspring of one who had grappled so fiercely
through the night?

Buechner discovered that even saints renowned for their holiness
were not so different from his own fictional creations, and not so different from the flesh-and-blood people around him, or from himself.
The books of memoirs-in-process continued to flow as he kept prob-
ing his past and his present, mining for grace.

If you tell me Christian commitment is a kind of thing that has
happened to you once and for all like some kind of spiritual plastic surgery, I say go to, go to, you're either pulling the wool over
your own eyes or trying to pull it over mine. Every morning you
should wake up in your bed and ask yourself: "Can I believe it
all again today?" No, better still, don't ask it till after you've read
The New York Times, till after you've studied that daily record of

the world's brokenness and corruption, which should always stand side by side with your Bible. Then ask yourself if you can believe in the Gospel of Jesus Christ again for that particular day. If your answer's always Yes, then you probably don't know what believing means. At least five times out of ten the answer should be No because the No is as important as the Yes, maybe more so. The No is what proves you're human in case you should ever doubt it. And then if some morning the answer happens to be really Yes, it should be a Yes that's choked with confession and tears and . . . great laughter.

(From *The Return of Ansel Gibbs*)

Thirty years have passed since the Buechners moved to the house in rural Vermont and Fred settled into his writing routine. The property had passed down to Fred's wife, and she domesticated it with outdoor things: flowers, a huge vegetable garden that feeds the deer as well as the family, horses, chickens, a pig "who grew to the size of a large refrigerator," goats, some cattle. To the household Fred mainly contributed a collection of books, "which, unlike people, can always be depended upon to tell the same stories in the same way and are always there when you need them and can always be set aside when you need them no longer." He converted part of a barn into a kind of library to hold his many volumes, and for years that barn served as his writer's refuge where he would retreat to fashion his own books.

Eventually, Buechner added a study onto the back of the house, a bright, airy room looking out onto a pond, a jagged line of stone fences, a stand of birch, a valley, a three thousand-acre preserve of hardwoods. "I call it my 'magic kingdom,' " he says, and little wonder. Here are displayed Buechner's most valued books, many re-bound in oiled leather and gold leaf: first editions of John Donne's *Sermons* and Foxe's *Book of Martyrs,* an original copy of Dickens's *Christmas Carol,* others by Ben Jonson, Joseph Conrad, F. Scott Fitzgerald, Oscar Wilde. It takes several shelves just to hold the many first editions, in various languages, of Buechner's cherished Oz collection. Shelves by the windows hold other objects of delight and whimsy: a kaleidoscope, paired magnets that "suspend" in air, Dorothy's ruby slippers, a model of Humpty-Dumpty, a gargoyle.

In this room he sits in an upholstered chair by the fireplace, feet propped on an ottoman, and writes on unlined notebook paper with a felt-tip pen. "If you made a video of a writer's life, it would be hopelessly boring," he says. "I sit in this chair and make marks on a page. That's all you can see. I am sinking into my self, of course, into the place where dreams and intuitions come from. It is a holy place. But to an observer, I am not doing much at all."

Not a single other dwelling is visible from Buechner's study: leaning on an invisible pulpit, he addresses an invisible audience. Likewise, the results of Buechner's labors remain mostly hidden. He sells thousands of books, but hears from only a small sampling of readers. Some tell him his books saved their faith, or that he was the first Christian writer who seemed authentic. I was present at Wheaton College when a troubled young student stood in a large hall and said into a microphone, "Mr. Buechner, I would like to say that your novels mean more to me than the cross of Christ itself." Buechner was flustered and embarrassed—how could anyone reply to such a remark? What the student probably meant was that Buechner's novels had presented truth in a more penetrating way than he had ever heard before, especially in church.

Once, upon returning to Vermont after a winter holiday, Buechner found this message on his answering machine: "You don't know me but I am a fan of yours. I just wanted to tell you I have twice in the last six weeks contemplated suicide, and it was because of your books that I didn't do it." Given Buechner's family history, that message lodged like an arrow: hearing it, he said, "meant more to me than winning the Nobel Prize."

Because of scattered responses like these, Buechner does not downplay his pastoral role by elevating the "art" of his fiction and dismissing his nonfiction as somehow less valuable. Writing is his ministry: vicarious, indirect, mediated, perhaps, but ministry nonetheless. "I used to hang my head at such responses and say, 'God, if you only knew who I am.' Now I'm more likely to say, 'Yes, I'm a fool, hypocrite, weirdo, but God in his mercy chose me to present himself to you.' We have this treasure in vessels of clay . . . Mine is a disorganized, unstructured kind of ministry, but it is, I hope, a legitimate one."

Still, apart from these few messages from readers, Buechner remains largely disconnected from the people to whom he ministers. He has not found a satisfying church nearby. "I've found that most ministers preach out of their shallows more than out of their depths," he says. "I rarely go to hear them and when I do, I feel guilty about my negative reaction. So many churches remind me of dysfunctional families, full of loneliness and buried pain, dominated by an authority figure. Except for a marvelous Episcopal church I attended near Wheaton, I have found no church that truly ministers to me. Al-Anon support groups come closest to what I wish the church would be."

Most battles of faith, therefore, Buechner fights alone. He has no community of Christian friends nearby. Devotional writers whom others admire—Kathleen Norris, Henri Nouwen, Thomas Merton—for the most part fail to move him. He finds spiritual nourishment in poets such as John Donne, George Herbert, and Gerard Manley Hopkins, but as a source of artistic inspiration he usually turns to other novelists: Graham Greene, William Maxwell, Flannery O'Connor. Increasingly, he struggles with melancholy.

"I had my seventieth birthday, and it was the only one that really made an impression," he says. "Forty, fifty, sixty—those birthdays slid right by. This one made me feel shadowy and sad, geriatric. My great friend the poet James Merrill died. We knew each other for 55 years. We wrote our first books together one summer in Maine. Yet I don't want to write out of the shadowy part of myself, but out of the part that is still young and full of joy. I think of the lovely fairy-tale plays Shakespeare wrote in his old age: *The Winter's Tale, The Tempest.* I think of the last self-portraits of Rembrandt, suffused with golden light.

"One project, a novel based on Mary Magdalene, depressed me so badly that I abandoned it. And then one day came a miracle of grace. I was reading the Apocryphal Book of Tobit, a Hebrew fairy tale about a dog and a journey and a fish, a tale full of magic. Joy welled up. That night, or early the next morning about 4:45 A.M., I got out of bed and began a retelling of the story of Tobit and his son Tobias. Nothing I have written ever gave me such pleasure, and I finished it in a month and two days. It is called *On the Road with the Archangel.*

"Every once in a while a book comes along like that, a gift of grace. Like an artesian well, almost all you have to do is let it flow out under its own power. At least for yourself, the writer, it comes with such life of its own that it almost bowls you over. When that happens, I feel as if the book is gathered in the palm of my hand. It is there, I am holding it. Of course you have to work very hard to get the language and the form right, but the one thing you don't have to do is struggle to bring it to life. The gift comes first, and then the labor."

Buechner's chronicles of a spiritual journey have, like Annie Dillard's, achieved the rare feat of attracting readers from two polarized worlds, the Eastern elite and conservative Christians. His work divides evenly between fiction and nonfiction (around fifteen books of each), and Buechner notes that the two genres roughly fit his contrasting audiences: the fiction speaks to the "cultured despisers" of religion while his nonfiction, more overt, finds its primary audience among those already committed to the faith.

This straddling feat has cost him and is, in fact, the central ambiguity of his career. "I am too religious for the secular reader and too secular for the religious reader," Buechner laments. Secular reviewers, noting him to be an ordained Presbyterian minister, sometimes prejudge his work. Buechner admits that seeking ordination was probably the dumbest move he could have made for his writing career. "The world is full of people—many of them, I regret to say, book reviewers—who, if they hear that a minister has written a novel, feel that they know, even without reading it, what sort of a novel it must be. It must be essentially a sermon with illustrations in the form of character and dialogue, and, as such, its view of life must be one-sided, simplistic, naive, with everything subordinated to the one central business of scoring some kind of homiletical bull's-eye. I protest that, in my case anyway, this simply is not so."

On the other hand, conservative Christian readers wonder why the Christian message in Buechner's novels remains so subtle, and why he insists on portraying characters as so, well, *human,* complete with sex lives and a disturbing penchant for sin. Buechner responds that he writes of people with feet of clay because they are the only kind of people he has met, including himself.

Writers, like farmers and fishermen, tend to dwell on the disappointing aspects of their work. Buechner has not made a breakthrough in sales on the level of, say, Scott Peck or Thomas Moore. He sinks into instant depression when he visits a "Book Superstore" that contains not a single copy of his thirty-odd books. He winces when he reads in the *New York Times* a reviewer's comment describing him as someone "whom I wrongly did not read because I thought he was a propagandist." And he tires of answering the letters from seminary students asking why he felt it necessary to include the scene of incest in *Godric,* or why he made the hero-evangelist of his Bebb novels a sexual exhibitionist. Furthermore, Buechner objects to the label "Christian novelist" often slapped on him, insisting it only applies in the sense it would apply if a physicist wrote a novel: of course the author's outlook would suffuse the novel, and its content may well touch upon the field of physics, but that would hardly make it a "physics novel," any more than a novel written by a woman necessarily makes it a "woman's novel."

Yet in more ways than he is prone to admit, Buechner has indeed succeeded in straddling two worlds. He has maintained close friendships with literary giants such as the poet (now deceased) James Merrill and his former student John Irving, who acknowledged his debt to Buechner in the preface to *A Prayer for Owen Meany.* He gives readings at the New York Public Library. His novel *Godric* was nominated for a Pulitzer Prize. Meanwhile, Frederick Buechner and conservative Christians have got much better acquainted. Christian colleges adapt his novels into plays and invite him to their campuses to give readings. Ministers quote him from the pulpit, and fledgling writers study his prose style. I have a hunch, in fact, that Buechner has become the most quoted living writer among Christians of influence. Appreciation of his craft continues to grow—who else gets equally laudatory reviews in *Christianity Today* and *The Christian Century,* as well as the *New York Times Book Review?*

For those of us who labor in the same vineyard, who likewise make a living by shuffling words around on paper, Buechner offers a living model of writing as a form of faith-expression. I have many shelves loaded with books written by Christians. Most of them, I regret to say, would hold little appeal to anyone not already committed to the faith they espouse. People of faith stumble across God everywhere: in nature, in the Bible, in daily acts of Providence. God seems amply evident. But the secular mind sees no such evidence, and wonders how is it even possible to find God in the maze of competing claims. Unless we truly understand that viewpoint, and speak in terms a faithless person can understand, our words will have the quaint and useless ring of a foreign language.

I learned from Buechner the advantage of saying too little rather than too much. As he wrote in *The Eyes of the Heart,* "I have seen with the eyes of my heart the great hope to which he has called us, but out of some shyness or diffidence I rarely speak of it, and in my books I have tended to write about it for the most part only obliquely, hesitantly, ambiguously, for fear of losing the ear and straining the credulity of the readers to whom such hope seems just wishful thinking. For fear of overstating, I have tended especially in my nonfiction books to understate, because that seemed a more strategic way of reaching the people I would most like to reach who are the ones who more or less don't give religion the time of day."

Christian literature often gives off the scent of rationalization. The author starts with an unshakable conclusion and then sets out to travel whatever logical course might support that conclusion. Much of what I read on depression, on doubt, on suicide, on suffering, on homosexuality, seems written by people who begin with a Christian conclusion and who have never been through the anguished steps familiar to a person struggling with depression, doubt, suicide, suffering, or homosexuality. No resolution could be so matter-of-fact to a person who has actually survived such a journey.

When I began writing openly about my faith, I concluded that I had only one thing to offer: honesty. I had heard enough church propaganda growing up. I would cling to the stance of a pilgrim, not a propagandist, describing life with God as it actually plays out, not as it is supposed to play out. Not everyone agrees. A publisher once asked me to consider changing a book title from *Disappointment with God* to something cheerier, perhaps *Overcoming Disappointment with God*. I thought about it, and decided to keep the title, because disappointed people were the ones I most wanted to address.

I nearly despaired of the usefulness of any writing about faith until I discovered Buechner. It seemed to me at the time that Christians were reading primarily for the experience of nodding agreement, "Yes, that's true," whereas great literature makes us stop and ponder: "I've never imagined it that way before." For Buechner, faith was an act of discovery, not a packet of orthodoxy dispensed from on high. He made me slow down and pay attention, first to the words and then to the thoughts behind them. He did not use life as an illustration of his point; his point, rather, named what he had already portrayed about life. As William James wrote in *The Varieties of Religious Experience*, "The truth is that in the metaphysical and religious sphere, articulate reasons are cogent for us only when our inarticulate feelings of reality have already been impressed in favor of the same conclusion."

To speak to a reader's inarticulate feelings of reality is a writer's greatest challenge. We live odd lives, we writers. We sit in small rooms with little sensory input, contemplating the words before us at that moment. In effect, we fabricate in those words the semblance of time and materiality while disconnected from them both. Writing is the most vicarious of acts. I write about skiing while not skiing, about eating while not eating, about love while not loving, and worship while not worshiping.

The first book of Buechner's that I read, *Telling the Truth*, gave me hope that even in the vicariousness of the writing act, truth can be told. The tedious process of arranging and then rearranging words on a page—the alphabet of grace—can, like a catalyst in a chemical reaction, create for a reader a startling new reality. Through Buechner's own pen, the old story of Hosea and Gomer becomes first a juicy tale of cuckolding and gullibility, and then an unforgettable parable of God's grace. The grotesque and irreducible character of Leo Bebb becomes a reminder that God can work through traitors and perverts, and in one sense only works through traitors and perverts. Buechner's introspective gaze into a writer's oh-so-dull life reveals that boredom fits like a deceptive mask over fathomless mystery. By attending to his life, I pay attention to my own—the act of vicariousness fulfilled.

GETTING STARTED WITH FREDERICK BUECHNER:

With thirty books to choose from, the newcomer to Buechner may well need a roadmap. I still like *Telling the Truth* as a concise introduction to his thought and style; *Peculiar Treasures* offers another fine example of his prose style. *Listening to Your Life* collects excerpts of several of his works in the format of daily meditations. Buechner expresses his own life most personally in a series of memoirs: *The Sacred Journey, Now and Then, Telling Secrets, The Eyes of the Heart*. In the field of fiction, he is best known for the novels based on the character Leo Bebb, conveniently collected into one volume, *The Book of Bebb*. Do not ignore *Godric* and *Brendan*, however, which display Buechner's stylistic ability at its best, or his most recent novel *The Storm*, which has echoes of Shakespeare's *The Tempest*.

I doubt that anyone born in the last thirty years could possibly imagine the fear we lived under, those of us moving through adolescence at the height of the Cold War. For our school science projects we made bomb shelters, digging deep holes in our backyards and stocking them with our favorite comic books and snack foods. We watched educational films on the effects of thermonuclear war and learned, to the accompaniment of a bouncy soundtrack, the "Duck and cover!" technique of crawling under our school desks to lessen exposure to radioactive fallout. I lived in Atlanta, Georgia, just within range of Cuba, and during the Cuban missile crisis each homeroom period began with a "Duck and cover" exercise.

My brother and I read aloud to each other horrifying accounts of what Communists did to their enemies. They pulled out your fingernails and toenails, or jammed bamboo splinters up the nail beds. They tied you down and slowly dripped water on your head until you went crazy. They set loose spiders and rats and poisonous snakes on your naked body. They cut off your fingers, one by one. They buried you alive. When they took over a town, they lined up all the occupants and examined hands; if yours showed any calluses, that meant you belonged to the worker class and they just might let you live. If you could speak Russian, or Chinese as the case may be, they also might let you live. Otherwise, they would torture you for a few days and then kill you.

In a determined effort to stay alive, the

Chapter 12

SHUSAKU

ENDO

A PLACE

FOR

TRAITORS

two of us launched countermeasures. We scouted nearby woods for hideouts the enemies might not find. Hadn't some Southerners survived General Sherman's assault by hiding out like that for months at a time? We raked leaves with barehanded vigor in order to develop blisters and calluses on our schoolboy hands. Still afraid, we decided to study the Communists' languages. My brother signed up for a course in Russian and I took Chinese so that, no matter which direction the attackers came from, we would at least have a chance to talk them out of killing us. (Stories from my Chinese teacher, an upper-class refugee who escaped during Chairman Mao's reign of terror, did little to allay my fears.)

Church further fueled our terror, adding gruesome accounts of what Stalin and Mao had done to the Christians. Soldiers would march into a church service, line up all the believers, and demand that they denounce Christ. Those who agreed, they would immediately reward with presents and food. Those who refused, they would kill, slowly and cruelly, in front of the terrorized congregation.

"What would you say?" our pastor demanded. "Would you stand firm for your faith, or would you betray the one who died for you?" It was a terrible question for anyone to contemplate, much less a four-teen-year-old plagued with questions about his faith. I practiced Chinese calligraphy and raked leaves as if my life depended on it, because I believed it surely did.*

M uch later, after I had grown up and forgotten all my Chinese, after the threat of nuclear war had receded, I came across historical accounts of a similar persecution that occurred several centuries ago. At one point in history Japan seemed the most fruitful mission field in Asia. Francis Xavier, one of the seven original Jesuits, landed there in 1549 and spent two years establishing a church. Within a gen-

---

*Today, pastors ask their teenagers the same question, holding up Columbine High School martyr Cassie Bernall as the model of courageous faith. Only now the enemy threat comes from within, rather than overseas.

eration the number of Christians had swelled to three hundred thousand. Xavier called Japan "the delight of my heart . . . the country in the Orient most suited to Christianity."

As that century came to an end, however, the shoguns' suspicion of foreigners, exacerbated by the divisions among Christians, led to a change in policy. The shoguns expelled the Jesuits, and required that all Christians renounce their faith and register as Buddhists. Twenty-six crucifixions soon followed and the age of Japanese Christian martyrs began.

The *fumie* plaque—a bronze portrait of Jesus, or the Madonna and child, enclosed in a small wooden frame—became the ultimate test of faith. Japanese who agreed to step on the *fumie* were pronounced apostate Christians and set free. Those who refused, the shoguns hunted down and killed, in the most successful extermination attempt in church history. Some were tied to stakes in the sea to await the high tides that would slowly drown them, while others were bound and tossed off rafts; some were scalded in boiling hot springs, and still others were hung upside down over a pit full of dead bodies and excrement. I had been raised on inspiring stories of martyrs advancing the cause: "The blood of Christians is the seed of the church," said Tertullian. Not so in Japan, where the blood of the martyrs was nearly the annihilation of the church.

Nearly, but not entirely. In the late nineteenth century, when Japan finally permitted a Catholic church in Nagasaki to serve Western visitors, priests were astonished to see Japanese Christians streaming down from the hills; they were Kakure Kirishitans, or crypto-Christians, who had been meeting in secret for two hundred and forty years. Worship without benefit of a Bible or book of liturgy had taken a toll, however: their faith survived as a curious amalgam of Catholicism, Buddhism, animism, and Shintoism. Over the years the Latin words of the mass had devolved into a kind of pidgin language. *Ave Maria gratia plena dominus tecum benedicta* became *Ame Maria karassa binno domisu terikobintsu,* and no one had the slightest idea what these sounds meant. Believers revered the "closet god," bundles of cloth wrapped around Christian medallions and statues, which were concealed in a closet disguised as a Buddhist shrine.*

In one of history's terrible ironies, the second atomic bomb exploded directly above Japan's largest community of Christians, destroying Nagasaki's cathedral. Clouds had obscured the intended city, forcing the bombing crew to turn toward a secondary target. A museum in the rebuilt city traces the history of Christianity in Japan, featuring relics from the age of Japanese Christian martyrs.

In the 1950s, the very period when I was growing up in fear of nuclear holocaust, a young writer named Shusaku Endo used to visit this museum in one of the two cities that had actually experienced such a fate. Drawn to the story of the martyrs, he would stand gazing at one particular glass case, which displayed an actual *fumie* from the seventeenth century. Black marks defaced the bronze portrait, which was so worn down he could barely make out the figure of Mary holding Jesus—the result, Endo learned, of human toes, the accumulated impressions made by thousands of Christians committing the *fumie*.

The *fumie* obsessed Endo. Would I have stepped on it? he wondered. What did those people feel as they apostatized? What kind of people were they? Catholic history books recorded only the brave, glorious martyrs, not the cowards who forsook the faith. They were twice damned: first by the silence of God at the time of torture and later by the silence of history. Endo vowed that he would tell the story of the apostates—and through novels such as *Silence* and *The Samurai* he kept that vow.

When I first discovered Shusaku Endo, I sensed an immediate bond, for he had grown up possessed by the same fear and self-doubt that had so troubled me in my youth. Standing in Hell Valley, a site where many Japanese Christians had been martyred, he concluded that probably he too would have denied his faith rather than endure such pain.

---

*Around thirty thousand of these Kakure Christians still worship today, and eighty house churches carry on the tradition of the "closet god." Roman Catholics have tried to embrace them and bring them back into the mainstream of faith, but the Kakure resist. "We have no interest in joining his church," said one of their leaders after a visit from Pope John Paul II; "we, and nobody else, are true Christians."

As he further reflected, Endo realized what had drawn him so forcefully to the museum display case. The story of the Japanese Christians in the seventeenth century had disturbing echoes in his own life in the twentieth. Though he had never faced the wrath of the shoguns, ever since childhood he had felt a constant, unrelieved tension over his faith. Externally he was a Christian; what was he underneath?

At the age of ten, Endo had returned to Japan from Manchuria with his mother, who was fleeing a bad marriage. Suffering from the pain and social rejection of a divorce—a rarity in Japan—his mother found solace in the devout faith of her sister and so she converted to Catholicism. She faithfully attended mass each morning. In order to please his mother, Shusaku submitted to baptism as well. But had he meant it? Was he in fact the reverse image of the Kakure, a Christian who had gone through the externals while secretly betraying Christ?

"I became a Catholic against my will," he later decided, likening his faith to an arranged marriage, a forced union with a wife chosen by his mother. He tried to leave that wife—for Marxism, for atheism, even contemplating suicide for a time—but his attempts to break away always failed. He could not live with this arranged wife and he could not live without her. Meanwhile, she kept loving him, and to his surprise eventually he grew to love her in return.

I recognized in Endo's groping toward faith an odd parallel with my own, lived out in a very different context. During high school years I attended a fundamentalist church I now see as almost cultic. I prayed the prayers, went forward at the altar calls, and recited the testimonies, but inside I could not stop doubting. Did I truly believe, or was I merely mimicking the behavior of those around me? I learned to excel at such behavior, and mostly it brought me rejection and shame.

Even now those scenes of hot shame surge up. Standing before a high school Speech class trying to explain why I wouldn't be able to accompany them on a class trip to view Laurence Olivier's movie version of *Othello* (too "worldly"). Asking a leering coach's permission to miss the square-dance lessons in Physical Education on religious grounds (also too worldly). Carrying a thick red Bible around on top of my school books so that perhaps someone might ask me about my faith. Sitting on a garish red-and-white bus, piano-equipped and marked in large letters "Youth For Christ Bible Club," as it lazily circled the parking lot, stirring up scorn. Listening to a Biology teacher sarcastically explain to the class why my 20-page term paper had failed to demolish Charles Darwin's 592-page *Origin of the Species*. Shame, alienation, and inferiority defined my adolescence. Like Endo, I grew up feeling outcast.

Later, when I realized that church had taught me lies as well as truth, I felt lost, homeless, adrift. For what had I sacrificed my pride and prepared for martyrdom? A religion of racists, anti-intellectuals, and social misfits? Reaching for another analogy, Endo likens his pilgrimage of faith to a young boy squirming inside a suit of clothes. He searches in vain for a better fitting suit, or perhaps a kimono. Endo said he was constantly "re-tailoring with my own hands the Western suit my mother had put on me, and changing it into a Japanese garment that would fit my Japanese body." I too tried on different suits of clothes, and could never find one to replace the Christian suit I had been dressed in as a child.

Endo's life story reads like the plot of one of his novels. As a child in Manchuria he had lived as an alien, a despised Japanese occupier. Returning to Japan, where the Christian church comprised far less than 1 percent of the population, he suffered once again the anguish of an alien. Classmates bullied him for his association with a Western religion. World War II intensified this sense of estrangement: Endo had always looked to the West as his spiritual homeland, but these were the people now vaporizing the cities of Japan.

After the war he traveled to France to study French Catholic novelists such as François Mauriac and George Bernanos. Yet France hardly made him feel welcome either: as one of the first Japanese overseas exchange students, and the only one in Lyons, he was spurned this time on account of race, not religion. The Allies had cranked out a steady stream of anti-Japanese propaganda, and Endo found himself the target of racial abuse from fellow Christians. "Slanty-eyed gook," some called him. He learned, as I did, that Christians have manifold ways of betraying their faith. Some publicly renounce it. Others, more subtly, live in ways that contradict it.

During his three years in France, Endo fell into a depression. Worse, he contracted tuberculosis, had to have a lung removed, and spent many months laid up in hospitals. He concluded that Christianity had, in effect, made him ill. Rejected in his homeland, rejected in his spiritual homeland, Endo underwent a grave crisis of faith.

B efore returning to Japan from his studies in Europe, Endo visited Palestine in order to research the life of Jesus, and while there he made a transforming discovery: Jesus too knew rejection. More, Jesus' life was *defined* by rejection. His neighbors ran him out of town, his family questioned his sanity, his closest friends betrayed him, and his fellow citizens traded his life for that of a common criminal. Throughout his ministry, Jesus purposely moved among the poor and the rejected: he touched those with leprosy, dined with the unclean, forgave thieves, adulterers, and prostitutes.

This insight into Jesus hit Endo with the force of revelation. From the faraway vantage point of Japan he had viewed Christianity as a triumphant, Constantinian faith. He had studied the Holy Roman Empire and the glittering Crusades, had admired the grand cathedrals of Europe, had dreamed of living in a nation where one could be a Christian without disgrace. Now, studying the Bible in its homeland, he saw that Jesus himself had not avoided "dis-grace." Many of the depictions of Jesus in Western culture were merely projections of Roman images of glory and imperial power. Jesus himself came as the Suffering Servant depicted by the prophet Isaiah: "despised and rejected by men, a man of sorrows, and familiar with suffering. Like one from whom men hide their faces . . ." Surely this Jesus, if anyone, could understand the rejection Endo himself was going through.

I must say that when I first encountered this Jesus, it hit me too with the force of revelation. As I studied the gospels, I noticed a pattern so consistent it almost reduces to a mathematical formula. The more ungodly, unwholesome, and undesirable the person, the more that person felt attracted to Jesus. And the more righteous, self-assured, and desirable the person, the more that person felt threatened by Jesus. Just the opposite of what most people assume! Evangelical Christians hold up the ideal of a balanced, solid citizen who believes in family values and hangs out with "the right kind." Consider who Jesus hung out with: a prostitute, an unclean man with leprosy, a moral outcast, a Roman centurion, a mixed-race woman with five divorces. Meanwhile the Pharisees—upright citizens who studied the Scriptures and scrupulously obeyed the law—the ruling establishment, the pillars of society: all these saw Jesus as a threat.

I discovered the Jesus of reversal, through Endo, just as evangelicals were gaining national attention and political power. It occurred to me that a phrase like Repentant Majority or Forgiven Majority might be a more correct way of describing Christians than Moral Majority. Such a label would credit God for any trace of goodness, thus assuring that, in Paul's phrase, "no one can boast." Instead, we convey an unctuousness that drives away the very people to whom Jesus directed his appeal: "Come to me, *all you who are weary and burdened,* and I will give you rest," he said. I could find no prod toward success or superiority in the invitations of Jesus. Grace, like water, flows to the lowest part.

How ironic, I thought, that a Japanese man rejected by the Christian West was introducing me to this Jesus. I began to read Shusaku Endo in search of the Suffering Servant, who understood rejection as well as anyone who has ever lived. As a young person in a fundamentalist church, I had known rejection and shame from the broader culture. As a struggling Christian I had received rejection from the church itself: it wanted me to conform and not quibble, to believe and not question. Now, in Jesus, I met someone whose message centered on the rejects.

Jesus told stories about lost sheep and prodigal sons, about bizarre banquets where only the poor and sick bother to attend. Truly, as the American slaves used to sing, "Nobody knows the trouble I've seen—nobody knows but Jesus." I began to believe that Jesus welcomed reluctant followers, even traitors, even me. My books *The Jesus I Never*

Knew and *What's So Amazing About Grace?* came into being as I pondered this new side of Jesus, and the sheer wonder of God's grace.

After his research in Palestine, Endo returned to his native land with his faith intact, yet sensing the need to reshape it, to fashion a suit of clothes that would better fit. "Christianity, to be effective in Japan, must change," he decided. He became a novelist, in fact, in order to work out these issues in print. A lean, sickly man, wearing thick glasses, on the fringe of society, he slipped easily into the bookish life of a writer. He began cranking out novels at the rate of one per year, and his pace hardly slowed until his death in 1996.

I first visited Japan in 1997, so I missed any opportunity to interview Shusaku Endo. I found that the paradox of his life continues to this day. By and large, the Christian community does not acknowledge him as one of its own. He had doubts about key doctrines, which made other Christians suspicious of him. Whenever I mentioned him in one of my lectures, a Japanese Christian would come up afterward and solemnly advise me that Endo might not be the best example to use.

In yet another irony, Endo's lifelong fixation on rejection and alienation brought him success and acclaim in the wider culture. He became Japan's best-known living writer, his books translated into twenty-five languages, his name making the short list for the Nobel Prize for Literature. Graham Greene called him "one of the finest living novelists," and luminaries such as John Updike and Annie Dillard joined the chorus of praise. In his later years, Endo served as a cultural icon in Japan, prominent in newspapers and magazines and for a time even hosting a television talk show. In a nation where Christians still do not exceed 1 percent of the population, it seems remarkable that Endo's major books all landed on the best-seller lists, for no important modern novelist worked so exclusively with overt Christian themes.

Endo speaks to the inner person, where lie buried the feelings of shame and rejection that the average Japanese must endure in a culture that honors appropriate and proper behavior, that is unfailingly polite and civil on the outside. Ask any Japanese the difference between *honne,* what takes place on the inside, and *tatemae,* what others see on the outside, and they will nod knowingly. Ask any American, for that matter, or any European or African. Endo explores the crevices of failure and betrayal every person on earth lives with, and often seeks to hide. In doing so, Endo sheds new light on the Christian faith—at once a harshly revealing light that exposes long-hidden corners, and also a softening light that erases shadows.

From the very beginning, Endo sought to probe the differences between the Eastern and Western views of the world. He had been schooled in the Catholic literature of the West, which assumes a Supreme Being separate from creation. Most Japanese, however, believe in no such Supreme Being, and as a result the profound themes of God, sin, guilt, and moral crisis that underlie much Western literature have little relevance to the average Japanese reader.

In the early novels Endo portrays Japan as a kind of swampland (and sometimes a literal swamp) that swallows up all that is foreign, including Christianity. One of his earliest works, *Yellow Man,* shows a French missionary abandoning his priesthood in order to marry a Japanese woman, and then later choosing suicide. The priest wonders aloud whether his God "can sink roots into this wet soil, into this yellow race." In *Volcano,* written a few years later, the foreign priest not only defects but turns seducer, enticing others to give up their faith. Behind these figures looms the silhouette of a lone young man standing before a display case in a Nagasaki museum.

In time, though, the novelist Endo seemed to find a path out of the swampland. Japanese writers have the custom of spinning off light, entertaining works in between their more serious books. In these "entertainments," serialized in periodicals, a new figure emerged from Endo: the good-hearted fool, a Japanese comic version of Dostoevsky's *The Idiot.* Endo's *The Wonderful Fool* presents a bumbling, horse-faced missionary who would easily win an "ugly American" contest were it not for the fact that he is French—Gaston Bonaparte, to be precise, a descendant of the famous emperor. Gaston offends his hosts, commits a cultural *faux pas* every five minutes or so, and seems attracted to all the wrong kind: a stray mongrel, a prostitute, an old hermit, a murderer. Nevertheless, his bumbling/loving actions rekindle life for everyone he touches: the closing scene takes place in a swamp where the love of Gaston moves the murderer—named Endo!—to repentance.

In *The Samurai* and *Silence,* the clash of cultures works itself out in the form of tragedy, not comedy. Both novels reflect actual events and characters from the early 1600s, when shoguns were tightening the noose around the Christian community in Japan. *The Samurai* takes place just as the shoguns are reconsidering their policy of open exchange with the West. A priest leads four samurai on a trade mission to Mexico and Europe, where, hoping to enhance the success of their mission, the samurai become nominal Christians. During their time abroad, however, Japan closes its borders, and upon their return they are executed as traitors. (Overtones of Endo's own life—the nominal baptism, the trip abroad, rejection for a faith he barely believes— abound.)

At least one of the samurai, though, may grasp the true meaning of a martyr's death. His servant Yozo speaks to him of Jesus: not the triumphant, resurrected Christ, rather the rejected One whom Endo himself had come to know on his visits to Palestine:

> I suppose that somewhere in the hearts of men, there's a yearn-
> ing for someone who will be with you throughout your life,
> someone who will never betray you, never leave you—even if
> that someone is just a sick, mangy dog. That man became just
> such a miserable dog for the sake of mankind.

The samurai dies with these words from Yozo ringing in his ears: "From now on he will be beside you. From now on he will attend you."

Critics regard the other novel set in this historical period, *Silence,* as Endo's masterpiece. Its prose is spare and clean, the plot marches inexorably toward a tragic conclusion, the characters achieve a depth rare in Endo's fiction, and indeed the entire atmosphere is suffused with the power of myth. *Silence* follows a Portuguese priest, Rodrigues, on a dangerous mission to Japan. Word has filtered back to Jesuit headquarters that the most famous missionary in Japan, Father Ferreira, has apostatized. Rodrigues, who studied under Father Ferreira in seminary, cannot believe that the great man, his own mentor, would renounce the faith after twenty years of courageous service. He sets sail to find Ferreira, knowing that he likely will not return alive. (All this is based on actual historical characters and events from 1635.)

Upon arrival in Japan, after a harrowing journey, Rodrigues hears the confessions of secret Christians—members of the underground Kakure church—who have not seen a priest in years. One of them, a despicable, cunning fisherman, turns Rodrigues in to the shogun for a reward. Rodrigues holds fast to his faith under torture, even when he faces an unbearable moral situation. Groups of Christians are paraded before him. If he steps on the *fumie,* he is told, they will be set free. He refuses, and they are taken away and killed before his eyes. "He had come to this country to lay down his life for other men, but instead of that the Japanese were laying down their lives one by one for him." Still, no matter what barbarous methods the shogun uses, Rodrigues will not renounce his faith.

As the title intimates, the theme of silence pervades the novel. Over one hundred times Rodrigues sees the haunting face of Jesus, a face he loves and serves; but the face does not speak. It remains silent when the priest is chained to a tree to watch the Christians die, silent when he asks for guidance on whether to commit the *fumie* to set them free, and silent when he prays in his cell at night.

At first it seems *Silence* will pay homage to what has propelled the church through the centuries: the intrepid faith of heroic martyrs. Rodrigues, a priest without guile, has voluntarily taken on a suicidal mission. But in *Silence,* Rodrigues's love and faith extend beyond martyrdom, extend even to the point of apostasy.

One night Rodrigues hears a sound like snoring. The sound, actually moans of pain, comes from Christians hanging upside down over pits, their ears slit so that blood will drip and they will die a slow, agonizing death. These too can be set free, if Rodrigues will only recant. Rodrigues has been warned about this torture by Ferreira, who visited him in his cell. To his horror, he learned on that visit that the great missionary Ferreira had indeed recanted, after just five hours of hanging in the pit. Ferreira urges Rodrigues, too, to step on the *fumie*. It is just a symbol, an external act. He need not really mean it. It will save so many lives . . . And so in the end the priest Rodrigues forfeits his own faith for the love of others.

Endo later complained that *Silence* was misinterpreted because of its title. "People assume that God was silent," he said, when in fact God does speak in the novel. Here is the decisive scene when silence is broken, at the very moment when Rodrigues is contemplating the *fumie*.

"It is only a formality. What do formalities matter?" The interpreter urges him on excitedly. "Only go through with the exterior form of trampling."

The priest raises his foot. In it he feels a dull, heavy pain. This is no mere formality. He will now trample on what he has considered the most beautiful thing in his life, on what he has believed most pure, on what is filled with the ideals and the dreams of man. How his foot aches! And then the Christ in bronze speaks to the priest: "Trample! Trample! I more than anyone know of the pain in your foot. Trample! It was to be trampled on by men that I was born into this world. It was to share men's pain that I carried my cross."

The priest placed his foot on the *fumie*. Dawn broke. And far in the distance the cock crew.

When *Silence* first appeared, in 1966, many Japanese Catholics responded with outrage. Protective of their martyred forebears, they objected to the "romanticization" of apostates like Ferreira and Rodrigues. How easily we forget that the church was founded by disciples who betrayed their master. None was willing to stand by Jesus as the religious and political authorities condemned him to death. At his moment of greatest need, the disciples fled in the darkness. The boldest of the lot, Peter, was the very one who cursed and denied him three times before the cock crew. It was for traitors that Jesus died.

In his own defense, Endo locates the theme of the novel in the transformation of the face of Jesus, not in the transformation of the characters. "To me the most meaningful thing in the novel is the change in the hero's image of Christ," he says. Formerly, Rodrigues had believed in a Jesus of majesty and power. The image of Jesus that had appeared to him more than one hundred times was pure, serene, heavenly. Gradually, though, as Rodrigues's mission fails—and indeed causes the death of many Japanese—the face of Jesus begins to change into one marked by human suffering. What must it have been like for Jesus himself, knowing as he must that the faith he would set loose on the world would result in the persecution and martyrdom of so many throughout history, including so many Japanese? "Brother will betray brother to death, and a father his child . . . All men will hate you because of me . . ."

Weary, hunted, near despair, Rodrigues catches a glimpse of his own reflection in a pool of rainwater, a glimpse that becomes an epiphany:

> There reflected in the water was a tired, hollow face. I don't
> know why, but at that moment I thought of the face of another
> man . . . the face of a crucified man . . . heavy with mud and
> with stubble; it was thin and dirty; it was the face of a haunted
> man, filled with uneasiness and exhaustion.

From that point on, the novel uses words like *suffering, emaciated, worn down,* and *ugly* to describe the face of Jesus. And when the silence finally breaks, just as Rodrigues is about to step on the *fumie,* this face speaks, from the center of the *fumie.* "Trample!" says the face already "worn down and hollow from the constant trampling."

The scheme behind Endo's transformed image of Jesus comes to light in his nonfiction work *A Life of Jesus.* The book sold three hundred thousand copies and for many Japanese remains their primary introduction to the Christian faith. Shusaku Endo believes that Christianity has failed to make much impact on Japan because the Japanese have heard only one side of the story. They have heard about the beauty and majesty: Japanese tourists visit Chartres and Westminster Abbey and with their digital cameras record images of that glory; Japanese choirs and orchestras perform the religious masterpieces of Handel and Bach. But somehow the Japanese have missed another message: of a God who "made himself nothing, taking the very nature of a servant"; of a Son of God who wept, as if helpless, when he approached Jerusalem.

Endo explains that his point of contact with the Japanese centers on the experiences of failure and shame because in his culture these leave the most lasting impact on a person's life. People raised in a Buddhist culture, Endo feels, can best identify with one who suffers with us and allows for our weakness. For Endo himself, the most poignant legacy of Jesus was his undying love, even for—*especially* for—people who betrayed him. When Judas led a lynch mob into the garden, Jesus addressed him as "Friend." His nation had him executed; while stretched out naked in the posture of ultimate disgrace, Jesus roused himself for the cry, "Father, forgive them." To those scandalized by the apparent apostasy of his characters Ferreira and Rodrigues, Endo points to the two great founders of the Christian church: Peter denied Christ three times, Paul led the first persecution of Christians. If grace had not encompassed those two, the church might never have gotten off the ground.

Why is Christianity virtually the only Western practice that has failed to take root in Japan, which so quickly adopted baseball, McDonald's, and rock music? Following another thread of thought, Endo traces its failure to the Western emphasis on the fatherhood of God. Therapist Erich Fromm says that a child from a balanced family receives two kinds of love. Mother love tends to be unconditional, accepting the child no matter what, regardless of behavior. Father love tends to be more provisional, bestowing approval as the child meets certain standards of behavior. Ideally, says Fromm, a child should receive and internalize both kinds of love. According to Endo, Japan, a nation of authoritarian fathers, has understood the father love of God but not the mother love.

An old Japanese saying lists the four most awful things on earth as "fires, earthquakes, thunderbolts, and fathers." On my trips to Japan, many have told me of their authoritarian fathers who never apologize, who remain emotionally distant, who show nothing resembling love or grace, who offer much criticism and little if any encouragement. One woman told me she had actually plotted to kill her father at the age of thirteen, after he sexually abused her. Afraid of capital punishment, she went away to study in America instead. When her mother died, he demanded that she return to care for him, and under Japanese custom she felt obligated. "Last month for the first time in my life, my father thanked me for something I had done," she told me. "I consider that a real victory."

For Christianity to have any appeal to the Japanese, Endo concludes, it must stress instead the mother love of God, the love that forgives wrongs and binds wounds and draws, rather than forces, others to itself. ("O Jerusalem, Jerusalem, you who kill the prophets and stone those sent to you, how often I have longed to gather your children together, as a hen gathers her chicks under her wings, but you were not willing!") "In 'maternal religion' Christ comes to prostitutes, worthless people, misshapen people and forgives them," says Endo. As he sees it, Jesus brought the message of mother love to balance the father love of the Old Testament. A mother's love will not desert even a child who commits a crime; it forgives any weakness. To Endo, what really impressed the disciples was their realization that Christ still loved them even after they had betrayed him. To be proven wrong was nothing new; to be proven wrong and still loved—that was new.

A Life of Jesus fills in the portrait of the mother love of Jesus:

> He was thin; he wasn't much. One thing about him, however—
> he was never known to desert other people if they had trouble.
> When women were in tears, he stayed by their side. When old
> folks were lonely, he sat with them quietly. It was nothing miraculous, but the sunken eyes overflowed with love more profound
> than a miracle. And regarding those who deserted him, those
> who betrayed him, not a word of resentment came to his lips.

No matter what happened, he was the man of sorrows, and he prayed for nothing but their salvation.

That's the whole life of Jesus. It stands out clean and simple, like a single Chinese ideograph brushed on a blank sheet of paper.

Traditional Christians will find Endo's portrayal of Jesus incomplete. He says nothing of Jesus' miracles and, frankly, they seem almost irrelevant to his aims. He leaves out scenes that show Jesus' authority and power. He is presenting a Jesus the Japanese can relate to, and for them all tokens of power make Jesus intimidating and difficult to accept. Similarly, Endo gives a limp rendering of the resurrection, which to him poses a barrier to Japanese belief. To critics who judge his theology harshly, he replies, "My way of depicting Jesus is rooted in my being a Japanese novelist. I wrote this book for the benefit of Japanese readers who have no Christian tradition of their own and who know almost nothing about Jesus."

Yet we who grow up hearing about Jesus have much to learn from Endo as well. I remember addressing the topic "Culture Wars" before a large gathering that was tilted toward the liberal Democratic persuasion and included a strong Jewish minority. I had been selected as the token evangelical Christian on a panel that included the presidents of the Disney Channel and Warner Brothers, as well as the president of Wellesley College and the personal attorney for Anita Hill, who had testified so strongly against Supreme Court Justice Clarence Thomas. I felt like wearing a T-shirt with a bull's-eye target painted on it, for all of them had stories to tell of powerful Christian lobbies that had battled them.

Southern Baptists were boycotting Disney, evangelicals were expressing outrage over a blasphemous art exhibit at Wellesley College, and Anita Hill was still getting angry letters from conservative Christians years after her appearance before Congress. The youngest panelist, Lucinda Robb, granddaughter of President Lyndon Johnson and daughter of Senator Chuck Robb, told of a bruising campaign against Oliver North, in which right-wing Christians picketed their every appearance. "I thought we were Christians," Lucinda told me. "We grew up with Billy Graham as a frequent visitor, and we have always been active in church. We truly believe. But these demonstrators treated us like we were demons from hell."

When my turn came to speak, I mentioned that on such issues I seek guidance from the life of a Jew from the first century, who was also involved in a culture war. A rigid religious establishment hounded him throughout his time on earth, worried that his revolutionary message might upset the ruling authorities. And surely the pagan empire he lived under gave him cause for offense. Rome had practices—slavery, mass executions, infanticide, public gladiator games—that no modern state would tolerate. Jesus relied on one main weapon to "fight" the culture wars: sacrificial love. Among the last words he spoke before death were these: "Father, forgive them, for they do not know what they are doing."

After the panel, a television celebrity came up to me whose name every reader would recognize. "I've got to tell you, that stabbed me right in the heart," he said. "I was prepared to dislike you because I dislike all right-wing Christians and I assumed you were one. You can't imagine the mail I get from right-wingers. I don't follow Jesus— I'm a Jew. But when you told about Jesus forgiving his enemies, I realized how far from that spirit I am. I fight my enemies, especially the right-wingers. I don't forgive them. I have much to learn from the spirit of Jesus." The power of Jesus' sacrificial love was at work yet again.

Toward the end of his career, Endo turned to more personal, even autobiographical themes. In 1988 his novel *Scandal* appeared, which, rather shockingly, presents as the central character a famous Catholic writer in Japan who is accused of frequenting the red-light district of Tokyo. The reader is never quite sure whether this writer, with his obvious resemblance to Endo, is being set up by his accusers, has a shadow side, or is experiencing some kind of doppelgänger. Endo lays bare the treachery of his own soul. "Don't overestimate me," he tells his readers. "It's as much as I can do just to deal with my own problems. I can't take on the responsibility for your lives too."

As a writer, I find *Scandal* the most courageous, and in many ways the most moving, of Endo's novels. Writers of faith have a tendency to sanitize their characters, to portray them with a kind of glow about them. This tendency directly contradicts the example of the Bible, which depicts the flaws in its great characters—Abraham, Moses, David, Peter, Paul—with brutal realism. In this sense, Endo is one of the most biblical of all modern fiction writers, for the theme of betrayal surfaces in every one of his major books. In *Scandal*, Endo himself is the traitor.

"A novelist cannot write about what is holy," Endo says. "He cannot depict the holy Christ, but he can write about Jesus through the eyes of the sort of people who stepped on the *fumie*, or the eyes of his disciples and others who betrayed the Christ." He might have added that the novelist can only write about Jesus through the eyes of the novelist himself, for in the end Endo did not stray far from his own autobiography. Inside the elderly, esteemed man of letters was still a little boy struggling to make his foreign suit of clothes fit a Japanese body.

One of Endo's short stories, "Mothers," tells of a man who visits a group of Kakure Christians on a remote island in search of some truth about himself. These crypto-Christians, devoted to Mary, with an acute sense of historical failure, appeal to the visitor. He senses in them something of the longing he felt as a child, unable to communicate well with his own mother. "Sometime I catch a glimpse of myself in these Kakure, people who have had to lead lives of duplicity, lying to the world and never revealing their true feelings to anyone."

In a recurring dream, the narrator lies in a hospital, heavily drugged. As he fades in and out of consciousness he sees that beside him, patient, doggedly loving, sits his mother—no one else, just his mother. In lucid moments he ponders her intense faith and his own waywardness. "The more she compelled me to share her faith, the more I fought her oppressive power, the way a drowning child struggles against the pressure of the water."

As the narrator thinks these thoughts, listening to the hum of life-support machines, shifting mistily between the present and the past, preparing for a future he cannot imagine, his mother sits beside him, silent, waiting.

GETTING STARTED WITH SHUSAKU ENDO:

Start with *Silence,* Endo's acknowledged classic. I deeply admire *Scandal* also. One of his last novels, *Deep River,* revisits many of the themes of the earlier novels—trips abroad, a shattered faith, the bumbling fool—but explores the new territory of comparative religions through the eyes of a Japanese tour group visiting India. Many readers find Endo's fiction repetitive or difficult to relate to, perhaps because of cultural differences; these might prefer the short stories collected in *The Final Martyrs.* His *A Life of Jesus* helps explain the point of view expressed in the novels.

In 1983 the priest and university professor Henri Nouwen first encountered Rembrandt's painting *Return of the Prodigal Son* in the form of a poster pinned to the back of a door. Perhaps because he had just completed an exhausting lecture tour on Central American justice issues and was nearing emotional collapse, the painting touched him as he had never before been touched. He wanted nothing more than to take the place of the ragged son kneeling before the father, to bathe in the golden light, to feel the tender weight of the father's hands on his shoulders. He wanted nothing more than to go home—wherever that might be.

Born in the Netherlands, Nouwen had an affinity for paintings by his compatriots, especially Rembrandt and Van Gogh. Three years later, when offered a chance to visit Russia, he quickly agreed, in part because it gave him the opportunity to view Rembrandt's painting in person. Twice within a week he entered the Hermitage Museum in St. Petersburg and sat for several hours before the masterpiece, which Rembrandt had painted on huge scale, larger than life. Dwarfed by the painting, Nouwen watched it change hour by hour with the sunlight, drinking in every detail of the characters in their spare setting.

A short time later, after resigning his professorship and making a radical change in his life, Nouwen wrote the slim book *The Return of the Prodigal Son: A Story of Homecoming.* By moving into a community of the physically and mentally disabled in Toronto, Canada, he

Chapter 13

HENRI

NOUWEN

❧

THE

WOUNDED

HEALER

hoped he had found his true home at last. The painting continued to captivate him, and Nouwen began to see his own story in terms of Jesus' parable of the prodigal. Ten years after the move, his life ended with a kind of poetic unity for he was working on a television special on the painting in 1996, making preparations to visit the Hermitage with a Dutch camera crew, when he suffered the heart attack that ultimately killed him.

As he reflected on the parable during his life, Nouwen found himself identifying most naturally with the responsible and obedient elder brother. From the age of five, after all, he had desired to be a priest, and had acted out the role with a toy altar, tabernacle, and vestments. Trained in Holland as a psychologist and a theologian, then ordained as a priest, Nouwen spent his early career years fulfilling ambitions. He studied at the Menninger Clinic, taught at Notre Dame and Yale, and traveled widely as a conference speaker. Broadly ecumenical, he might speak to leftist Catholic liberation theologians and hand-waving charismatic evangelicals on the same day. (Robert Schuller, the popular TV pastor, turned over his Crystal Cathedral pulpit to Nouwen for three consecutive television programs.) He ignored Rome's rules about restricting Eucharist to fellow Catholics and celebrated it daily with friends, students, or strangers wherever he went.

After teaching at elite universities and writing sixteen books, Nouwen had a résumé to die for—which was the problem, exactly. The pressing schedule and relentless competition were suffocating his own spiritual life. He made a couple of six-month retreats at an abbey in upstate New York, then withdrew to South America, scouting a possible role for himself as a missionary in the developing world. In Peru he lived in a slum in northern Lima, a parish of one hundred thousand people. The family he stayed with had few possessions, but Nouwen felt their love through the children who crawled all over him, giggling, squirming, playing games with the strange priest who spoke their language like a child. The children literally hugged life back into him, he would later say. He discovered a paradox, that the poor and oppressed have a more profound sense of God's love than Westerners who live materially privileged lives.

"How little do we really know the power of physical touch," wrote Nouwen during his sojourn in Peru. He had just visited an orphanage where the children, starved for affection, fought for the privilege of touching him. "These boys and girls only wanted one thing: to be touched, hugged, stroked, and caressed. Probably most adults have the same needs but no longer have the innocence and unself-consciousness to express them. Sometimes I see humanity as a sea of people starving for affection, tenderness, care, love, acceptance, forgiveness, and gentleness. Everyone seems to cry: 'Please love me.' "

Living in the homes of the poor, Nouwen learned that we minister to the needy not only to take Jesus to them but also to find Jesus within them. Jesus said "Blessed are the poor," not "Blessed are those who care for the poor." By living among them, Nouwen received that blessing and began to recover from the damage caused by stress. Even so, the time in South America convinced him that his calling did not lie there. After six months he accepted a new position at Harvard University.

While living in Peru, Nouwen received news from Holland that his sister-in-law had given birth to a daughter with Down's syndrome. He wrote the family these words, unaware that in a few years they would seem a prophetic insight:

> Laura is going to be important for all of us in the family. We have never had a "weak" person among us. We all are hardworking, ambitious, and successful people who seldom have had to experience powerlessness. Now Laura enters and tells us a totally new dependency. Laura, who always will be a child, will teach us the way of Christ as no one will ever be able to do.
>
> (From *Gracias!*)

The pressures of fame, his teaching schedule at Harvard, and personal issues that became increasingly weighty combined to push Nouwen to the point of a complete breakdown within three more years. Finally he fell into the arms of the L'Arche ("The Ark") community, who work with the seriously disabled. He received a visit from the director of a L'Arche home, Jan Risse, on a mission from the group's founder. Jan visited Nouwen for a few days, cooked meals for him, and helped him in very practical ways. Nouwen kept expecting the inevitable request to give a lecture, write an article, offer a retreat. No such request came. L'Arche was bringing Nouwen grace pure and simple, with no strings attached.

Jan's visit made such an impression that Nouwen asked his bishop for permission to join a L'Arche community in France. For the first time in his life, he sensed God calling him to do something. He wanted to learn "what seminary and theology didn't teach me: how to love God and how to discover the presence of God in my own heart." The nourishment he felt from the community in France was what led him to become priest in residence at Daybreak, an affiliated home in Toronto.

From the outside, Nouwen's move from a university position to a home for the mentally challenged seemed noble, the ultimate act of a virtuous older brother. As Nouwen made clear in his writings, though, he reached the decision out of failure, spiritual darkness, and deep wounds. He went there not to give but to gain, not out of excess but out of need. He went in order to survive. Cast always in the role of the responsible elder brother, he had fallen prey to the very temptations that afflicted his prototype in Jesus' parable. "The lostness of the resentful 'saint' is so hard to reach precisely because it is so closely wedded to the desire to be good and virtuous," he concluded.

> I know, from my own life, how diligently I have tried to be good, acceptable, likable, and a worthy example for others. There was always the conscious effort to avoid the pitfalls of sin and the constant fear of giving in to temptation. But with all of that there came a seriousness, a moralistic intensity—and even a touch of fanaticism—that made it increasingly difficult to feel at home in my Father's house. I became less free, less spontaneous, less playful . . .

The more I reflect on the elder son in me, the more I realize how deeply rooted this form of lostness really is and how hard it is to return home from there. Returning home from a lustful escapade seems so much easier than returning home from a cold anger that has rooted itself in the deepest corners of my being.

(From *The Return of the Prodigal Son*)

In Rembrandt's painting, the elder brother stands at a distance from the father, coolly observing the embrace of his scoundrel brother. Staring at the figure, Nouwen wondered if Rembrandt should have titled the painting *Return of the Lost Sons,* for the elder was in many ways more lost than the prodigal, unable to overcome his own pride and resentment and enter into the celebration of his brother's return.

"I love Jesus but . . ." Nouwen wrote in the journal recording his decision to move to Daybreak. "I love Jesus but want to hold on to my own independence even when that independence brings no real freedom. I love Jesus but do not want to lose the respect of my professional colleagues, even though their respect does not make me grow spiritually. I love Jesus but do not want to give up my writing plans, travel plans, and speaking plans, even when these plans are often more to my glory than to the glory of God."

In the end, Nouwen loosed the chains of independence, respect, and busyness, and moved from a prestigious institution to one few had ever heard of, to work not with the nation's leaders but with society's rejects. He did so in part because of a detail easily overlooked in Jesus' story: the father reaches out to both his children. Not only does he welcome the wayward son, he also goes out from the house to meet the responsible son who has heard the sounds of music and dancing. The same hands that embrace the prodigal wait to embrace and warm his resentful brother. Nouwen yearned for that embrace.

I first learned of Henri Nouwen in his elder-brother phase. I came across his small classic *The Wounded Healer* early in my career while doing research into suffering, and found its insights remarkable.

I read many more books over the years before meeting him in person. Nouwen has been accused of having had no unpublished thought, and indeed some of his thoughts have been published more than once in different forms, and sometimes in booklets dressed up to look like books. Nevertheless, he served me as a wise older brother, a pioneer who nimbly explored trails of thought I found myself eager to follow.

"Somehow I believed that writing was one way to let something of lasting value emerge from my little, quickly passing life," Nouwen once wrote, a sentiment that expresses what every writer feels. Writing was an act of discovery for him as well as for his readers:

> Most students think that writing means writing down ideas, insights, visions. They feel that they must first have something to say before they can put it down on paper. For them writing is little more than recording a pre-existent thought. But with this approach true writing is impossible. Writing is a process in which we discover what lives in us. The writing itself reveals what is alive . . . The deepest satisfaction of writing is precisely that it opens up new spaces within us of which we were not aware before we started to write. To write is to embark on a journey whose final destination we do not know.
>
> (From *Reflections on Theological Education*)

I know well the typical inward course of the writing journey. Most writers are introspective, introverted, and not the kind of people you would invite for a fun evening. Most prefer relating to a word processor over relating to a live person. Not Nouwen. While churning out a book or so each year, he also maintained a frenetic pace as international speaker, professor, and priest, and eagerly invited others to join him on the journey.

Once when I was dining with a group of writers, the conversation turned to letters we get from readers. Richard Foster and Eugene Peterson mentioned an intense young man who had sought spiritual direction from both of them. They had responded graciously, answering questions by mail and recommending books on spirituality. Foster learned that the same inquirer had also contacted Henri Nouwen. "You won't believe what Nouwen did," he said. "He invited this stranger to live with his community for a month so he could give him spiritual direction in person."

You would have to be a writer to appreciate fully Nouwen's action. We writers jealously protect our schedules and privacy. A few years ago I moved from downtown Chicago to rural Colorado specifically to put space between myself and the madding world outside. Yes, we may accept speaking engagements, answer letters, and even return phone calls from curious readers, but always we cultivate a private domain that no one else may enter. Henri Nouwen broke down such barriers of professionalism. He carried on an active correspondence with five hundred people, and encouraged many of them to make personal visits.

I know several people who looked to Nouwen as their long-distance spiritual director. He responded at length to their questions, never giving the impression that they were interrupting his life or keeping him from more important things. One of them, Bob Buford, recalls, "He approached me, as he approached everyone he met, as if I were the most interesting person he'd ever met." He had the gift of giving full attention, all of himself, to whomever he was with.

As I now hear other people reminisce about Nouwen, I am stabbed with conviction. When someone calls and talks too long, I turn to my computer, cover the mouthpiece to hide the insect-click noises, and start shuffling items around in my Microsoft Outlook calendar program. My wife will tell a story at dinner and I'll ask about a detail that, she'll gently remind me, she just mentioned two minutes ago. How difficult I find it to move from the inner life, where most of a writer's life takes place, to the world of other people. In contrast, Nouwen erred on the side of other people. His writing may have suffered as a result, but many individuals profited.

Nouwen once defined the task of spiritual director: "You're in a big room with a six-inch-wide balance beam in the center. Now the balance beam is only twelve inches off the fully carpeted floor. Most of us act as if we were blindfolded and trying to walk on that balance beam; we're afraid we'll fall off. But we don't realize we're only twelve inches off the floor. The spiritual director is someone who can push you off that balance beam and say, 'See? It's okay. God still loves you.' "

In many ways, Nouwen did that for me. I began to take risks in my writing because he led the way, laying bare his own neuroses and failures for the world to see. I began to look upon people not as an interruption of my work but as the reason for it. I began to see myself, with Nouwen, as the elder brother standing at the edge of a party resentful of guests who had not paid their dues. With his encouragement, I also saw the father's hands outstretched to me.

Late in his life, Nouwen wrote about how difficult it was for him to return to his family in Holland. They had been devout Catholics as he grew up, and took delight in his decision to become a priest. Now, however, most of the family had lost all spiritual interest. If he christened a niece or nephew during one of his visits, the adults patronized him with a "This is fine for you, but of course we don't believe it" tone. He felt like a performer who was far from entertaining.

Reading such accounts, I realized why Nouwen made so few complaints against a church that irritated him with many of its policies. For him, the church for all its faults represented a haven of hope and comfort. He saw the results of non-faith in his own family, materially prosperous but spiritually void, and in the students at elite universities, floundering with no answers to their questions about meaning. Nouwen never became a propagandist for the church, but he did point the way toward direct communion with God. Faith was a lifeline for him, the one still point in his turning world.

Not until after Nouwen's death did others learn the full story about the turmoil going on inside him. His writings contain many clues, and that alone may explain their extraordinary reception among both Catholics and Protestants, not to mention unbelievers: he gave the impression of opening up his heart, holding nothing back. He managed to nourish others' faith while dealing with personal turmoil—indeed, *because* he wrote so openly about that turmoil.

Quoting Gordon Allport, Nouwen once described "heuristic faith," or faith that is held tentatively until it can be confirmed. Nouwen offered for me an example of heuristic faith. He clung to what he believed, even when the circumstances of his own life argued against it. He trusted the character of God even when his life grew dark and God's hand seemed invisible. He continued to function as a responsible elder brother even when, looking inward, he knew himself to be a prodigal.

> So I am praying while not knowing how to pray. I am resting
> while feeling restless, at peace while tempted, safe while still
> anxious, surrounded by a cloud of light while still in darkness,
> in love while still doubting.   (From *The Road to Daybreak*)

A former member of the Daybreak community said, "When I think of Henri, I think of two "books": one is the book that Henri wrote forty times, yet couldn't quite live; the other is the book that Henri lived for almost sixty-five years, yet couldn't quite write. The second book waits to be written, as the meaning of Henri's life and wisdom reveal themselves now, after his death." Nouwen himself lamented, "People who read your ideas tend to think that your writings reflect your life."

Nouwen's biographer, Michael Ford, interviewed more than a hundred people who knew Nouwen well. Many of them circled back to the theme of dissonance in his life, especially the dissonance between what he wrote in print and said onstage and how he acted in person. He would give inspiring addresses about the spiritual life, then collapse into an irritable funk. He would speak of the strength he gained from living in community, then drive to a friend's house, wake him up at two in the morning, and, sobbing, ask to be held. His phone bills usually exceeded his rent as he called around the world, disregarding time zones, in desperate need of companionship. If a friend failed to compliment him, waited too long to respond to a letter, or neglected to invite him out for coffee after a lecture, he would sulk for days, nearly immobilized by rejection. In short, he felt called to present a message of inner peace and acceptance that he himself never realized.

Ford concludes that Nouwen was "a multi-gifted man of boundless generosity, charm, and pastoral vision, but also a deeply insecure person of anguish, pain, and craving." His biography reveals a secret that Nouwen kept from all but a few people during his life: the priest was a celibate homosexual. As a result, he longed for intimate relationships yet recoiled from them out of fear where they might lead. Ford says, "I came to realize just how central Nouwen's long-repressed homosexuality had been to his struggles and how it had probably been the underlying stimulus for his powerful writings on loneliness, intimacy, marginality, love, and belonging."

I have known several people in ministry who struggle with issues of sexual identity, knowing themselves to be gay and feeling trapped, with no acceptable way to admit it, let alone express it. I know of no more difficult path for a person of integrity to tread. Now I go back through Nouwen's writings and sense the deeper, unspoken agony that underlay what he wrote about rejection, about the wound of loneliness that never heals, about friendships that never satisfy.

Nouwen sought counseling from a center that ministered to homosexual men and women, and he listened as gay friends proposed several options. He could remain a celibate priest and "come out" as a gay man, which would at least release the secret he bore in anguish. He could declare himself, leave the priesthood, and seek a gay companion. Or he could remain a priest publicly and develop private gay relationships. Nouwen carefully weighed each course and rejected it. Any public confession of his identity would hurt his ministry, he feared. The last two options seemed impossible for one who had taken a vow of celibacy, and who looked to the Bible and to Rome for guidance on sexual morality. Instead, he decided to keep living with the wound. Again and again, he decided.

The priest or pastor is constantly tempted to see himself as the answer-giver, the spiritual authority, the dispenser of grace and not its recipient. To fight that temptation, the temptation of the elder brother, Nouwen centered his writings on his failures and inadequacies. He usually expressed the wound in terms of restlessness, loneliness, and rejection, rather than sexuality. Risking gossip, he wrote of emotional attachments to friends that only his priestly vows kept him from consummating. He spoke of the alienation he felt when he left his family and country and moved to the United States, then to South America, then to Canada. A misfit within his own secularized family in Holland, he searched constantly for a true home.

He once described the wound of loneliness as resembling the Grand Canyon: a deep incision in the surface of existence that has become an inexhaustible source of beauty and self-understanding. That insight typifies Nouwen's approach to ministry. He did not promise a way out of loneliness, for himself or for anyone else. Rather, he held out the promise of redemption through it. For readers and listeners, perhaps, the wound became a source of beauty and understanding. For Nouwen himself it rarely represented anything but pain.

Though he could never resolve the restlessness, he learned to manage it as some people must learn to manage a chronic physical pain: ". . . you do not run away from it but feel it through and stand up in it and look it right in the face." If so, you may find in the middle of the pain some hidden gift, a source of hope. Nouwen confessed that in his own life the true gifts were often concealed in the places that hurt most. The pain forced him to God, where he discovered and rediscovered a source of strength "from someone who holds me, who loved me long before I came into life, from someone who will love me long after I have died."

The Road to Daybreak chronicles Nouwen's decision to move to Daybreak in search of some comfort and solace, in search of a true home. One reviewer, Harold Fickett, wrote that he found it disappointing to read that the same problems described a decade earlier in *The Genesee Diary*—deficient friendships, unrequited love, hurt feelings at perceived slights—continued to plague Nouwen. Fickett went on to explain, "It's disappointing in exactly the same way it's disappointing to be ourselves—the same person with the same problems who learns and then must relearn again and again the basic lessons of religious faith. Nouwen does not spare himself or us the embarrassment of this perennial truth."

Fickett has put his finger on a defining characteristic of Nouwen: indeed he does not spare himself, or his readers, the embarrassment of truth, no matter how bad that truth makes him look. Much suffering, Nouwen said, stems from memories, buried deep inside, which release a form of toxin that attacks the center of one's being. Good memories we display in the form of trophies, diplomas, and scrapbooks; other, painful memories remain hidden from view, where they escape healing and cause enduring harm.

Our instinctive response to such wounding memories is to act as if they did not happen, to not talk about them and think instead about happier things. But by the deliberate act of not remembering we allow the suppressed memories to gain strength and maim our functioning as human beings. Nouwen had the courage to shine the light on some of those deep places, to expose the wounding memories within himself. "The only true healer," he said in a memorable phrase, "is a wounded healer."

My one extended conversation with Nouwen came just after he had returned from San Francisco, where he had served for a week in an AIDS clinic. At the time, I knew nothing of Nouwen's personal sexual issues. He told me what he had seen in the Castro district. The word "gay" seemed to him very out of place there, at the height of the AIDS crisis. Young men were dying every day, and thousands more walked around terrified that they were carrying the virus. Even as shops displayed gaudy T-shirts and sexual products ranging from the playful to the obscene, fear hung like a fog over the streets. Not only fear, he said, but also feelings of guilt and anger and rejection.

In the clinic Nouwen listened to personal stories. "I'm a priest—that's my job. I listen to people's stories. They confess to me." He told me of young men banished from their own families, forced to hustle on the street. Some of them had hundreds of partners whom they had met in bathhouses, whose names they had never learned, and from one of those partners they had contracted the virus that was now killing them. Nouwen looked at me, his piercing eyes bright with compassion and pain. "Philip, those young men were dying—literally dying—because of their thirst for love." He went on to tell me individual stories he had heard there. The accounts all had in common a search for a safe place, for a safe relationship, for a home, for acceptance, for unconditional love, for forgiveness—Nouwen's own quest, I now realize.

Nouwen's comment about thirst lodged inside me, and over time worked a transformation in my spirit. As a writer associated with the evangelical magazine *Christianity Today,* I had regular contact with people who led the religious right. I had been invited to the White House with a group of twelve evangelicals to answer a question from Bill Clinton, "Why do Christians hate me?" Some of my friends saw themselves as crusaders in a great culture war. They vividly described the threat posed by "immoral" and "ungodly" people.

Through Nouwen's eyes, I saw a new way to look at such people: not as immoral and ungodly, but as thirsty—as people dying for love. Like the Samaritan woman at the well, they had drunk their fill of water that did not satisfy. They needed Living Water. After that conversation with Nouwen, whenever I encountered someone whose behavior offended or revolted me, I would pray, "God, help me to see this person not as repulsive, but as thirsty."

The more I prayed that prayer, the more I began to see myself on the same side as the one who had repulsed me. I, too, have nothing to offer God but my thirst. Like the elder brother in the parable, I can never experience the cleansing flow of God's grace or enter the family celebration if I stand outside the banquet hall, arms folded in a posture of moral superiority. God's grace comes as a free gift, but only one who has open hands can receive a gift.

In the end, I learned Henri Nouwen's contribution, as a priest and a writer. He offers no unique insight into human personality, no wisdom that could not be gleaned elsewhere from other authorities. He offers instead the humble posture of the prodigal son.

His own deep wound exposed the hypocrisy of his natural stance as the elder brother. Loneliness, temptation, rejection, alienation—all these worked to produce in him an undeniable thirst. He had to come to terms with himself as the prodigal in relentless pursuit of home.

> Faith is the radical trust that home has always been there and always will be there. The somewhat stiff hands of the father rest on the prodigal's shoulders with the everlasting divine blessing: "You are my Beloved, on you my favor rests."
> Yet over and over again I have left home. I have fled the hands of blessing and run off to faraway places searching for love! This is the great tragedy of my life and of the lives of so many I meet on my journey. Somehow I have become deaf to the voice that calls me the Beloved, have left the only place where I can hear that voice, and have gone off desperately hoping that I would find somewhere else what I could no longer find at home.
> (From *The Return of the Prodigal Son*)

Since childhood I have felt a fierce and no doubt unfair resistance against traveling evangelists, preachers, and devotional authors who convey a tone of moral superiority. Too many times they have misled me; too many times they have fallen off the pedestal on which I placed them. I listen, though, to someone who presents himself or herself as one sinner talking to another. I listen to someone who begins with a confession of thirst, of homesickness.

In *Making All Things New,* Henri Nouwen wrote what could stand as an epitaph for his journey:

> Poverty, pain, struggle, anguish, agony, and even inner darkness may continue to be part of our experience. They may even be God's way of purifying us. But life is no longer boring, resentful, depressing, or lonely because we have come to know that everything that happens is part of our way to the house of the Father.

In countless personal appearances, in more than forty books, and most of all in his daily life, Nouwen demonstrated that flaws and faithfulness do not supplant each other but coexist. We all bear wounds. His came from anxiety over sexual identity and a hypersensitivity to rejection. Mine come mostly from family and church. Others come from chronic illness or deep pain. We can live as victims, blaming God or someone else for our misfortune; or, following Nouwen, we can allow those wounds to drive us to God. After spending half a year among Trappist monks at an abbey in New York, Nouwen asked himself whether the intense time with God solved his problems, made him a different, more spiritual person. He had to answer no. He realized that a monastery is not built to solve problems but to praise God in the midst of them.

Once, while serving as chaplain to L'Arche community in France, Nouwen listened all day to people confessing their secret lives in the Sacrament of Reconciliation. As he heard their stories of guilt and shame, he felt overwhelmed by their sense of isolation. He wanted to draw together all who had confessed and ask them to share their stories with each other, so that they could discover how much they had in common. Each one thought only he or she struggled with a particular pain or doubt; in reality, they were confessing a shared humanity.

Nouwen the priest, with no life partner with whom to share his inner secrets, took the risk of revealing them—most of them, at least—to the rest of us. He knew that by hiding our pain, we also hide our ability to heal. "No one person can fulfill all your needs," he reminded himself in a journal kept during the year of his strongest sexual tension. "You have to move gradually from crying outward—crying out for people who you think can fulfill your needs—to crying inward to the place where you can let yourself be held and carried by God, who has become incarnate in the humanity of those who love you in community."

Daybreak, where he spent the last decade of his life, became that community for Nouwen. It was an awkward transition at first. Accustomed to addressing large crowds of admirers, he found it jarring to speak to people who could not understand big words, who grunted, drooled, and made spastic movements during his homilies. If a resident named Bill did not like the priest's sermon, he would interrupt mass to tell him so. Nouwen found that his beautiful words and arguments had little relevance to what the residents were going through. To these damaged bodies and damaged minds, his prestigious résumé meant nothing. They couldn't even read his books. All that mattered was whether he loved them.

A priest who knew nothing of normal household duties—cooking, ironing, caring for children—he found himself all thumbs when asked to care for disabled residents. In time, though, he did come to love these people. And in the dawning of compassion for the broken bodies around him, he began to sense at last how God could love a broken person like himself.

> It took me a long time to feel safe in this unpredictable climate, and I still have moments in which I clamp down and tell everyone to shut up, get in line, listen to me, and believe in what I say. But I am also getting in touch with the mystery that leadership, for a large part, means to be led. I discover that I am learning many new things, not just about the pains and struggles of wounded people, but also about their unique gifts and graces. They teach me about joy and peace, love and care and prayer—what I could never have learned in any academy. They also teach me what nobody else could have taught me, about grief and violence, fear and indifference. Most of all, they give me a glimpse of God's first love, often at moments when I start feeling depressed and discouraged.   (From *In the Name of Jesus*)

Nouwen became so attached to the people in his home, and so dependent on them, that he began taking them with him on his speaking trips. Whereas other well-known speakers might command an honorarium of five or ten thousand dollars, Nouwen would ask for just five hundred (which he would sign over to Daybreak) and a plane ticket for himself and a companion. A reporter for *The Wall Street*

Journal remembers attending one such engagement in North Carolina. When Nouwen invited his friend Bill—the same one who interrupted mass—to the microphone to speak, the reporter thought to himself that people had come a long way to hear Henri Nouwen, not Bill.

In order to give Bill support, Nouwen stood next to him on stage. Bill looked out over the audience, and suddenly all his words failed him. He was overcome. He simply laid his head on Nouwen's shoulder and wept. Much that Nouwen said has passed from the memory of that North Carolina audience; the memory of Bill resting his head on a priest's shoulder has not. "I tell you the truth, anyone who will not receive the kingdom of God like a little child will never enter it," said Jesus. "And he took the children in his arms, put his hands on them and blessed them."

Daybreak assigned Nouwen one person to look after in particular: Adam. (Their relationship is celebrated in Nouwen's book, *Adam: God's Beloved,* published posthumously in 1997.) Adam was the weakest and most disabled person in the community. Although in his twenties, Adam could not speak, dress or undress himself, could not walk alone or eat without help. Instead of counseling Ivy League students and juggling a busy schedule, Nouwen had to learn a new set of skills: how to feed, change, and bathe Adam, how to support his glass as he drank, how to push his wheelchair over a road full of potholes. He ministered not to leaders and intellectuals but to a young man who was considered by many a vegetable, a useless person who should not have been born. Yet Nouwen gradually learned that he, not Adam, was the chief beneficiary in this strange, misfitted relationship.

From the hours spent with Adam, Nouwen gained an inner peace that made most of his other, more high-minded tasks seem boring and superficial. As he sat beside that silent child-man, he realized how obsessive, how marked with rivalry and competition, was his prior drive toward success in academia. From Adam he learned that "what makes us human is not our mind but our heart, not our ability to think but our ability to love. Whoever speaks about Adam as a vegetable or animal-like creature misses the sacred mystery that Adam is fully capable of receiving and giving love."

This is what Henri Nouwen learned from Adam:

Keep your eyes on the one who refuses to turn stones into bread, jump from great heights or rule with great temporal power. Keep your eyes on the one who says, 'Blessed are the poor, the gentle, those who mourn and those who hunger and thirst for righteousness; blessed are the merciful, the peacemakers and those who are persecuted in the cause of uprightness' . . . Keep your eyes on the one who is poor with the poor, weak with the weak and rejected with the rejected. That one is the source of all peace.

(From *World Vision* magazine)

When Nouwen sat in the Hermitage Museum in St. Petersburg, Russia, meditating on Rembrandt's great painting, he had no trouble identifying with the elder brother, for that had been his natural stance in life, trained from youth to be a virtuous priest. He had no trouble identifying with the prodigal either, for inner turmoil had forced him to confront his true self, his truly needy self, and fling himself on the mercy of the father. It was when he projected himself onto the character of the father that he recoiled. To him, the father had always been a powerful, distant character, one to inspire fear.

Not in Rembrandt's painting, however. The right hand placed on the prodigal's shoulder is soft and tender, a feminine hand. The father's head tilts gently to the side, and he bends over to close the distance between himself and his son; as he does so, his warm red cloak billows out like the wings of a sheltering bird. Nouwen thought of Isaiah's feminine image of God: "Can a woman forget her baby at the breast, feel no pity for the child she has borne? Even if these were to forget, I shall not forget you"; and of Jesus' maternal cry about a hen gathering her chicks under her wings. His image of God the Father needed sharp correction, he realized.

As he meditated further, he gained a new insight into the parable:

the mystery that Jesus himself became something of a prodigal son for our sakes. "He left the house of his heavenly Father, came to a foreign country, gave away all that he had, and returned through a cross to his Father's home. All of this he did, not as a rebellious son, but as the obedient son, sent out to bring home all the lost children of God. . . . Jesus is the prodigal son of the prodigal Father who gave away everything the Father had entrusted to him so that I could become like him and return with him to his Father's home."

At last, Nouwen found a way to identify with the father in Rembrandt's painting. People called him "Father" all the time, especially when he wore a robe or clerical collar. He could accept that title in the way the parable portrayed it, the father being the one who beckons home both the elder brother and the prodigal. I cannot remain a child forever, thought Nouwen. God is inviting me to become like himself, to show the same compassion to others that he is showing to me. He is calling me to reach out to the broken and the needy, to welcome them to God's family. That realization spurred his difficult decision to leave Harvard and move to Daybreak.

Nouwen was the first person I knew to use the phrase *downward mobility*. In a 1981 article in *Sojourners* he wrote against the uncontrolled drive for prestige, power, and ambition—in other words, the upward mobility—characteristic of American culture. "The great paradox which Scripture reveals to us is that real and total freedom can only be found through downward mobility. The Word of God came down to us and lived among us as a slave. The divine way is indeed the downward way."

By moving to Daybreak, Nouwen acted out God's pattern of downward mobility. It went against all his instincts, he admitted. Leaving a tenured position at an Ivy League school to settle among a community of the mentally challenged made no sense by any modern measure of success. When I first heard the news, I smiled at Nouwen's choice to live as a "holy fool." How wrong I was. He did not reach that decision as an act of self-sacrifice; he chose it for his own sake.

In fact, what others saw as a pattern of downward mobility in his career path, Nouwen himself saw a form of "inward mobility." He withdrew in order to look inward, to learn how to love God and be loved by God so that he could beckon others into that love. He described his intent by citing a passage from Robert Pirsig's *Zen and the Art of Motorcycle Maintenance*:

> Pirsig describes two kinds of mountain climbers. Both place one foot in front of the other, breathe in and out at the same rate, stop when tired, and move forward when rested. But the "ego-climber" misses the whole experience. He does not notice the beautiful passage of sunlight through the trees. He looks up the trail to see what's ahead even though he just looked for the same thing a second ago. "His talk is forever about somewhere else, something else. He's here but he's not here. What he is looking for, what he wants, is all around him, but he doesn't want that because it *is* all around him."   (From *The Genesee Diary*)

Nouwen had been living his spiritual life in the manner of an ego-climber. Books to read, skills to learn, talks to give, letters to answer—these things pressed in on him so that he could not notice God all around him, and meanwhile he was straining to peer ahead, farther down the trail. When he asked advice of Mother Teresa, she counseled, "Spend an hour a day in contemplative prayer and commit no conscious sins." Nouwen had difficulty carving out an hour a day, but at Daybreak he did manage half an hour a day. He began to conceive of prayer differently: not as a time to talk but to listen, a quiet, attentive time of "listening to the voice that says good things about me." For someone as insecure and riven with doubts as Nouwen, that was a hard discipline.

When he moved to Daybreak, Nouwen wondered about the negative effects of withdrawal. Would he suffer from living "out of the loop"? Instead, like Thomas Merton, he found a life of withdrawal need not lead to isolation. One author who has written extensively on hermits draws a parallel to scientists who work alone in pursuit of cures for diseases, which will eventually help many. Most of Nouwen's followers found his work growing more relevant, not less, during his time at Daybreak.

I met Henri Nouwen in person only once, on a visit to Daybreak. First we talked in his office, swapping publisher stories and comparing some of the topics we each planned to write on. Somewhat embarrassed, I mentioned that I was finishing a book titled *Disappointment with God*. Instead of frowning at the title, he grew positively excited, gesticulating nonstop with his hands and telling me of his own experiences of disappointment. At one point he jumped to his feet, rushed over to the wall, and removed a print of a Van Gogh painting. "Here, this is what I mean," he said. "This captures the mood. It's yours. Take it as my gift."

When lunchtime came, I tucked my newly acquired artwork under my arm and followed him on a wooden walkway that led across construction mud to the room where he lived. It had a single bed, one bookshelf, and a few pieces of Shaker-style furniture. The walls were unadorned except for a print of another Van Gogh painting—Nouwen had recently contributed to a book called *Van Gogh and God*—and a few religious symbols. A staff person brought in a bowl of Caesar salad, a flask of wine, and a loaf of bread. No fax machine, no computer, no Daytimer calendar posted on the wall—in this room, at least, Nouwen had found serenity. The church "industry" seemed very far away.

Thoreau wrote that "Most of the luxuries, and many of the so-called comforts of life, are not only not indispensable, but positive hindrances to the elevation of mankind. With respect to the luxuries and comforts, the wisest have ever lived a more simple and meagre life than the poor. . . . None can be an impartial or wise observer of human life but from the vantage ground of what we should call voluntary poverty." Glancing around, mentally comparing Nouwen's setting to my own office full of machines, books, and *things*, I felt a twinge of envy. Yes, he had secretaries to handle correspondence and a religious sister to prepare his meals. Yes, a vow of poverty eliminated worries about IRS tax payments and royalty statements, and a vow of obedience simplified his process of decision-making. But wasn't that the point? He had shed these encumbrances out of commitment to something higher.

And what was that something higher? All morning Nouwen had been talking about his friend Adam. "You are here on a very special occasion!" he told me excitedly. "Today is Adam's birthday!" (In his Dutch accent, it came out "birfday.") "He turns twenty-six, and his parents and brothers will be here for a very special celebration of Eucharist."

Already that day, Nouwen told me, he had spent nearly two hours preparing Adam. I had read Nouwen's own description of this daily process:

It takes me about an hour and a half to wake Adam up, give him his medication, carry him into his bath, wash him, shave him, clean his teeth, dress him, walk him to the kitchen, give him his breakfast, put him in his wheelchair and bring him to the place where he spends most of the day with therapeutic exercises. . . .

He does not cry or laugh. Only occasionally does he make eye contact. His back is distorted. His arm and leg movements are twisted. He suffers from severe epilepsy and, despite heavy medication, sees few days without grand-mal seizures. Sometimes, as he grows suddenly rigid, he utters a howling groan. On a few occasions I've seen one big tear roll down his cheek.

(From *World Vision* magazine)

After lunch we adjourned to a small chapel for the service. With solemnity, but also a twinkle in his eye, Nouwen led the liturgy in honor of Adam's birthday. Adam, unable to talk and profoundly retarded, gave no sign of comprehension although he did appear to recognize that his family had come to share the event with him. He drooled throughout the ceremony and grunted loudly a few times.

I must admit I had a fleeting doubt as to whether this was the best use of the busy priest's time. I had heard Henri Nouwen speak, and read many of his books, and recognized all that he had to offer. Could not someone else take over the manual chores of caring for Adam? Back in his office, when I cautiously broached the subject with Nouwen himself, he informed me that I had completely misinterpreted him. "I am not giving up anything," he insisted. "It is I, not Adam, who gets the main benefit from our friendship."

The rest of the afternoon Nouwen kept circling back to my question, as if he hardly believed I could ask such a thing. He kept bringing up various ways he had benefited from his relationship with Adam. Truly, he was enjoying a new kind of spiritual peace, acquired not within the stately quadrangles of Yale or Harvard, but by the bedside of incontinent Adam. Listening to him, I felt convicted of my own spiritual poverty, I who so carefully arrange my writer's life to make it efficient and single-focused.

It had been difficult at first, Nouwen admitted. Physical touch, affection, and the messiness of caring for an uncoordinated person did not come easily. But he had learned to love Adam, truly to love him. In the process he had learned what it must be like for God to love us— spiritually uncoordinated, retarded, able to respond with what must seem to God like inarticulate grunts and groans. Indeed, working with Adam had taught him the humility and emptiness achieved by desert monks only after much sacrifice. The time he spent caring for Adam had become an invaluable time of meditation.

Nouwen has said that all his life two voices competed inside him. One encouraged him to succeed and achieve, while the other called him simply to rest in the comfort that he was *the beloved* of God. Only in the last decade of his life did he truly listen to that second voice. Ultimately Nouwen concluded that, "The goal of education and formation for the ministry is continually to recognize the Lord's voice, his face, and his touch in every person we meet." Reading that description, I understand why he did not think it a waste of time to invite a seeking stranger to live with him for a month, or to devote hours each day to the menial care of Adam.

As I recently thumbed through the books on my Nouwen shelf, I came across three books that he had inscribed to me after my visit. "Thank you for giving me the courage to keep writing!" he had written in one. I had left Daybreak feeling convicted and ashamed, an intrusive journalist wasting a busy priest's time. Nouwen, though, had harbored a very different memory, of a fellow-seeker, one beloved of God.

Like a father, he had welcomed me into the community of God. Even now, after his death, he gives that gift to me afresh.

As Nouwen points out, "God rejoices. Not because the problems of the world have been solved, not because all human pain and suffering have come to an end, nor because thousands of people have been converted and are now praising him for his goodness. No, God rejoices because one of his children who was lost has been found."

I miss Henri Nouwen. For some, his legacy consists of his many books, for others his role as a bridge between Catholics and Protestants, for others his distinguished career at Ivy League universities. For me, though, a single image captures him best: the energetic priest, hair in disarray, using his restless hands as if to fashion a homily out of thin air, celebrating an eloquent birthday Eucharist for an unresponsive child-man so damaged that most parents would have had him aborted. A better symbol of the Incarnation, I can hardly imagine.

Henri Nouwen's legacy lives on. While in the very process of assembling these reflections, I came across two others that I include as a kind of postscript to his life.

The first, I learned about while speaking of Nouwen at an international book fair in Frankfurt, Germany. A Dutch publisher came to me afterward and said, "Oh, but you don't know the rest of the story. You mentioned how Henri felt like such a misfit in his family, and how their spiritual emptiness grieved him. Even now, after his death, that is changing. His brother, who for many years headed up the largest Dutch tourist association, stood before a meeting of diplomats, ambassadors, members of parliament, and other dignitaries. He told of sitting at Henri's funeral and hearing people from many countries—Canada, the United States, France, Belgium, the Netherlands—speak of Henri's impact on their lives. 'I realized that compared to Henri, I have nothing,' he said. 'And as I sat there listening the difference became clear—Henri had God. That made all the difference.' He went on to tell of his wife's death from cancer, and then the death of his father, who barely outlived Henri. Then in a humble spirit he told of the changes he was now making in his own life, to better prepare for death, to restore a relationship with the God whom Henri knew so well. So you see, perhaps Henri wasn't such a misfit after all."

The second recollection occurred at a church service I wandered into in a beach town in California. The term "low church" aptly describes their worship culture: a leader dressed in baggy surfboard clothes (for a few after-service waves) sets down his guitar, leans over the podium and asks, "Hey, does anybody have anything to share today?"

That particular morning, as it happened, three young women came prepared to reminisce about Henri Nouwen, whose book *Life of the Beloved* they had read together in a small group.

The first speaker, Elizabeth, had a sheaf of notes, which she followed closely. She told of her determined efforts to become a superachiever. In high school she strove to make all A's, to win a state tennis championship, to head up the Student Council, to join every club she could. She won her school's "Super Seahawk" award. Reading Nouwen's book, she recognized herself in his own superachieving phase. She realized that she, like Nouwen, had all the while been thirsting for God's love, and trying desperately to earn it. From him, she got a glimpse of what it might mean to see herself as God's beloved, as one loved from the beginning of time, with no need to prove herself worthy.

The second speaker, Kate, carried a laptop computer to the podium, and started working the mouse to find her manuscript. That morning, her printer had refused to cooperate. "This is kind of a symptom of my life," she said. "Everything always goes wrong." Unlike Elizabeth, she had no résumé of superachievement. In fact, her counselor once told her, "Kate, I see some people with a Messiah complex, people who think they can save the world. You have a Satan complex. You think you are singlehandedly destroying the world." She truly believed herself cursed, incapable of goodness. From Nouwen she was learning for the first time to imagine herself as blessed, not cursed.

Kate made a few self-effacing comments and shut down her laptop computer as everybody laughed. Then Cathy stood up. Her lip trembled, and tears formed in the corners of her eyes. The congregation grew still. "Most of you don't know my story. I was molested as a child. Then in college I was drugged and raped. I kept asking, 'Why me?' I had tried to be good. I went to church every week and all that. So I just gave up. I took to alcohol to cover the pain. Of course it just brought on more pain, so I drank more alcohol. I was on a spiral to nowhere, feeling old before I had finished being young. One day I stopped by my old church just to see what might have changed inside. In the empty building, without planning to at all, I began to pray. I started bawling like a baby.

"Not everything got resolved that day, of course. The pain did not go away. It was my brokenness that I was confronting in church, not my healing. But through Henri Nouwen I learned that suffering and joy can go together, that God can use everything in our lives, even the pain that never goes away. I learned to claim my brokenness.

"Am I glad these bad things happened to me? No. But I do realize they have helped make me the person I am today. I can be a true friend to others. I can offer a safe place for other people going through tough times."

Cathy closed her talk with her own paraphrase of Luke 4, a dramatic scene where Jesus enters the synagogue and announces, "The Spirit of the Lord is upon me. He has sent me to heal the *brokenhearted*."

For several minutes after she sat down no one moved, except to reach for tissues and handkerchiefs. The traffic outside, the sunny day, the plans for Sunday at the beach—none of that mattered anymore. God was in that place.

Then the three women who had spoken stood and offered communion elements to each other. "This is Christ's body, broken *for you*," Kate said, handing bread to Elizabeth. "Christ's blood, shed *for you*," Elizabeth said, holding out a cup to Cathy. And the rest of us formed two ragged lines down the center aisle, to eat and to drink of God's brokenness.

GETTING STARTED WITH HENRI NOUWEN:

Seeds of Hope collects in one volume a selection of readings from Nouwen's work, and offers a good introduction for those who don't mind reading passages out of context. I recommend *The Return of the Prodigal Son* and *Life of the Beloved* as introductions to his introspective yet oddly comforting work. *The Genesee Diary, The Road to Daybreak* and *Sabbatical Journey* record more personal and autobiographical reflections. Of Nouwen's many other books I enjoy especially *Gracias!* and *Intimacy. Nouwen Then* and *Wounded Prophet* give reflections on Nouwen from those who knew him.

Writers have the prerogative of focusing on one thing for months, even years at a time. Recently, I have thought about little else than the thirteen people in this book and how they have affected me. Doing so was a wonderful tonic, one I would recommend in smaller doses to anyone. Make a list of the people who have shaped your life for the better, and try to figure out why.

As I review the list in total, I see flawed, not perfect people. Several of them, a psychiatrist would probably diagnose as unstable. Each one had longings that went unfulfilled, dreams that never entered reality. I learn from them how to handle my own longings. Do they drive me on, toward the person I want to become and haven't, toward the God I want to know? Or do they depress me, make me tired and cynical? From these mentors, I have learned to sense longings as intimations of something more, worthy of my ceaseless even if futile pursuit, and to resist the temptation to settle for less.

Søren Kierkegaard said, "With the help of the thorn in my foot, I spring higher than anyone with sound feet." Some of the people profiled in this collection demonstrate that proverb as well. I would add only that we also need the help of those who show us what direction to spring. For me, these people point the way.

I have dealt mostly with my past in this book, for these guides set me on my own pilgrimage at a crucial time when my beliefs were taking shape. As for the present—well, that's the subject of most of my other books . . .

EPILOGUE

RECOVERING FROM CHURCH ABUSE

Philip Yancey says he "spent most of [his] life in recovery from the church" (page 1). And he is candid about the racist views he acquired in a society and church that were pervaded by prejudice and legalism. Talk about what, if anything, made you begin to wonder about the truth of things you learned in church. What feelings and emotions have marked your questioning?

Did you at any point experience a contradiction between the church's teachings and its actions?

What denomination were you raised in? What are your happiest memories of church? The saddest, the most painful?

Yancey talks about people like millionaire Millard Fuller, who abandoned his life of luxury to found an organization to build houses for people who cannot afford them (page 8). How does such willingness to live one's faith go against the grain of a secular world? What role does the church play in who you are today?

MARTIN LUTHER KING, JR.

Philip Yancey describes growing up in the apartheid conditions of the South in the 1950s and 1960s (page 13). Even if we have not grown up in such an obviously racist climate, few of us escape some form of it. What racial assumptions did you grow up with? What made you begin to understand them as something other than "right" or "normal"?

Martin Luther King, Jr., now stands accused of personal moral flaws, yet he was a powerful agent for equality and change. How can we reconcile the two sides of his character? Does one side somehow negate or lessen the other?

Can you think of other men and women with seemingly contradictory public and personal behaviors? What makes you forgive or accept such a duality?

Does accepting questionable moral practices in a leader weaken the moral fabric of society?

What is the difference between passivity and nonviolence? Do you see a place for nonviolence in the contemporary world? Why or why not?

G. K. CHESTERTON

C. S. Lewis wrote: "A young man who wishes to remain a strong atheist cannot be too careful of his reading" (page 44). What does this statement mean to you? Have you been exposed to such transforming reading?

Yancey's brother reacted to their confining upbringing by embarking on a "grand quest for freedom." His brother's failures showed Yancey "the destructive power of casting off faith with nothing to take its place" (page 44). Have you been through such a freedom quest? Talk about the relationship of faith and freedom. Why is freedom such a frightening concept for some people?

Nature contains both majestic beauty and unspeakable cruelty. What does Chesterton mean when he said, "Nature is not our mother; Nature is our sister"? (page 51)

Why do you think we experience pleasure? What role does it play in God's creation? Why does the church focus so strongly on the dangers of pleasure?

Chesterton weighed three hundred to four hundred pounds (page 56), showing one example of how a sensual pleasure such as eating may ultimately be destructive. How can we savor pleasure and avoid destructive excesses?

Chesterton propounded faith with great wit. How would Christians of today benefit from Chesterton's sense of humor?

DR. PAUL BRAND

From Paul Brand, Philip Yancey learned, "It is indeed possible to live in modern society, achieve success without forfeiting humility, serve others sacrificially, and yet emerge with joy and contentment" (page 67). Do you believe this kind of life is attainable and desirable? What makes a person who could have fame, wealth, and prestige choose a life of anonymity and scarcity? Can you think of such models? Is this model inspiring or intimidating?

Yancey acknowledges that the problem of pain has been a theme in his work. How would you define this problem? How can we reconcile the idea of a loving God with the existence of pain in the world? Can you think of reasons to be grateful for pain? How can we view pain as a gift?

Do you believe God is trustworthy? Why? Why not?

Paul Brand learned from his parents "that love can only be applied person-to-person" (page 75). Why does it often seem easier to care about groups than individuals?

What did Jesus mean when he said, "Happy are they who bear their share of the world's pain: In the long run they will know more happiness than those who avoid it"? (pages 85–86)

DR. ROBERT COLES

"Vicariousness is, after all, a writer's business," Yancey writes (page 89). How does a reader know when to trust the vicarious experience a writer presents?

Six-year-old Ruby Bridges was escorted daily through an angry mob, "attending a vacant school to sit alone all day in her classroom" (page 97). Imagine yourself in her place. In her parents' place. What gives a person the strength to endure such an ordeal? What would you say to a parent who allowed a child to endure an experience like this? Have you ever had to act courageously for a cause?

Robert Coles believed that, for the poor, religion "was no crutch but rather a source of inspiration" (page 102). Karl Marx said, "Religion is the opiate of the masses." What makes one view more convincing to you than the other?

What do we learn from Jesus' parable of the prodigal son in which the father loves the errant and the dutiful son equally? How would you advise a parent in a similar situation, with one "good" child and one "bad" child? Where does the concept of "tough love" fall in such a scenario?

Do you think wealth makes people less compassionate? What do we gain/lose by our relative affluence?

LEO TOLSTOY AND FEODOR DOSTOEVSKY

Through Tolstoy and Dostoevsky, Yancey developed an "understanding of the tension between Christian ideals and reality" (page 121). Can you identify beliefs and behaviors that create this gap? What figures, if any, have helped you come to terms with life as Christians say it should be lived and life as it is lived?

Tolstoy's desire to live his faith caused his family pain and suffering. Talk about the dangers and virtues in having ideals you cannot live up to.

What does it take to say "attack *me* rather than the path I follow"? (pages 131–132) How can you separate one from the other?

Dostoevsky lived through a mock execution that changed his life. Talk about near-death experiences or national catastrophes or any traumatic event that may have changed you somehow.

Through Dostoevsky, Yancey came "to understand grace, not as a theological concept but a living reality worked out in a world of ungrace" (page 139). What do "grace" and "ungrace" mean to you?

At the beginning and end of this chapter, Yancey poses a basic question about faith: "Why doesn't it work?" How would you answer or refute him?

MAHATMA GANDHI

Gandhi said that a leader "is only a reflection of the people he leads" (page 157). Think about leaders in your life, not only national and state leaders, but the leaders in your community. What do they reflect about society?

In a world that is global and materialistic, how can one person make a difference? What prevents most of us from exerting the power of a Gandhi?

How would the United States respond if a national figure announced he/she was going on a fast to promote a cause? Say, if a leading senator pledged to fast to death unless Congress enacted campaign finance reform? If Laura Bush pledged to fast to death until all children were assured of an adequate education?

How would your life change if you renounced material possessions or radically simplified your life? How does the need for possessions shape us as individuals and as a society?

What makes a person a saint? What happens when a saint appears in our midst?

What are the similarities between Martin Luther King, Jr., and Mahatma Gandhi? The differences? Is one more appealing to you than the other? Why?

DR. C. EVERETT KOOP

Ronald Reagan appointed Koop surgeon general on the basis of his strong antiabortion position. Yet Koop became the center of controversy when he announced that "the scientific studies do not provide conclusive data about the health effects of abortion on women" (page 193). How can this statement be reconciled with his long-standing and continued opposition to abortion? How do you respond when apparent facts do not support your beliefs or your church's teachings?

Conservatives often call for less government control of things like the environment and business, but advocate government control in areas like abortion and sexuality. Liberals call for more government control of the environment and business, but less in areas like abortion and sexuality. What role can faith play in reconciling these apparent polar opposites? How do you normally react to people who have strong feelings about positions different from yours?

Koop had to learn to distinguish the immoral from the illegal (page 199). How does a person of faith accomplish this?

How is it possible to hate the sin and love the sinner? Is sin an outdated concept?

JOHN DONNE

When he thought he was dying, John Donne struggled with the meaning of suffering in *Devotions*. Why do you think God lets us suffer? What can we learn from God's becoming human and enduring the pain and humiliation of the Crucifixion?

Even if you believe the Incarnation is a myth, why has this story retained such a powerful hold on human imagination for two millennia?

Why do we take health for granted and look for meaning in suffering?

Many of us grew up with very specific notions of life after death. Do you have a vision of an afterlife? What is heaven like? Hell? How has your view evolved since childhood?

ANNIE DILLARD

Philip Yancey was raised in a strict, fundamentalist milieu, Annie Dillard in a more laid-back social one. Yet both have made a lifelong journey of spiritual inquiry. How does childhood experience shape adult faith?

Talk about your experience of nature. What have you learned from it?

What books have guided you on your faith journey? What do "secular" books offer that overtly "religious" books do not? And, vice versa, what do religious books offer that secular ones do not?

Annie Dillard enjoys some aspects of conservative Christian worship. What kind of religious services are you drawn to? What makes you uncomfortable? What can you learn from experiencing either sort?

FREDERICK BUECHNER

Buechner rejected rational explanations of a conversion experience, viewing it instead as "an exemplar of the 'crazy, holy grace' that wells up from time to time" (page 250). What is your understanding of a conversion experience?

Buecher believed "that God is alive and present in the world" (page 252). How do you perceive God interacting with history? What is the point of searching for God in history?

A number of people Yancey writes about in this book, including himself, made deliberate attempts to simplify their lives. What are the challenges inherent in such a decision? What are the gains? The losses?

At a critical juncture—the death of a loved one, the loss of a job, a debilitating illness—a friend expresses trust in God. What is your response?

SHUSAKU ENDO

What do you remember of your fears during the Cold War? If you are too young to remember, how do you respond to stories about fear of the atomic bomb, the Cuban missile crisis, the Communists' torture of their enemies? What are we afraid of today? What do our fears tell us about the world we live in?

Endo was drawn to the stories of the Japanese Christian martyrs (page 276). How have stories of martyrdom affected you? How has your response changed over time?

What makes a person an "outsider"? How do we identify people who "are not one of us"? How do we treat them?

Yancey suggests that Christianity's emphasis on father love prevented the Japanese from embracing it as eagerly as many other Western phenomena. Some contemporary theologians oppose language that attributes gender to God. How has your understanding of God's gender—male or female—informed your understanding of the divine?

Why do "writers of faith have a tendency to sanitize their characters" (page 291) when so many great characters in the Bible are deeply flawed?

HENRI NOUWEN

What do you think of a man like Nouwen who abandoned a life of celebrity and acclaim to take responsibility for the care of a profoundly disabled man?

Where many would see downward mobility, Nouwen saw "inward mobility" (page 311). How can abandoning a public life of teaching in favor of a much more private life in a small community be seen as embracing God's gifts rather than abandoning them?

Nouwen never publicly acknowledged his homosexuality. Most Christian churches are divided over issues around gay ordination and gay marriage. Should members of the clergy openly acknowledge their homosexuality? How would the members of your church react to a gay minister? To gay marriage?

PHILIP YANCEY has written sixteen books, including the bestsellers *Reaching for the Invisible God*, *What's So Amazing About Grace?*, and *The Jesus I Never Knew*. His works have sold over five million copies and have garnered many prizes, including *Christianity Today* Book of the Year and two ECPA Book of the Year Awards. He lives in Colorado with his wife, Janet.

ABOUT

THE

AUTHOR